Epicurus and the Singularity of Death

Also available from Bloomsbury

Health and Hedonism in Plato and Epicurus, by Kelly Arenson
Plato and Plotinus on Mysticism, Epistemology, and Ethics, by David J. Yount
Plato's Trial of Athens, by Mark A. Ralkowski
Rewriting Contemporary Political Philosophy with Plato and Aristotle, by Paul Schollmeier
The Philosophy of Death Reader, edited by Markar Melkonian

Epicurus and the Singularity of Death

Defending Radical Epicureanism

David B. Suits

BLOOMSBURY ACADEMIC
LONDON • NEW YORK • OXFORD • NEW DELHI • SYDNEY

BLOOMSBURY ACADEMIC
Bloomsbury Publishing Plc
50 Bedford Square, London, WC1B 3DP, UK
1385 Broadway, New York, NY 10018, USA
29 Earlsfort Terrace, Dublin 2, Ireland

BLOOMSBURY, BLOOMSBURY ACADEMIC and the Diana logo are trademarks of
Bloomsbury Publishing Plc

First published in Great Britain 2020
This paperback edition published in 2021

Copyright © David B. Suits, 2020

David B. Suits has asserted his right under the Copyright, Designs and
Patents Act, 1988, to be identified as Author of this work.

For legal purposes the Acknowledgments on p. vi constitute an extension
of this copyright page.

Cover design: Louise Dugdale
Cover image: Bust of Epicurus (Photo by Araldo de Luca/Corbis via Getty Images)

All rights reserved. No part of this publication may be reproduced or transmitted
in any form or by any means, electronic or mechanical, including photocopying,
recording, or any information storage or retrieval system, without prior
permission in writing from the publishers.

Bloomsbury Publishing Plc does not have any control over, or responsibility for, any
third-party websites referred to or in this book. All internet addresses given in this
book were correct at the time of going to press. The author and publisher regret any
inconvenience caused if addresses have changed or sites have ceased to exist,
but can accept no responsibility for any such changes.

A catalogue record for this book is available from the British Library.

A catalog record for this book is available from the Library of Congress.

ISBN: HB: 978-1-3501-3404-1
PB: 978-1-3502-7756-4
ePDF: 978-1-3501-3405-8
eBook: 978-1-3501-3406-5

Typeset by Deanta Global Publishing Services, Chennai, India

To find out more about our authors and books visit www.bloomsbury.com and
sign up for our newsletters.

Contents

Acknowledgments — vi

1. The Epicurean View of Death — 1
2. Radical Epicureanism — 23
3. Premature Death and the Complete Life — 37
4. Counterfactual Comments — 67
5. Death and Deprivation — 81
6. A Critique in Four Dimensions — 113
7. Killing — 123
8. Immortality — 155
9. Will He Nill He — 177
10. Suicide — 197

Bibliography — 211
Index — 219

Acknowledgments

In my ethics class one day years ago, when I was presenting Epicurus's argument that "death is nothing to us", I suddenly stopped and began to write down some quick notes (soon forgetting that I was standing at the lectern in front of a class), because I realized that Epicurus's argument was far better than I had previously given it credit for. In the following months my hasty notes started to form a growing set of ideas. Not long thereafter I mentioned to Frederik Kaufman that I was planning to write an article about Epicurus's view of death, and he pointed me to an article of his own that was soon coming out in *Midwest Studies in Philosophy*,[1] a collection that, it turned out, contained still other valuable essays on the philosophy of death. I was eventually led to Fred Feldman's *Confrontations with the Reaper*. Because it presented a strong case against Epicurus, it had an important influence on the development of my own ideas in defending Epicurus. I purchased a copy of *The Metaphysics of Death*, edited by John Martin Fischer (who has himself frequently contributed to the literature in the area). That book, which every student of the philosophy of death should own, contains many of the now-classic articles which are still being referred to in publications today. I was especially pleased with Harry Silverstein's presentation of some of the fundamental issues in his "The Evil of Death". But the most influential articles in Fischer's collection were two by Stephen Rosenbaum, "How to Be Dead and Not Care: A Defense of Epicurus" and "Epicurus and Annihilation",[2] both of which helped me to understand Epicurus a bit better and also to realize that there really were defenders of Epicurus in the modern world.

My studies in the philosophy of death resulted in a few published articles and now the present book, in which I hope to have given the Epicurean view some additional support.

---

[1] Frederik Kaufman, "Thick and Thin Selves", 94–97. (Complete bibliographic information on this and all other sources in this book is provided in the Bibliography.)

[2] Rosenbaum also published a valuable article in the *Midwest* collection that Kaufman referred me to: "Appraising Death in Human Life: Two Modes of Valuation". That article was followed some years later by a companion piece, "Concepts of Value and Ideas about Death". Altogether, he has published almost a dozen articles presenting and defending the Epicurean view of death.

Acknowledgments

* * *

For their comments and suggestions on some of my work which became draft chapters of this book, I want to give special thanks to Christine Sage Suits, John T. Sanders, Katie Terezakis, John Capps, Evelyn Brister, Frederik Kaufman, and Wade Robison.

1

The Epicurean View of Death

Prelude[1]

One ugly revolutionary day a priest, a politician, and an Epicurean are to receive capital punishment for their crimes. The three men are brought to the guillotine to await their turn for execution.

First is the priest, condemned to death for practicing a religion not legalized by the state. He is weeping and trembling as his head is placed in the restraining stock, because he has a fear of death, even though he also believes in an afterlife. The executioner triggers the device, and the blade high above starts to drop. But instantly it stalls. The executioner curses and kicks the machine, but he is unable to coax the blade to drop any further. The priest calls out that obviously God has interceded with a miracle. The executioner, also being superstitious, and having no better explanation for the failure of the machine, and not wanting to anger the Almighty (and therefore immediately regretting his cursing), lets the priest go free.

The executioner manages with some effort to pull the rope to lift the guillotine blade the short way back up to its trigger position.

Next is the politician, wearing expensive clothes made dirty by a short stay in prison. He has been condemned because he participated in the opposition to the ruling powers. He should have known better. As his head is placed in the stock, he, too, is trembling in the face of death. He believes that his life is made better by public acclaim and by the acquisition of wealth and power (all for the good of "society as a whole", he was wont to say). He believes that death will deprive him of all the goods that he would have been able to get. The executioner triggers the guillotine, but once again as soon as the blade starts to drop, it stalls. Thrilled with his good fortune, the politician exclaims that he must be released because it would be illegal to be put twice in jeopardy of his life. The executioner, possessing a few popular beliefs about the law, reluctantly agrees, and so the politician is set free.

The guillotine blade is with some effort coaxed back up to its starting position as the Epicurean is brought forward. He has been condemned because he is an Epicurean,

---

[1] The following is a variation on a story whose variations probably outnumber the years since it was invented. I have been unable to locate the original version.

which is, according to the ruling powers, an immoral doctrine, promoting a materialistic view of the world and leading people to attend to the quiet satisfaction of themselves and their friends instead of to virtue and the state, especially to the present ruling power. Before the Epicurean's head is placed into the restraining stock, he glances up at the guillotine blade and its mechanism. "Aha! I see the problem", he says, pointing up. "See that? The rope keeps binding because it slips off the pulley. It's an easy fix."

1 The argument

Nothing. That is the conclusion of Epicurus's argument designed to inform you about what the prospect of your own death should mean to you. But how are we to understand that remarkable conclusion? Does he mean that in the face of death you ought to just shrug your shoulders, not caring whether you live or die? We will examine his argument in some detail, but first there are two cautions. By "death" he does not mean the process of dying, but rather having died—nonexistence after having existed. All living things eventually die (or so we may suppose), after which they are dead—permanently. Epicurus was alive, but then he died, and so now he is dead. You are alive, and some day you will die and therefore be dead. The second caution is that he is not talking about how your death might affect other people. He means that your mortality—the fact that you will die at some time in the future—ought to be of no concern for you now.

Epicurus's claim is remarkable because obviously most people are afraid of, or in some way seriously concerned about, their own future death. Some people worry that because of their death they will miss out on whatever they might have experienced had they continued to live. Some people are concerned about how others might think of them after death. Some people are worried because they do not know what will happen after death.

But according to Epicurus, as we will see, death is annihilation, and so when your nonexistence comes about, whatever happens thereafter can be of no concern to you. (For example, you certainly will not be embarrassed *after* death, even if you died with your pants down.[2]) And so as you contemplate your future

---

[2] "Once a raid came suddenly in the twilight and caught me sitting comfortably in the officers' head, down in the little valley behind the tents. There was nothing to do, no point in running up to the foxhole; I simply sat there with my pants around my ankles, and went about my business. It was very quiet, and then, with a sudden ripping sound, a Japanese fighter swept over the trees by the mess hall, very low. I could see the blinking of his machine guns as he rushed toward me and then swung toward the parked planes on the field. Then he was gone. [. . .] I pulled up my pants and walked up the valley to the tent. Only then did I think how embarrassing it would have been to die down there, on the toilet, with my pants down" (Samuel Hynes, *Flights of Passage: Reflections of a World War*

absence from the world, if you realize that it will be neither a good thing nor a bad thing for you, you ought not to be concerned in advance.

Is that view reasonable? I think it is, and this book is an attempt to present and defend that view and some of its implications. My goal is to convince you that none of the bad things (and none of the good things) that you have heard about the prospect of death are correct. But I hasten to add that the therapy for whatever anxieties about death that you may have will not consist in some kind of religious instruction about life after death or a promise of eternal bliss. It is much simpler, and also in some respects more complex, than that.

Let's begin with Epicurus's own words in his *Letter to Menoeceus*[3]:

> For all good and bad consists in sense-experience, and death is the privation of sense-experience. Hence, a correct knowledge of the fact that death is nothing to us makes the mortality of life a matter for contentment, not by adding a limitless time [to life] but by removing the longing for immortality. For there is nothing fearful in life for one who has grasped that there is nothing fearful in the absence of life. Thus, he is a fool who says that he fears death not because it will be painful when present but because it is painful when it is still to come. For that which while present causes no distress causes unnecessary pain when merely anticipated. So death, the most frightening of bad things, is nothing to us; since when we exist, death is not yet present, and when death is present, then we do not exist. Therefore, it is relevant neither to the living nor to the dead, since it does not affect the former, and the latter do not exist.

The argument may seem a bit convoluted, so I want to reorganize it in order to make its structure more explicit. I will offer some comments on each of the parts, along with advertisements here and there about what will be available in later chapters. (In Chapter 2, I will reinterpret the argument in order to emphasize certain aspects of it.) The argument has six premises (which I have labeled α, β, γ, δ, ε, and ζ) and a final conclusion (η).

(α) *"All good and bad consists in sense-experience."* What is good or bad for a person must always have reference (explicit or implicit, direct or indirect) to the person's experiences. I am taking a small liberty here by understanding "sense-experience" as, more simply, experience, because that will allow us to avoid the trap of thinking that Epicurus is speaking merely of bodily sensations of pleasure

---

II Aviator, 204). (Complete bibliographic information on this and all other sources in this book is provided in the Bibliography.)

[3] This *Letter* and two others were preserved by the third-century CE biographer Diogenes Laërtius in Book 10 of his *Lives of Eminent Philosophers*. I make use of the translation by Brad Inwood and L. P. Gerson in *The Epicurus Reader*.

and pain, such as the pleasurable taste of chocolate or the painful stubbing of a toe. Although he is a materialist (see premise β), Epicurus is comfortable, just as we moderns often are, with speaking of bodily pleasures and pains on the one hand, and mental pleasures and pains on the other (see, for examples, PD 18, 20, and 30[4]). The pleasures of the soul, provided especially by philosophy, are experiences more to be prized than pleasures of the flesh.

Epicurus is called a hedonist (and, often, an egoistic hedonist) because he says that one's goal is pleasure (ἡδονή, *hēdonē*). But while hedonism is usually said to be the view that pleasure is good (or that one ought to strive for pleasure) and pain is bad (or one ought to avoid pain), Epicurus's version is not that simple. In the *Letter to Menoeceus*, shortly after presenting his argument that "death is nothing to us", Epicurus makes a curious but important claim about his view of pleasure:

> So when we say that pleasure is the goal we do not mean the pleasures of the profligate or the pleasures of consumption, as some believe, either from ignorance and disagreement or from deliberate misinterpretation, but rather the lack of pain in the body and disturbance in the soul. For it is not drinking bouts and continuous partying and enjoying boys and women, or consuming fish and the other dainties of an extravagant table, which produce the pleasant life, but sober calculation which searches out the reasons for every choice and avoidance and drives out the opinions which are the source of the greatest turmoil for men's souls. [See also *PD* 3]

One might complain that "lack of pain in the body and disturbance in the soul" is a peculiar notion of pleasure. Scholars have puzzled over how best to understand Epicurus's use (or, rather, his several different uses) of *hēdonē*. We will return briefly to the issue in Chapter 3, but for the purposes of this book there is no need to pursue the meaning of *hēdonē* much further than to suggest that lack of pain in the body (*aponia*) and lack of disturbance in the soul (*ataraxia*), with special emphasis on *ataraxia*, constitute a state of *satisfaction*. So although Epicurean hedonism includes the view that pleasure in the ordinary sense, and considered in itself, is good, and pain in the ordinary sense, and considered in itself, is bad, it is not the view that more pleasure is always to be sought and more pain is always to be avoided; nor is it the view that we ought to maximize a balance of pleasure over pain. It is, rather, a view that the good life is a life without serious

---

[4] PD = Principal Doctrines (or *Kuriai Doxai*), forty short paragraphs from some of Epicurus's works (most of which have not survived) as reported by Diogenes Laërtius. Again, I use the translations by Inwood and Gerson.

complaints; it is a style of living wherein one is not in mental turmoil or visited with frequent anxiety, regrets, and fears. The good life is a way of living such that one does not always yearn for more, or feel anxiety at not having more; one does not long to escape one's present lot or feel dissatisfied with one's present and probable future conditions. If one is confident that any problems can be easily dealt with, and that this satisfactory living will not disintegrate (from either internal or external causes) into dissatisfaction, one has *ataraxia*—peace of mind, serenity. It is this living-while-satisfied that is our *telos*.

(β) "*When death is present, then we do not exist.*" According to Epicurus's materialist ontology, there is an infinity of subvisible, indestructible atoms moving in infinite space, colliding, combining, and separating. In large combinations they form objects visible to us. (See his *Letter to Herodotus*.) We ourselves are aggregations of atoms. Our modern materialism, although far more intricate both empirically and theoretically, is very roughly similar to Epicurus's, and so we find it easy to agree with the materialistic view, as long as we do not attend to the finer details we have discovered, such as subatomic things and forces.

Because we, like all living things, are complex material objects, we are subject to damage and malfunction. The death of a living thing happens when the important processes of coordinated organic functioning have failed. It is not important here to be very demanding as to the criteria for when death occurs; they will change at least slightly in different contexts. Even a materialist does not claim that death is the complete destruction of the body—or anyway, not necessarily.[5] Unaided by present technologies, the apparent inactivity of the organism, especially the cessation of heartbeat and respiration, might satisfy serious investigators that death has occurred. When a corpse is burned up, buried, or autopsied, someone probably thought that the person had died. (And if it was not already dead, then we presume that after the cremation, burial, or autopsy, whatever is left over is not then a living animal.) The permanent cessation of the usual kinds of rich interactions of the organism with its environment may occur either suddenly or gradually. If it occurs gradually, then there is a period of time during which it is not clear whether death has occurred, especially when by virtue of its gradual nature it is not clear that the loss of interaction will be both total and permanent. (Coming into existence as an organism interacting in typically rich ways with its environment also raises issues of vagueness.) A person who died is sometimes

---

[5] See Fred Feldman, "The Termination Thesis", for a useful discussion of a few puzzles about the idea of annihilation.

called a dead person. I want to say that personality has vanished; there is no longer an organism with a psychology, even if body parts remain, and so I will sometimes emphasize that aspect of death by saying that the previously existing person has become an *experson*.

The death of a person, as the failure of the important organic functions of the parts that previously composed the person, is no different in principle from the destruction of nonliving things such as machines. If an automobile is crushed and the resulting bits and parts piled in a heap, it would be silly to claim that the automobile still exists, or anyway exists as the kind of thing you would want an automobile for, such as transportation or racing or an afternoon tour of the countryside. Whatever now exists is not an integrated functioning of automobile parts. *Something*, of course, exists, but it is a scrap heap, and not an automobile. The automobile no longer exists.

I put a log onto the fire. After a while it is finished burning, and it is no longer there. What has happened to it? Gone up in smoke, it has; and down in ashes. Then is it both up and down at once? No; it is nowhere at once. See all those atoms? They used to be parts of a log. Now they no longer form anything recognizable. Well, perhaps heaps of ash and wisps of smoke are familiar collections, but most of the atoms are scattered abroad to who knows where.

Or consider a small nuclear bomb that was lying on the surface of the moon near the center of the crater Copernicus. It was a gun-metal gray titanium alloy box about 100 cm × 200 cm × 100 cm with a mass of 150 kg. So the bomb had various properties and relations. Then it was detonated. Now where is it? What is its size? Color? Mass? Such ordinary attributes and relations are no longer applicable, because there is no longer a bomb. Perhaps nothing obvious is left of that atomic device. In that case, the term "dead" seems inapt, whereas "dead" can comfortably apply to electric circuits that can no longer carry current, light bulbs that no longer work, and plant and animal bodies that have stopped functioning in the usual ways. In such cases, when we can identify what the remains are the remains of, then the term "dead" can be useful. Still, "dead" is not like many contingent attributes of functioning things. "Dead" is not another attribute of "rabbit" in the way "afraid", "fast", "hungry", "missing an ear" are. A dead rabbit is a corpse not capable of usual rabbit behavior, but in unguarded moments we might think of a lifeless rabbit as though it were still a regular rabbit but missing a few of its previous properties and now with a new and special attribute. A dead person is at most a corpse no longer capable of personality, but if there is still a body, we sometimes have a tendency to use the term "dead person" as though there were an odd kind of person with a special attribute.

Context is important. What is a body? A king wants bodies for his army, but he will not be satisfied with dead bodies. It may be that dead doves and dead roses would not count as doves or roses if they were used in response to the bride-to-be's desire to line the aisle with roses and to end the ceremony by releasing a dozen doves. Wouldn't she say "That's not what I meant"?

True, people are bodies, but bodies that behave in certain ways—the ways we find important for loving, hating, and admiring; they have jobs, or are retired, or are unemployed. Such vital properties vanish at death, which is why I say that death is the annihilation of the person.

One way to prove that Bea exists (as a person) is to point: there she is, and she has what we ordinarily call properties (she has a certain mass, is quick-witted, enjoys jokes about politicians) and participates in many relations (she is sitting at a table, conversing with friends, ordering chocolate cake for dessert), and she is capable of having other properties and relations. Now shake her hand, have a conversation with her, go dancing with her, share a cab, hire her as an accountant. One way to describe what it means for Bea to have become nothing is to say that she is now nowhere to be found even if you were to look everywhere in the universe. Although you might find a corpse that used to be part of Bea-the-person, you can no longer have a conversation with her, go dancing with her, or hire her to do your taxes. Bea-the-person is now nothing because she, or rather what is left of what used to be her, cannot interact in the usual person-ways with anything. What presently exists in the universe does not include Bea. That is what it means to say that Bea-the-person has become nothing. Personality has been annihilated, and whatever does not exist can have no actual qualities at all.

(γ) Therefore, *"Death is the privation of sense-experience."* Death as we usually understand it is a final and unalterable disruption of organic functioning, which means the loss of sentience. Only existing things can be sentient, and from premise β we learn that death is nonexistence. Someone might ask, "How can we be so sure that nonexistent things have no sensations?" The question seems to be the kind of thing one might ask in response to a claim that plants do not have emotions. The question "How can we be so sure?" seems to admonish us to be careful lest we fail to look closely or lest we be led astray by prejudices. But in the case of the claim that only existing things can feel (and think), we are dealing not with an empirical issue but with a conceptual one.

(δ) *Therefore, death is not relevant to the dead.* That is to say, there is neither good nor evil for the experson in being dead. Nothing is of concern for a dead person, since a dead person is not an actual person; it is a non-functioning has-been (or, rather, whatever remains, if anything, is not a sentient being, even if it might function in some other way—as a teaching tool for students of anatomy, for example).

(ε) *"That which while present causes no distress causes unnecessary pain when merely anticipated."* There are two ways of thinking of pain in prospect. To put the matter plainly, it is a contradiction to say that one anticipates pain (or, more generally, dissatisfaction or adversity) from that which one truly believes will not produce pain. (Of course, it is not necessarily silly or unreasonable to be afraid of what one *believes* will be painful or distressing even though in fact it turns out to be not so. We all make mistakes.) Second, one might be concerned because of a possible loss of pleasure. In some cases a rude interruption to an enjoyable occasion can cause frustration; in some cases not. Sometimes one is prepared for the ending of a pleasant experience; sometimes not. One lies comfortably in bed, perhaps awakened by the morning sun, but wanting the moment to endure; there is no pressing need to rise. Later on, one climbs from bed, no longer wishing the earlier moment to endure, nor regretting its end. On other mornings one forces oneself to get up, wishing mightily for some excuse to fall back under the covers.

But it is unreasonable to be afraid of that which one believes will in no way be troublesome either now or later (neither troublesome in any positive sense nor troublesome in the sense of experiencing a loss of pleasure or the consequences of such a loss). If, then, you believe that you will cease to exist at your death, then you ought to believe that being dead will in no sense be aversive, and consequently (but here is a conclusion which some people find difficult to accept, and about which more will be said later on) you ought not to be concerned in advance.

(ζ) *"When we exist, death is not yet present."* We may take this as a mere tautology: living beings are not nonliving.

(η) *Therefore, death is not relevant to the living.* Being dead must be nothing to you now as a living thing, because you are not dead; and the thought of your future death, which will be nothing to you when you are dead, ought not to concern you in advance. Epicurus does not aim to deny that the prospect of death does cause anxiety in many people. It is because he has seen how the prospect of death can be troublesome that he uses his argument to try to banish such anxiety—to show how such anxiety is based upon a misunderstanding of death: "a correct knowledge of the fact that death is nothing to us makes the mortality of life a matter for contentment".

So the passage from the *Letter to Menoeceus* contains two main arguments. The first attempts to show that *being* dead *cannot* be in any way either satisfying or dissatisfying. The second attempts to show that the *prospect* of being dead *ought* not to be either attractive or repellant—that there is no good reason either to welcome death or to be afraid of it. The second relies upon the first, and is no doubt the more difficult of the two conclusions to accept.

2 Old habits

Where does the common sentiment that one's death is important get its force? This may be one part of an answer: People fear death because they see it is a permanent condition, and so it is a momentous divide from which there is no escape; there is no undoing it. To be sure, any decision—any act—is in some sense undoable: once it has been done, it remains true that it has been done. But almost all acts are undoable in a rather commonsensical way, namely, that one can be put into a position similar to one's earlier condition. If, for example, I throw away my favorite shirt, then I can later on buy a similar shirt. If I do not accept the current job offer, then I can find another, probably very similar, job elsewhere. And so it is with almost all ordinary choices and actions. Even what happens to me is usually reversible: a rock knocks me on the head, but my scalp heals; I catch a cold, and later I recover. But some conditions are more difficult to reverse. The more the consequences of actions and events are thought to be difficult to undo, the more time is spent thinking about them, worrying about them, defending against them, regretting them. Death, of course, appears to be at the extreme end of that scale—the irrevocable event par excellence. It is no wonder, then, that having conceived the nature of death as the extreme version of an undoable event, people are filled with so much anxiety about it.

There is another source of concern. It is a feature of a mature mind—you can see this develop in children as they grow—that one takes more and more into account when framing one's decisions and expectations. More and more, one's decisions become infused with "what-ifs" that were not there before. Experience begins to teach the young mind that various consequences occur, and one has to take these consequences into account. There are pleasures of the mind and the body to be tended to and savored, but present actions overflowing with present pleasures will later on give rise to hesitations and to further expectations and desires. A desire for a playmate might be well satisfied today, but tomorrow one's companion is going to be a partner in other activities as well, and what about that? That is the burden—of having to live more and more in the future. So burdened are we with the futurity of our thoughts that eventually the thought of having no future at all will weigh on us. This happens when one is leaving childhood and is beginning to practice an adult care for the future. When this skill is laid down, it encounters the distant limit of death, so that one has to both live in the future and realize that at some point there will be no future to live in. That realization, some people say, is so unsettling that it gives rise to a *denial* of death. Peter Berger, for example, remarks on "Man's 'no' to death".[6] It is better, I think, to propose not a denial of death but rather an expectation that things will proceed in the usual ways in which we have always experienced them. We are creatures of habits; we are not denying death so much as expecting a future, and that expectation meets a strange resistance when thinking of one's own annihilation.

Another basis for the discomfort one feels when contemplating one's own death could be the thought that death is a way of losing the world, especially the social world, as though the world were going on without one, leaving one behind. Perhaps one has some vague images of an increasing distance as relatives or friends move on into their own futures, as though one could stretch out a hand and try to keep in touch with them, or raise one's voice and try to call to them, but to no avail. One is being left alone, all alone, denied all the desirable interactions that had for so long been one's life and its meaning.

It is not always to be expected that a rational understanding of something will cause our emotional responses to change. It is, for example, hard to imagine that a fervent believer in a supreme being could at one stroke give up that belief on the basis of what someone else takes to be logically unassailable considerations; the action of some people's faith is apparently utterly opposed to logical suasion. Deeply held desires can be starting points for, rather than conclusions of, argumentation. A woman has an addiction that causes her time and money (and sometimes anxiety when she is not confident that she will be able to satisfy the next occasion of craving). She has been advised to be rid of the destructive habit, and she understands the reasons; she also knows that some people in her situation have managed to free themselves from the addiction. But she is at the same time worried that getting rid of the offensive habit will put her in various kinds of pain. When she is offered a cure, she is both attracted to it and repelled by it—attracted, because if it is successful she might be better off; repelled, because it means that if it is successful she will be without that which

---

[6] *A Rumor of Angels*, 64.

she in fact now craves. She imagines what it would be like, right now, to not have what she right now craves: it would be cause for anxiety and perhaps even a bit of panic. This seems to me to be a parallel with the anticipation of death. A person knows (intellectually, or abstractly) that she will not exist after death, yet she is seriously concerned that when she dies, then of course she will not be able to enjoy access to those persons, things, activities, and projects that she now in fact cherishes.

In addition, there can be stories that encourage us to imagine a continuation of the person beyond death. In a charming Platonic myth, a man, Er,

> died in war; and on the tenth day, when the corpses, already decayed, were picked up, he was picked up in a good state of preservation. Having been brought home, he was about to be buried on the twelfth day; as he was lying on the pyre, he came back to life, and [. . .] he told what he saw in the other world. [*Republic* 10.614b]

This is convenient. First we have the authorial stipulation that Er was alive, then dead, and then alive again. Then we have the authorial stipulation that Er in fact was in another world when he was dead. If you tell even the most outrageous tales about resurrections and afterlives, you will start some people to wondering: "What do you think happens after you die?" Epicureans are at a disadvantage in not having stories or myths about an afterlife. For an Epicurean, there is no speculation about what death might *really* be like. There is no story that can be told about a person who comes back from death in order to report on what takes place there. It would make no sense to say "Death is annihilation. Now once upon a time a person was annihilated and then came back to life and reported that death was absolute nonexistence."[7]

We can have many reactions to the thought of death, but sometimes we can change some of our more visceral responses, just as we can in the case of other things and events when we have opportunities for reflection. Some of our immediate feelings can be checked, turned aside, hidden, or covered over with some polite camouflage. With practice, one can learn to not have a fear of high places, of flying, or of falling. One can come to positively enjoy such experiences. To be sure, being dead is not the sort of thing that one can practice. But Epicurus believes, what I hope to show in this book, that one can contemplate death philosophically and come to understand that there is nothing about it to fear.

---

[7] But consider the curious case of A. J. Ayer as described by Abigail L. Rosenthal, "What Ayer Saw When He Was Dead".

3 Deprivation

Many philosophers object to Epicurus's position. Death—that is, the prospect and meaning of our own death—cannot, they say, be nothing to us. Although the mass of publications in recent decades being anti-Epicurean would seem to indicate that Epicurus's conclusion has yet to meet its equal rival, the "deprivation" view—that death deprives a person of goods that would have been available had death not occurred—seems to be a strong favorite. (That death is not annihilation seems to have few supporters among philosophers.) I will have much more to say about this in Chapter 5. For now, let's try a little thought experiment.

Imagine that for most of Lex's adult life he was a lawyer, but there came a time when he abandoned the practice of law and took up a life devoted to something else. One can imagine how his life might have been, had he not given up practicing law when he did. One can imagine all the goods in a lawyerly life (for there can be goods in such a profession) counterfactually extended beyond his actual lawyerly career. Can one say that it is a pity, a shame, too bad for Lex that his career as a lawyer ended when he took up a different occupation? Can it be claimed that the end of his legal career was a bad thing for him? (It might, of course, be judged, either by Lex or by others, that his career switch was unfortunate for some other people, but that is a different issue.)

The question is certainly ambiguous. We might try to make out three versions of a claim that Lex's career switch was bad for him: (1) Lex judges that his switch in professions was a mistake; he regrets his decision. (2) Someone else judges that Lex's going on in law would have been better for him than what is available in the new career, even if Lex himself does not realize it. In both senses there is a comparison of his new life as it is (and as it will probably continue) with his old life as it probably would have continued. Finally, (3) someone judges that in his new career Lex will now be denied the goods of a continued lawyerly life, and that is too bad, even though no comparison with his new life is made.

The third sense is the interesting one for our purposes, because it is most analogous to a person's apparently missing out on the goods of a counterfactually extended life, where, because of death, there is no alternative life for comparison with the counterfactual. That is, we can examine two cases: one wherein a lawyer switched careers and became something else instead, and another wherein a lawyer died and became nothing.

To say that someone "missed out" on something or did not get something good is ordinarily to imply that it was bad that he did not get it. To say that something is bad is often, but not always, to encourage the implication that something else is or would have been better, and to say that something is good is often, but not always, to imply that something else is or would have been bad, or at least not as good. Such implications are stronger when there is an explicit mention of some alternative. But ordinarily what is known to happen to a person happens in a context of alternatives. All narration bulges with counterfactuals. (More about that in Chapter 4.) And even when one tries one's best to dispassionately list a simple history of events, it is difficult to resist the urgings of alternatives at every step. Hence, nearly every evaluation of something that happens to a person is made in a context (implicit if not explicit) of alternatives that could have borne different evaluations.

Ordinarily, when we say that because Lex switched careers he missed out on the goods that he would have received, we are comparing two things—two sets of consequences, two lives, two ways of going on in the world—and we are evaluating one way as better (or worse) than the other. This is the ordinary way of understanding alternatives. If, then, we say that Lex's death caused him to miss out on the goods that he would have received had he continued to live, we have a tendency to think in the ordinary way, and the ordinary way is a comparison, as though continuing to live were one alternative way of going on in the world, and being dead were another. We can try to remind ourselves that being dead is not really a way of going on, and that being dead is not the sort of situation to be compared to any other, because it is no situation at all for the experson. But when we then say that to have died is to have missed out on something, we are nevertheless encouraging just such a comparison.

"Lex decided to switch careers. Had he not switched, he would have experienced many good things." We might want to actively fight the implication that his career switch put him into a worse situation. We can head off such an impression by saying something like "But because he switched, he experienced many good things too", or "Yes, but in his new career he is even happier". But when it comes to death, and not a career switch, there is nothing to fight with; the usual aids and comforts that we rely on are no longer there. We are thrown off balance, rather like being faced with a nit-picking attorney questioning a witness in court: "Yes or no: Did Lex miss out on some goods when he switched careers?" Of course he did, for even in the practice of law there are some goods. But the witness is afraid that a simple "yes" will leave the jury with the misimpression that Lex is therefore worse off for having switched careers. The implication is easy, natural, automatic; it is resisted by supplying a fuller explanation. But in the case of death there is no fuller explanation in the usual sense. "Yes or no: Did Lex miss out on some goods when he died?" A simple "yes" could leave the jury with the misimpression that Lex is therefore now worse off for having died. The hardest part is fully realizing that in the case of death we are no longer dealing with alternatives in any usual sense. Death is not an alternative to life; it is, rather, the eternal absence of alternatives *for Lex*; all comparisons permanently vanish. And because one of the elements to compare is missing, to say "He died and missed out on some goods" is rather like an incomplete sentence. An attentive juror will understand that the witness was forced to answer "yes" to the yes or no question of whether Lex missed out on some goods when he switched careers, and the juror will want to hear information from the other side of the story—to hear a confirmation of the implication that he is indeed in a worse situation now, or else to hear a denial of the implication, a "Yes, but—". Yet in the case of Lex's death, the juror will wait forever without getting further information; there will be neither confirmation nor disconfirmation of the implied evaluation. There can be neither "Yes, he is in a worse situation" nor "Yes, but he is even happier now", nor even "Yes, but really he's not so bad off." There is a weak implication of such possibilities, but in the case of death no comparison is possible.[8]

Lex's death was not bad for him. His death was not good for him either. His death was not even just as good as (or just as bad as) some alternative for him. His death was precisely nothing for him.

4 Death is not a solution

Someone has a problem with some object (or event or situation) because the object has a particular property (or participates in some relation). There are three ways to make it false that the person still has the problem. (1) The offending property is removed from the object or situation. (2) The object is destroyed. (3) The person is destroyed. Which one is chosen depends on the person's further goals and on what is possible. Stan's shirt has been stained by spaghetti sauce. Stan might choose the first approach if he wants to retain the shirt but without the stain. He might launder the shirt, and if the stain disappears, this will count as a solution of the problem for Stan. The second method might be chosen if the property is difficult to remove (or if for some reason the object has become such as to be useless if the property is now removed). If the stain on the shirt proves to be very stubborn, Stan might discard the shirt. This might or might not be a solution of the problem for Stan. (Probably the problem will be given a

---

[8] On some problems involved in comparing life to death, see Harry S. Silverstein, "The Evil of Death".

new description. If at first the problem is that there is an unwanted stain on the shirt, then, if laundering does not help and the stain has become permanent, the problem might be redescribed: there is an unwanted shirt.) Under what conditions might the third be chosen? Stan might commit suicide, but this cannot be a solution *for Stan*, which is to say that it cannot put Stan into a problemless situation as the first two can, because to be annihilated is to be in no situation at all. To think that the third approach can be a solution is to embrace a fallacy that I will describe in Chapter 5. And in Chapter 10 I will address the issue of suicide.

5 Length of life

In Chapter 8 I will deal with a few issues having to do with immortality. For now, let us consider a survey question that Robert Kastenbaum says was given to about 200 people over about seven years.

> Suppose that the world is just as we know it, with one exception. Death is no longer inevitable. Disease and aging have been conquered. Let us also suppose that air and water pollution have been much reduced through new technologies. Think about this situation for a moment. Now write down your response—just a few words. Would you prefer to live in this world without death, or would you prefer to live in the world as it is now? ["A world without death? First and second thoughts", 115]

This is a remarkable prompt. One suspects that the respondents would understand it in a particular way, yet there are ambiguities. The imagined world is to be just like the present world "with one exception". Is it possible to imagine a single change in the world without introducing others? Kastenbaum himself stipulates others: disease has been conquered; so has aging. These are distinct from death. Many people fall ill but do not die (from that illness). Everyone is aging, yet people are still alive. To remove death is therefore not necessarily to remove either disease or aging. We are also to imagine that "new technologies" have reduced air and water pollution. It looks like we are to consider not one change from the world as we know it, but four or five at least. But there are bound to be plenty of further plausible changes.

At first it is said that we are to imagine that death is not inevitable, but later it is asked if we "prefer to live in this world without death". The omission of "inevitable" in the second instance is very significant. A world without death would be a world most likely without hamburgers, and I am not sure I would vote for that. I am not opposed to swatting pesky mosquitoes or killing ruthless tyrants. Would it be impossible to harvest and eat carrots? Evidently if disease is conquered (but somehow not by killing living disease-causers), we would have created a world far too distant from our own that only a foolish adventurer would take a chance on it.

For Epicureans, death is of no concern, and neither is immortality. But what about prolonging life, if not without end, then at least by some finite amount? A life of more pleasure is often thought to be better than a life of less pleasure, and the acceptance of such a principle would seem to generate a desire to live longer, provided that one expects the extra time to be pleasurable. If Epicureans do not seek immortality, do they, as hedonists, seek to avoid *premature* death? The answer in the negative will be discussed in Chapter 3. A principle that recommends more pleasure over less pleasure (and hence a longer pleasurable life) is ambiguous. How, for example, is pleasure to be quantified? Are we to Benthamize our assessment? How are we to account for Mill's claim that quality outweighs quantity? Assuming we get past these matters, we may note that the principle is appealing because it seems to apply to our experiences—not always, perhaps, but anyway often enough to make the principle seem plausible. But principles extended beyond borders can sometimes suddenly fail. Usually the limits are implicit.

Jonathan Glover says that one reason why a longer life might be thought better than a shorter life is that

> other things being equal, more of a good thing is always better than less of it. This does not entail such absurd consequences as that an enjoyable play gets better as it gets longer, without limit. The point of the phrase "other things being equal" is to allow for waning of interest and for the claims of other activities. [*Causing Death and Saving Lives*, 122]

What Glover gives with one hand he takes back with some other. The *ceteris paribus* clause makes the entire comment inapplicable to length of life. When dead, one will have no interests, and nothing will be enjoyable to one, and this is so regardless of the length of life one led, just as it is so regardless of how long one has been dead. It is true that some people feel that life has begun to lose interest for them (it might more properly be said that they have lost interest in their various projects), but it does not follow that in the absence of such waning interests, a longer life is better. It only gives us the rather trivial conclusion that people enjoyed their various projects longer than they might have. Longer is better only in cases where one wishes that the activities would have continued or is pleased that they did not end earlier. Such attitudes are impossible in death, of course. Can one anticipate that an event will last a certain length of time, and wish, before the fact, that it would end up going on longer, anticipating, probably, more pleasure thereby? Of course. But what is being anticipated is that one will wish, after it is over, that it would continue. Such a wish is impossible in death.

Peter Unger offers a very plausible-sounding comment.

> I would far prefer twenty years of normal life, replete with much conscious experience, to sixty more years alive only in wholly non-conscious states. [*Identity, Consciousness and Value*, 7]

Plausible, yet how curious! For what reason is it considered better to have experiences (even if all of them are enjoyable) to no experiences? It appears that an important premise is:

> For my life to be of much value to me, I must enjoy conscious experience during much of my life. [7]

Which is to say that

> given the values we actually do have, a person's enjoying much conscious experience is a precondition of her life being of much value for her. [7]

That's fine. But those two premises do not by themselves get to the comparison (the preference) that Unger started out with. Perhaps something like this could help:

> It is meaningful to prefer something of value over something of no value, where "no value" is taken in the sense of being utterly neutral—something about which I care not a jot.

Now, that is quite plausible, and no doubt we can produce many good instances of it in our lives, because, after all, we are constantly choosing what we believe to be more valuable over what we believe to be less valuable.

But when we contrast experiences with no experiences, that new premise will not suffice. Having no experiences is not the same as having experiences of nothing. To have experiences which I care nothing about—which are of no value to me (assuming there are such things)—may properly be chosen over experiences of pain; and experiences of pleasure may properly be chosen over neutral experiences. But having no experiences at all is simply not a choice. (A person intent on suicide might be trying to get rid of pain and suffering; but that is not the same as choosing nothing. We will come back to this issue in Chapter 10.) So the choice in that premise must be between kinds of experiences, not between some experiences and none.

One cannot, therefore, coherently choose twenty years of experiences over sixty years of nonexperiences unless one imagines that those sixty years will somehow result in undesirable experiences thereafter. (Or else one is conceiving of nonexistence as a deprivation, about which more in Chapter 5.)

6 Death is of no concern

Peter Koestenbaum says:

> On the positive side, the inevitable corollary of the experience of the dread of the destruction of our world leads to a complete reevaluation and transformation of the meaning of our individual human existence. We become aware of the urgency to find meaning in life. ["The Vitality of Death", 148]

Why is that "positive"? Why can we not already have found "meaning" in our lives? For my own part, nearly everything I do has meaning—a purpose, a goal, usually something trivial. I suppose that I am like most people in now and then being in a state of limbo, especially when something important in my life has changed, as when I have finished a large project, and suddenly I find that my forward energy has nothing to push against. But I soon enough become engaged in still other projects which interest me. True, some people must have more than that; perhaps they metaphysicalize and take a point of view beyond all their projects and ask "What's the point of it *all*?"—a question I find disorientingly presumptuous (and to which I will return in Chapter 8).

> Of course, the process of getting old and the many and severe problems associated with it arise only because of the conviction that the death of myself is inevitable. [154]

This is not correct, at least in my own case. Getting old has its disadvantages, but the issue of death need not enter in at all. Rather, it is an issue of the loss of energy and vigor. I am a bit less physically robust than I used to be, and so I have to watch more carefully how and what I eat and how and when I exercise. It is not anxiety about a future death which I experience, but rather the slowing down, the failing or the loss of the capacities I had for so long enjoyed and took for granted. It might be the case that, as a matter of fact, these are the characteristics of a body on its way to eventual demise. But that fact is not what I attend to. When a romantic relationship breaks apart, I attend to what is lost, or what I could have had, and not to the fact that eventually I will die. When a dinner party is cut short because the host is suddenly called away on some urgent matter, and we must all leave, I attend to what good times are being lost, and not to the fact that I will eventually die. My eventual death, it seems to me, is pretty much irrelevant to the goods and the bads of my life. I cannot speak for Koestenbaum, of course; perhaps he is much more engaged with his prospective death than I am with mine. I wonder, though, whether it is necessarily a part of human nature, and whether it is in general a useful thing, to be so engaged.

Koestenbaum describes a woman who is not happy in her job, and he suggests that if she fully recognizes the inevitability of her own eventual death, she will develop the will to quit her job.

> She also recognizes, once she honestly focuses her attention on death, that time is running out, that she has but one life to lead, that if she throws away this life she will have lost, as far as she is concerned, *all there is!* [155][9]

She may well come to think this way. I suppose that many people do. But there is a conceptual confusion involved here. The idea of having only one *life* to lead, and the prospect of throwing it all way, and the prospect of therefore losing something of great value, result from misuses of the notions of what it is to have only one of something, what it is to throw it away, and what it is, therefore, to lose it. Ordinarily, when we have only one of something, and this something is very valuable, we are careful to make good and proper use of it. Perhaps I have a ticket to an event which has been sold out for months, and if I lose this ticket, I will not be able to attend. We face such situations throughout our lives. But these sorts of actual losses (and threats of losses) are not applicable when it comes to our lives as a whole. To miss out on something, or to lose something, is to be in a condition later on without that something. To anticipate such a loss is to anticipate regretting such a loss. (There are of course occasions when we anticipate regret, yet when the time comes, we do not after all regret what we did not take advantage of.) But in the case of death, there simply can be no loss in that sense. What is the "otherwise" clause which is implicit in the "you have only one life to lead, so you ought to make good use of it"? You ought to make

---

[9] Similarly, Steven Cave writes: "Knowing that life will have an end puts a limit on our time and so makes it valuable. The fact of mortality imparts to our existence an urgency and allows us to give it shape and meaning—we have reason to make this the best of all worlds, because we know there is no other" (*Immortality*, 306–7).

good use of it, otherwise . . . . Otherwise *what?* In the case of death, there is no "otherwise" *for the person who died.* (I will discuss this further in Chapter 7.)

This is not to say that a close attention to one's inevitable death will not encourage one to act differently, and perhaps more productively and enjoyably. Certainly that must happen to many people. It may, therefore, even be an item of good advice for such people. People also find encouragement in praying to supernatural beings and in carrying talismans and fetishes. But even if such beliefs provide comfort, that does not give them the power to provide a rational account of things.

> The realization of death places immediate and tremendous pressure upon her. It makes the problem of the meaning of life a problem of the first importance to her. She realizes that she has no time to waste, that she must face the facts, and that she must come to a decision. [155]

It may indeed do that. But growing old is also a motive—perhaps a more immediate and obvious motive, because it can bring with it actual experiences of various limitations. And all of us experience the passage of time in the form of deadlines. Attention to such common experiences may encourage us to focus on those aspects of our lives we find most wholesome. We can be motivated to action once we have learned to look past immediate pleasures and pains in order to see what lies ahead for us in our lives. This is *phronesis* (prudence, or good practical judgment), and its development marks the growth from infancy to youth to adulthood, and, perhaps for some people, to sagehood.

> Thus, our first point illustrating the vitality of death, and the point of departure from which all subsequent considerations derive their merit, is that authentic success and happiness in human existence demand uncompromising realism: we must understand and acknowledge the facts of life. And paradoxically, the most vitalizing fact of life is the utter inevitability of death! Man must constantly keep before his eyes the reality, the nature, and the inevitability of that fact. He must make every effort to understand exactly what his own death means to him. He must see the consequences of the knowledge that he is mortal. He must never let go of this insight. [155–156]

> We are always directly before the disintegration of our world, whether we happen to be thinking of it or not. [161]

But are we? In the case of our own death, we are certainly not perched on the brink of disintegration in the way we stand at the beginning of a hurricane, or at the end of the time allotted for a final exam in school, or at the funeral of a friend. These typical events in our lives are what give meanings to the ideas of disintegration, destruction, finality, loss, suffering, darkness, anxiety, turmoil, and terror. These events in life, which leave us in life, are experiences which cannot be the same kind of thing as our death. Death is not a darkness or a loss. Death is nothing like that, because unlike all other events, death does not leave us foundering, gasping, blind, and regretful in its wake. Death wakes us not at all, even though some people believe that it does, and find solace or meaning or courage in that belief.

* * *

The title of this book includes the phrase "the singularity of death". One of the reasons for saying that death is a singularity for each of us is that it happens to a person only once. Moreover, in a key respect it is unlike everything else that happens to a person; some of the usual ways of talking about the value of events in life (bad, good, harm, misfortune, etc.) no longer apply, or at least we must be cautious lest we assume too much. Death might seem to be a harm, a loss, a deprivation, a thwarting of desires, and so on. But a closer look at the alleged deprivation or loss reveals that usual patterns have been used to characterize unusual circumstances. Many writers try to show how death is an ordinary evil—ordinary in the sense that we can adequately describe the evil using familiar forms. In the following chapters I take issue with such views.

2

Radical Epicureanism

Prelude

My friend, who is a sort of metaphysical auto mechanic, advises me that my car might somehow be defective. Well, not defective, exactly, but somehow possibly bound to fare ill. I ask him whether I am pushing the engine too hard.

"No", he says.

Then are you saying that the body will rust, or the suspension fail, or something similar happen such that I will have to bring it in to the repair shop, or such that I will have to junk the car and get another?

"No."

Let me generalize as much as I can: Is there anything at all that I might eventually notice, or such that it might have some kind of effect that I might notice?

"No."

Then what do you mean that there might be something wrong—that the car might fare ill? How can there be something wrong if I will never experience it, nor any of its effects? What could possibly be the difference to me between my car's staying healthy and my car's "faring ill" in *your* strange sense of the term?

"Oh! Well, *you* will never notice the difference, since the difference will show up, if it shows up at all, only after you have sold the car or otherwise got rid of it. What's more, if there are to be any ill effects, direct or indirect, you will never be the worse for them."

What if I keep the car for 20 years?

"You will notice nothing."

But what if I sell the car tomorrow?

"There too the car might have problems. But, to repeat, you will not be able to experience them, or even learn about them. If the car fares ill, it will be when and only when you relinquish ownership such that you never again learn how the car fares, and such that however the car fares, it will have no effect, direct or indirect, on any portion of your life whatsoever."

I certainly am puzzled. You are apparently warning me of something that, by your own admission, can make no difference to me.

"The world does not revolve around you, you know. There are other people, and *they* can experience things too."

Then are you telling me to be careful lest I get rid of a car that subsequently causes problems for its new owner? You are advising me, therefore, to . . . to what? To have more frequent oil changes?

"Maybe. Or maybe more frequent oil changes would make things *worse*. As I say, you will not be able to know."

You mean it's possible that if I mistreat this car, then when the car has a new owner, it might be *better* off than had I not mistreated it?

"That's possible. See, you cannot know, one way or the other."

You're not giving me any helpful advice.

"I know. Sorry."

1 The argument, again

In the previous chapter I presented Epicurus's argument in the *Letter to Menoeceus* that "death is nothing to us". In this chapter I want to propose a restatement and elaboration of key elements of that famous passage. (Then I will take a quick look at a few objections, to be given additional discussion in further chapters.) Premises *A*, *B*, *C*, *D*, and *E* below are intended to support the conclusion *F*—a conclusion that will be slightly different from, but still in the spirit of, "death is nothing to us".

(A) *The Null Hypothesis*: A state of affairs which can have no effect on me, directly or indirectly, is no different, to me, from nothing at all. That is to say, something which occurs, but which can have no effect on any decisions I make, now or later—which cannot alter my appreciation of things, or change my mind, or cause me pain, pleasure, remorse, wonder, regret, joy, pride, and so on—is, for me, equivalent to that thing's not occurring at all.

As an extreme example of this, we can speculate that our universe will start to collapse back on itself in so many trillions of years, and eventually there will be nothing but a dot of superdense stuff which might explode and begin a new universe. Whether the superdense seed does spawn another universe, or whether it simply remains superdense forever, or whether there is only a temporary fizzle, or whether an accident of chaos produces nothing but inert stuff—whatever happens will be nothing to us, who will necessarily no longer be; nor will there continue to exist anything which we might have created. Even if a new universe will be formed within which there will be intelligences who speculate on whether they had predecessors, there is no way we can help them in their search for information about us, because all information about us will have been lost in the transition. Nothing of our present universe provides grounds for predicting the details of the new universe, just as nothing in our present universe allows us to retrodict into any universe prior to our own. Whatever there will be in the new universe is, as far as we can be concerned, equivalent to there not being a new universe at all. Of course, that is an extreme case; but the principle applies equally in the case of my own death.

(*B*) Epicurus's argument is often presented as an argument against the fear of death. While this is certainly a main conclusion, his argument is actually stronger than that. An important premise (ε in the previous chapter) is "that which while present causes no distress causes unnecessary pain when merely anticipated", and since the argument begins with "all good and bad consists in sense-experience", we can add another implication: "That which causes no *pleasure* when it comes is an empty *pleasure* in anticipation". So death has nothing to do with evil *or* good; not only is death not bad for us, it is not good for us either. We can make the argument stronger still: Since having died cannot create or change any of our experiences, and since what cannot come into our experiences is irrelevant to us, our death is in no way relevant to us. It is neither instrumentally nor intrinsically good or bad (nor, as we will see in Chapter 5, is it a loss or deprivation); it has nothing to give us; it takes nothing away from us; it cannot change any of our experiences, and it cannot give us new experiences. It is less relevant than a gnat, a mote of dust, a stray atom far away in space and time. What cannot change any of our experiences is precisely what nothing can do; hence, there is no prudential reason to treat our death as important for our life.

So the Null Hypothesis can be precisified to yield the *Hypothesis of Prudence*: Whatever satisfies the Null Hypothesis is of no prudential value to me. We can be even more precise:

> *The Hypothesis of Prudence Present*: I ought not now to care about any possible present occurrence which I know satisfies the Null Hypothesis.
>
> *The Hypothesis of Prudence Future*: I ought not now to care about any possible future occurrence which I know will satisfy the Null Hypothesis.

My interest here is in certain future events, and so my focus is on the second of that pair. I included the first for the sake of contrast. Still, the first one might seem to be rather peculiar. Could there be something present that I knew could have no effect on me? If I knew of such a thing, would it not ipso facto already have had, or be having, some effect (even if indirect) on me? Also, it would appear that the Hypothesis of Prudence Present cannot be ignored, for whatever might concern the Hypothesis of Prudence Future would later on have to do with the then-present. I will not pause to consider that matter closely here, because I want to discuss what attitude I ought to take toward all those possible future events which I know cannot affect me because they cannot become present for me, namely, all those events that may occur after my death. The Prudential Hypothesis deals with what I might reasonably be concerned about, and it says that the very idea of concern involves attitudes of value—care, hope, regret, anxiety, fear, and so on—in regards to how some thing or event might affect me (directly or indirectly). If I see no basis for any kind of concern about some thing or event, then such a thing or event has no value for me.

(C) *The Materialistic Hypothesis*: Death is annihilation. This was discussed at length in Chapter 1 (premise β).

(D) Once I am dead, all things will, for me, satisfy the Null Hypothesis. This might be somewhat misleading because of the awkwardness with which it is expressed. It is not as though there will be me, yet somehow nothing will affect me, or as though in death I will experience nothing. That way of expressing the matter presents me with a "me": there I am, as if right in front of myself, and I am dead, as though it were just another way of being, such as walking, or being offered a raise in salary, or in some other way participating in life. It is not easy to keep clearly before the mind that once dead, a person has ceased to be at all. It is difficult to find a more apt way of putting the matter, and in this we are perhaps not further along than some ancient Greeks for whom the possibility of a vacuum—a pure nothingness—was nonsensical: "What? The existence of nonexistence?!" We moderns have similar problems with articulating the nothingness of death. It is all very well from the outside, that is, from the point of view of a survivor of someone's death, because the survivor is still there. But the one who has died—where is he? What is death like for him? And to answer "Death is nothing at all for him" is to hint that there *is* a *him* and that therefore death must somehow be something *to him*, although in this case it goes by an odd and difficult-to-grasp name: nothing.[1]

(E) So I know that when I am dead, nothing will have any significance for me. Again, that is because there will be no me for anything to have significance for.

---

[1] Even to call it, as Anthony Brueckner and John Martin Fischer do, "an experiential blank" ("Why is Death Bad" and "The Asymmetry of Early Death and Late Birth") might hint that something could fill it up, as though it were a placeholder, temporarily empty. (Complete bibliographic information on this and all other sources in this book is provided in the Bibliography.)

(F) *The Indifference Conclusion*: Hence, I ought not now to care (i.e., I cannot now reasonably care) about the fact of my mortality or about any postmortem state of affairs.

There seem to be two kinds of indifference. I can be indifferent about the presence or absence of something—or, more generally, about which of two (or more) things or conditions obtain, in the sense that I do not care which one obtains, because I evaluate them, or their consequences for me, as being equally good (or equally bad or equally neither good nor bad) in both cases. I might, for example, be indifferent about which of two kinds of tea I might brew today. Or I might be indifferent about having tea at all. Obviously, the absence of tea and the presence of tea will have different consequences for me, but I might not care which ones are available to me today. In the second sense of indifference, I am indifferent because I cannot see that there can be any consequences at all for me, whether the situation obtains or not. I can be prudentially indifferent, for example, whether I die and the world continues, or whether I die and the world ends too.

* * *

That is how I want to interpret the Epicurean claim that "death is nothing to us". I do not say that Epicurus understood his own philosophy as incorporating the Null Hypothesis. If he had grounds for rejecting it, I find no clear indication of what they might have been. Still, the extant writings of Epicurus are so sparse that we must be prepared to be surprised by future finds. In any case, I think that the Null Hypothesis, or something very much like it, not only is reasonable in itself, but is also one of the components in the Epicurean attitude toward death, and the Indifference Conclusion is a straightforward gloss on Epicurus's premises α, γ, and ε of Chapter 1 ("all good and bad consists in sense-experience", "death is the privation of sense-experience", and "that which while present causes no distress causes unnecessary pain when it is still to come"). But just to be careful, I will not insist that the Indifference Conclusion and the consequences which I will adduce from it would be thoroughly congenial to Epicurus (although I think they ought to be). If they are not, then I will be defending a variation of the Epicurean attitude that death is nothing to us. I will continue to call a person who takes such an attitude an Epicurean, but more conservative readers might prefer to add a modifier: "Radical Epicurean", for example, or "Neo-Epicurean".[2]

---

[2] The following chapters are in part consistent with, but go beyond, some of what James Stacey Taylor defends, namely, "full-blooded Epicureanism". See his *Death, Posthumous Harm, and Bioethics*.

But the Epicurean view, as I have expressed it in the Indifference Conclusion, is not without problems. Let me give some attention to a few of them now; I will return to these and related issues in later chapters.

2 To thanatize

It might be thought that the Indifference Conclusion is its own undoing because it could be used in the following way. All things which at some point in my life I find to be significant will be of no significance to me once I am dead (because there will be no me); therefore, I ought not to care about them even now. And if that is so, then it appears that Epicureanism is recommending that no significance should be given to anything whatsoever—that not only our nonbeing but also our being, ought to be "nothing to us".

> To thanatize, we would have to renounce the many ties, concerns and projects that make us affirm life. No longer could we pursue any fulfilling desire that would be thwarted if we were to die. But it is precisely *these* goals whose satisfaction makes life worth living. These are the ones that give us a reason to think that living is good. Any aspiration capable of motivating us to live is one we can achieve only if we are alive; inevitably, then, any such hope would be frustrated by our deaths. In the end, then, to become indifferent to death, to adopt a death-tolerant personality, requires that we become indifferent to life. (Steven Luper, *Invulnerability*, 150–51)

But an "aspiration capable of motivating us to live" is one which a person has when she is in some circumstance wherein she is faced with the choice of living or dying; it is any situation in which she seriously contemplates suicide or letting herself die or be killed. Such situations are of course not common. The common situation is one wherein a person is motivated to begin or to participate in some project because she anticipates that working on the project (or else having or witnessing the fruits of the project) would bring her satisfaction or the relief of dissatisfaction. In such common situations the issue of death usually does not arise. She picks up a book because she anticipates that she will somehow profit from reading it. She gives to a local charity because she thinks there is a chance that she is making the neighborhood a bit better. She seeks a higher education because she anticipates that the fulfillment of many of her other goals will thereby be made more certain. All such endeavors might of course be cut short by her death; that goes without saying. Projects might also be cut short by her changing her mind about their value. But that she might change her mind, or the less likely possibility that she might die, are no reasons, by themselves, to refuse to embark on the project in the first place. The Epicurean advice is to fashion a satisfactory living for as long as it happens to last—a style of living wherein one is content with its several challenges, occasional rewards, intellectual stimulations, peaceful reposes, interactions with good friends, and freedom from superstitions. Even in an unusual situation—say, where the world is ending—an Epicurean might spend the remaining hours at her home weeding the garden, if that is what she enjoys.[3] Or suppose an Epicurean is faced with the guillotine. That she might die today instead of tomorrow or sixty years hence is irrelevant. It is precisely what does or could bring her satisfaction or dissatisfaction, directly or indirectly, which is significant to her.[4] When she is dead, necessarily nothing will affect her, and so *that*—the nothing of death, or the fact that all things past, present, and future will *then* be insignificant to her because there will be no her—is what she ought not now to fear or to have anxiety about or to be concerned about in any way.[5]

3 Wills

A will is an expression of a desire that after one's death one's property should be disposed of in specified ways. Such desires are, I imagine, virtually universal. Yet it would seem that according to the Indifference Conclusion an Epicurean ought not to care what happens to his property postmortem. Moreover, if an Epicurean does not care about what happens to his property, then will he also not care what happens to his friends and lovers after his death? Does the Indifference Conclusion not imply that buying life insurance would be imprudent because it could not benefit him, but only benefit certain persons after his death, when he cannot care at all (and so why care now about what cannot be cared about later)?

In short, how much of an ordinary person with the usual kinds of fundamental social concerns can an Epicurean be? How can an Epicurean be a *moral* being in

---

[3] This is just what one of the characters does as the world is ending in Stephen Baxter's wonderful short story "Last Contact".

[4] Epicurus says that this is so even in science: "Do not believe that there is any other goal to be achieved by the knowledge of meteorological phenomena, whether they are discussed in conjunction with [physics in general] or on their own, than freedom from disturbance and a secure conviction, just as with the rest [of physics]" (*Letter to Pythocles*; see also *PD* 11 and 12).

[5] Besides, the thwarting of a desire or hope or aspiration is bad for a person only if she ends up in a desire-thwarted or hope-thwarted or aspiration-thwarted condition. But death is precisely no condition at all.

any usual sense? Or must an Epicurean be a radically different character in society? If so, is an Epicurean to be emulated? Why would anyone want to be like that?

I will have more to say on these issues in Chapter 9, but for now we may wonder whether such problems might be solved by rejecting the Null Hypothesis while retaining, as much as possible, the remainder of Epicurus's argument. If the Hypothesis is rejected, then maybe there could be a way of claiming that "death is nothing to us" while at the same time appealing to ordinary sentiments about being concerned for what happens after one's death—not only for the disposition of one's property but also for the state of one's reputation, for the fate of one's loved ones, for the fate of future generations, for the fate of the world. It is the Null Hypothesis which seems to block all such concerns.

But I do not know how such an argument could be fashioned. It seems to me that if one's own death is nothing to one in any sense, then it must be nothing to one in all senses. Besides, I do not want to reject the Null Hypothesis or the Indifference Conclusion. I shall argue in Chapter 9 that even though Epicureanism does indeed have unusual consequences, such results are after all worthy of acceptance and that the reasons which might be offered against them are insufficient to work a *modus tollens* in order to reject the Indifference Conclusion.

4 Time

Some writers present the Epicurean view as involving an issue of time. Death, Epicurus says, is not bad for us now, when we are alive; and death will not be bad for us once we are dead; hence, there is no time at which death is bad for us. Ben Bradley says that Epicurus's real question is "*at what time* is a person's death bad for her?" (*Well-Being and Death*, 80; italics in original). So Bradley wonders about a "badness-at-a-time" relation.

> The question is not: When does the instrumentally bad event occur? The question is: When is the instrumentally bad event bad for its victim? When it comes to other bad events [sc. other than death], we do not think the time of the badness is the time of the instrumentally bad event. [*Well-Being and Death*, 86]

Here is one of Bradley's examples:

> Consider my toe-stubbing. The event went out of existence, but continued to be bad for me for a week afterwards. [*Well-Being and Death*, 80–81; see also "Eternalism and Death's Badness", esp. 273]

At what time was the toe-stubbing bad for him? The question is a bit confusing. The toe-stubbing can be dated, and so can the experience of pain. The toe-stubbing was bad insofar as it caused pain. The pain was bad while it lasted. But to ask for the "when" of the badness of toe-stubbing is ambiguous, if not simply perplexing.

It is true that Epicurus's argument makes temporal claims. But the real issue is not at what time something does or does not happen, nor at what time something is or is not bad for one. The important question is, rather, "How so? How is toe-stubbing bad for you?" The answer is easy: it causes pain. The pain might not occur as the toe-stubbing is happening, but if not, then the pain will arrive shortly thereafter. Perhaps there could be a question of time involved here; it would be "When are the bad experiences?", but not "When is the cause of the bad experiences bad for you?", even if both the cause and the experiences can be dated.

The case of annihilation is similar. Someone says "Death is bad for you". Epicurus might seem to put the issue in terms of time, but it amounts to asking "How so?" And the answer might be "It causes x", or "It makes x the case". And then, although we might inquire into the time of death, and although we might want to know the time (or period) of x, the crucial issue is not the time, but rather "What's bad about x?" or "How is x bad?" The "when" of x might or might not be useful in coming to identify the "how", but the important issue is the "how". If a good case could be made for the answer's being pain, suffering, or other aversive experiences, then there would be no need for any—or any further—information about the "when".

Bradley seems to be aware of this issue:

> The toe-stubbing is bad *because of* what happens at those times after the toe-stubbing. If not for the fact that it caused me to suffer harm at those later times, the toe-stubbing would not have been bad. [*Well-Being and Death*, 74–75]

This has it right (except for the odd shift in tenses). But then he says:

> Intuitively, we should say that my stubbing my toe [. . .] is (extrinsically) bad for me during my seven days of discomfort [. . .], but once I recover it is no longer bad for me. [88]

To ask "When was the pain bad?" is to ask "When did the pain occur?" But the toe-stubbing, not being bad in itself, is bad in the derivative sense of causing badness, and any question of "when" can be thought to ask for a dating of that cause or for a dating of the effects of that cause. Suppose the toe-stubbing to occur at 8:00 pm and the pain to begin a fraction of a second later and to last for seven days. Now the question "When was the toe-stubbing bad for you?" is obviously ambiguous, and one ought not to try to answer that question, but rather respond with "What, precisely, do you mean?"

It is an odd thing to say that a past toe-stubbing *is* even now bad. Why not say—what I am confident all English speakers would say without special prompting—"The toe-stubbing *was* bad for me because of the painful consequences, and the consequences are *still* bad for me (i.e., I'm still having pain)."

Bradley could hop around and say "Ow! Ow! This hurts! I wish the pain would stop!", but he would be thought foolish if he were to say "I wish the toe-stubbing would stop". If he did say such a thing, we would look at his toe and notice that it was not in contact with anything; we would tell him that the event had past; what remained was the toe-stubbing's bad consequences—in this case, some pain.[6]

5 Continuity

In his "Introduction" to *Our Stories*, John Martin Fischer finds problematic the Epicurean claim that death is nothing to us, because our ordinary view is that there is a kind of "*continuity* in the nature of harm"; there is "a spectrum of increasing intensity or significance", beginning with small pains, then damage to tissues, then loss of limbs or failure of organs. "Now suppose that (say) torture is so severe that it issues in the individual's death. It would seem natural that this would make the harm of the torture *even worse*" (15). This suggests to Fischer a division between what he calls Level One features that include "pain, suffering, and various kinds of impairment and damage", and a Level Two feature of "badness or misfortune" that supervenes on the Level One features. As the features at Level One increase in intensity, Level Two increases in severity of misfortune. But, he says, on the Epicurean view, "as the features that intuitively underwrite harm-attributions get more and more significant, this is reflected in

---

[6] It turns out that there are two good senses of "the toe-stubbing is still—or continues to be—bad for me", but they cannot be fit into Bradley's example. (1) He could reasonably complain "I wish the toe-stubbing would end" if in fact he kept bashing his toe repeatedly against some hard object. "I keep bashing my toe! I wish I could avoid that. It hurts when I do that. Oh! There, I did it again! When will it end? Ow! Ow!" That, I say, would be understandable. (2) Suppose Bradley stubs his toe and complains of the pain. I tell him "Well, that's very common. But you know, not all toe-stubbings are painful, and if you practice toe-stubbing (I'll show you how), you can eventually get to the point where toe-stubbing is not bad." So he practices in the way I indicate. Some months later I meet him and ask "How's it going with the toe-stubbing?" and he answers "Not good! The toe-stubbing is still bad for me—it's still causing me pain each time." In this case, of course, he is referring not to a single past instance of toe-stubbing, but rather to a continuing pattern that he has been unable to control.

greater harm *until we get to death*, where there is suddenly no harm at all" (15).⁷ Since continuity is more to be prized than discontinuity, we ought to reject the discontinuity arising from the Epicurean view.

I agree that discontinuity begs for explanation. We tend to notice and be suspicious of interruptions to familiar patterns. But I do not see that the Epicurean has proposed something in need of exceptional explanation, because the Epicurean view *does* follow an expected pattern. Granted that as the Level One features of pain and suffering increase, the Level Two feature of misfortune increases: a broken arm is a greater misfortune than a hangnail. Then at death, according to the Epicurean, the Level Two feature of misfortune ceases. But that is not a problem; such a cessation is precisely what is to be expected if Level Two is to somehow track Level One as Fischer recommends. Level Two misfortune ceases at death because the Level One features of pain and suffering cease there as well. If Level Two misfortune did increase at (or past?) the point of death, then one would expect that Level One pain and suffering would increase too. But death puts a stop to pain and suffering, and so it is the anti-Epicurean claim, and not the Epicurean view, that violates the expected pattern: the anti-Epicurean view sees a discontinuity if badness is supposed to have increased just when pain and suffering have vanished (and cannot return).

The Epicurean might allow Fischer to use the term "harm" to characterize death; at least it would not be improper to say that the body is damaged and therefore harmed. But that is not what the Epicurean is concerned about when he says that "death is nothing to us". The ultimate issue is whether our peace of mind is taken from us (which damage to tissue might do, but which death logically cannot do); or, to put it another way: "Why should I care?" At death there is severe damage to the organism, but that will be a condition of my body about which I need not ever care as long as I understand annihilation rightly. As Level One pain increases—from, say, a hangnail to a broken arm—so might my concern. But at death—at the terminus of Level One—there is no more pain, and no more possibility of pain, and so my concern vanishes too.

Moreover, in Level One Fischer has classified pain and suffering together with damage and impairment. But that encourages a prejudgment of the issues, because there seem to be two different categories lumped together as "Level

---

⁷ Similarly, Fred Feldman says, "it would be surprising if it were to turn out that we need two independent accounts of what is meant by statements to the effect that something is bad for someone: one account of the meaning of such a statement when the relevant object is something other than the person's death, and another account of the meaning of such a statement when the relevant object is the person's death. Surely the statement about death ought to be nothing more than an interesting instance of the general sort of statement" (*Confrontations with the Reaper*, 148f).

One". We can experience damage which is not (or need not be) pain or suffering nor the cause of pain or suffering. And there are mental sufferings which are unrelated to bodily damage or impairment. Both of these observations are parts of the Epicurean philosophy, and they show up prominently elsewhere as well (in Stoicism and Buddhism, for example).

Also, there is nothing unexpected about all sorts of radical "discontinuities" at death. We expect that at death there is suddenly no more aging; there is a loss of personality, sense of humor, desire for chocolate, and annoyance at politicians; doctors stop trying to cure the fatal disease; and there are many other familiar and commonsense "discontinuities" associated with death, all of which are consistent with the Epicurean view.

What happens if we follow Fischer and divide evils into standard types, such as unpleasant experiences, and nonstandard types, which include death (*Our Stories*, 15)? Well, it seems to me that we get to the Epicurean position in effect, even if different names are used. That is, if death is evil-like in some nonstandard way, it must be acknowledged that this nonstandard evil is nonstandard because, unlike standard evils, it cannot possibly involve pain or suffering. A generous Epicurean will let you have any name you wish, including "nonstandard evil", only he will insist that in return you agree to draw the proper conclusion about death, namely, that there is nothing to be concerned about, to fear, to regret, to avoid, to rue, to rage against. If that is accounted as a nonstandard evil, then it is so nonstandard that we ought to wonder why, aside from superstitions and old habits, anyone would want to call it any kind of evil at all.[8]

> I suggest that the appeal of continuity (understood and applied as above) might constitute at least a small consideration on behalf of the ordinary view that death can indeed be a bad thing for the individual who dies. [Fischer, *Our Stories*, 16]

But even if that continuity were acceptable, it would not answer the Epicurean challenge. When Epicureans say that "death is nothing to us", they do not mean to deny that there could be unusual or nonstandard ways in which to relate death to things and events in life, or that there might be all sorts of Cambridge changes that are expressed in the same forms that describe actual changes.[9] The claim,

---

[8] Cf. Rosenbaum's distinction between "concrete bad" and "abstract bad" in "Appraising Death in Human Life" and "Concepts of Value and Ideas about Death".

[9] A so-called Cambridge change is usually thought of as a relation in which something participates, as contrasted with a real change in or to that something. A man who breaks an arm undergoes a real change. If his wife dies, he "Cambridge-changes" from a husband into a widower. (But if *he* subsequently dies, does the dead wife "Cambridge-change" into a widow?)

rather, is that death (like an undetected, and necessarily effectless betrayal—a nominal betrayal only) is nothing to be concerned about.[10]

Instead, then, of saying that "the Epicurean will insist that [. . .] we should resist the underlying picture that favors continuity", Fischer ought to say that the Epicurean resists the underlying picture (or assumptions) that favor *the particular kind* of continuity which Fischer is advocating. We should instead accept a different continuity—the one which the Epicurean has been trying to point out. A claim that death is a deprivation might suggest the following kind of continuity: To be deprived is to be prevented from having good things which were in some way expected; events can deprive a person of adequate schooling, of a fulfilling career, and so on; and in the case of death, the person will get none of the good things which the person might have enjoyed had death not occurred. An Epicurean, however, will point out the salient *discontinuities* in that line of thinking. For example, as I will explain in greater detail in Chapter 5, all ordinary deprivations require a subject who is in a deprived condition; why make death a special case? Epicureanism can be seen to propose a different continuity: Your life experiences have taught you that you need not be fearful of events which you have good reason to believe you will not (indeed, cannot) regret; you know that it will be impossible for you to regret that you have died; therefore, etc.

* * *

So much then for an introduction to some of the issues that will occupy us in subsequent chapters. But before we get there, it is necessary to clear up an important misunderstanding about how Epicurus's conclusion that "death is nothing to us" applies to the case of premature death.

---

[10] For an extended argument on this issue, see my "Death and Other Nothings".

3

Premature Death and the Complete Life

Prelude

A devilish imp appears in a puff of smoke on my shoulder. "If you continue as you are now", it says in an admonishing tone, "investing your life in these grand projects, they will all come to naught sometime after your death. You are, therefore, in a harmed condition even now: a dark shadow of misfortune is cast backwards upon you from those postmortem failures. But of course, there is no way you can experience any effects of such postmortem misfortunes during your life; nor will you be able to know about or experience any effects of them after you have ceased to exist."

An angelic imp appears on my other shoulder in a halo of gentle light. "If you continue as you are now", it says in a reassuring tone, "investing your life in these grand projects, they will bear marvelous fruit sometime after your death. You are, therefore, in a blessed condition even now: a bright glow of fortune is cast backwards upon you from those postmortem goods. But of course, there is no way you can experience any effects of such postmortem successes during your life; nor will you be able to know about or experience any effects of them after you have ceased to exist."

A third imp appears in a flash of insight in my cerebral cortex. "Wouldn't it be pleasant to relax with a game of backgammon?"

1 The challenge

Most modern philosophers who are acquainted with Epicurus's works agree with him in holding some version of materialism along with some of the implications thereof. Epicurus says "when we exist, death is not yet present, and when death is present, then we do not exist" (*Let Men* 125), and that is understood by most philosophers to be a claim that when a person dies the person ceases to exist; there is no afterlife—no disembodied soul that continues somehow and that can have postmortem experiences (good, bad, or otherwise). Being dead, therefore, cannot be a bad thing, because there is no longer a person to fare well or ill. So at least part of Epicurus's argument that "death is nothing to us" seems to find a sympathetic audience among many philosophers.

But there is a great reluctance to follow Epicurus any further. In particular, one of the important anti-Epicurean claims is that since death is the permanent loss of life (and hence the prevention of further life), it is or represents a harm or misfortune, and so it is reasonable to have a fear of it (or to be worried, concerned, or unhappy about it). With only a few exceptions, modern philosophers who have anything to say about the Epicurean view that death really is nothing to be concerned about find it to be, at best, difficult to support (and at worst absurd) when the issue is not being dead, but rather death as loss of life. It then becomes an interesting philosophical exercise for them to explain how Epicurus goes wrong, and how the end of life can be a significant harm or misfortune and therefore not "nothing to us". The most popular approach (it is virtually the only game in town) is to try to show how death is bad when it is some kind of loss or deprivation of good things. There are variations on that theme, and we will examine them more closely in Chapter 5.

But a few philosophers think that the fuller Epicurean view—that is, beyond the simple claim that being dead cannot be bad—is not as unsupportable as it has sometimes been made out to be. In the present chapter I want to look at some attempts to rescue Epicurus from a particular challenge: Epicurus says that being dead cannot be bad, but he appears to say nothing about what people are most afraid of, namely, *premature* death.

2 Rescue attempts

It is important to note that this challenge to Epicurus is not concerned simply about length of life, but rather about a life that is somehow shorter than it ought to be—a life that is cut off before it reaches completion. A distinction can be made between, on the one hand, mortality—the fact that life is naturally finite—and, on the other hand, a particular life that ends too soon. The latter, according to the challenge, is an aspect of death that the Epicurean view does not deal with. A fine example of this criticism is found in Gisela Striker's influential remarks:

> What we are rightly concerned about when we are afraid of dying is completeness as opposed to incompleteness, and that is only incidentally a matter of sheer length of time. ["Commentary on Mitsis", 325[1]]

---

[1] Complete bibliographic information on this and all other sources in this book is provided in the Bibliography.

> While the fear of mortality is arguably irrational and might be allayed by arguments like those of Lucretius, those arguments have no force whatsoever in the case of premature death. [325]

> It seems to me that his [Epicurus's] arguments might have some merit if it were meant to address the fear of mortality, but it will not serve to establish that it makes no difference whether we have a very short or a very long life, simply because a very short life could not possibly be complete. [327]

Some writers, intending to help Epicurus out on this issue, have tried to show that he can after all handle the issue of premature death if we look to additional arguments and implications drawn from Epicurean texts.[2]

A Rescue attempt will first have to make more precise the rather vague notion of premature death. The idea of prematurity seems to have to do with something's ending too soon; it is cut short when it could have gone on longer. But cut off how—in what way? Here are a few closely related possibilities.

We might interpret "premature" as meaning "before a normal life span".[3] Unfortunately, there are average or expected life spans for different living things and in different environments. A human baby born today in Japan can be expected to live for 80 or 90 years, whereas a baby born in Afghanistan has a life expectancy of about half that. Bowhead whales are thought to be capable of living for two centuries. Carrots live for two years. Mayflies last for about a day. If the kind of organism and its environment are taken into account, then are we willing to say that an Afghani who died at forty-five did not die prematurely? If on the other hand we look to future developments in medicine and molecular nanotechnology, we might reasonably predict that average human life spans could increase without clear limits. What would "premature" mean then? It seems that "before a normal life span" is as unhelpfully vague as "premature".[4]

---

[2] Aspects of Rescue arguments can be found in these publications: Annas, *The Morality of Happiness*, chapter 15; Armstrong, "All things to All Men"; Braddock, "Epicureanism, Death, and the Good Life"; Erler and Schofield, "Epicurean Ethics"; Görler, "Storing Up Past Pleasures"; Hetherington, "Where is the Harm in Dying Prematurely?"; Lesses, "Happiness, Completeness, and Indifference to Death"; Luper, "Exhausting Life"; Miller, "Epicurus on the Art of Dying"; Mitsis, "Epicurus on Death and the Duration of Life"; Reinhardt, "The Speech of Nature"; Rosenbaum, "Epicurus on Pleasure and the Complete Life"; Sanders, "Philodemus and the Fear of Premature Death"; Tsouna, "Rationality and the Fear of Death"; Tsouna, *The Ethics of Philodemus*, chapter 10; Warren, "Epicurean Immortality"; Warren, "Lucretius, Symmetry Arguments, and Fearing Death"; Warren, *Facing Death*, chapter 4; Warren, "Removing Fear". Something nearly identical to Rescue arguments might apply to the Cyrenaics: see Kurt Lampe, *The Birth of Hedonism*: "living pleasantly is a final and comprehensive end. Moreover, if we could accomplish the goal of living pleasantly, there would be nothing further to desire" (88), and "this may be the kernel of the Cyrenaics' argument against the fear of death" (238, n84).

[3] Striker says that "premature" can mean "as yet far from having lived the lifespan of a normal human being" ("Commentary on Mitsis", 325).

[4] A similar point is made by Kirk Sanders, "Philodemus and the Fear of Premature Death", 221.

"Premature" could mean "before the life-story is finished". Some people think of a life (especially a human life) as having a kind of descriptive narrative. A story is expected to go on for a while and then end in some appropriate chapter, before which the story would be unfinished. So a premature death would be a death before the life's descriptive narrative is concluded.[5] But what is to be the story? There are all sorts. A person is born, grows up into a life of crime and violence, and, even before reaching middle age, falls victim to a policeman's bullet. That story has a discernable arc—a shape suitable for novels and movies. Or a person is born, grows up into an uninspired but contented life of utter sameness, and finally dies peacefully at a ripe old age. That story is boring. But what is to count as premature is still unhelpfully vague. Where is the prematurity in either story?

J. David Velleman offers an account. Events later in one's life can give meaning to earlier events and hence to the life story. This has important implications for premature death, for "by middle age, one finds oneself composing the climax to a particular story—a story that is now determinate enough to be spoiled".[6] The short version of the argument is this: A person "can care about what his life story is like, and a premature death can spoil the story of his life. Hence death can harm a person" (357).

But this is not convincing (even with the detailed discussion that Velleman gives us, but which I have omitted here). First of all, one wonders whether a life can be understood as narrative.[7] Perhaps some lives can, but when I look at my own life, I do not know whether there is one narrative that will gather up all the things and events of my life and make out of them a coherent story. It seems to me that all the actions, desires, ambitions, plans, experiences, persons, objects, and events that have so far had some significant effects on my further actions, desires, plans, and so on could make for a practically endless series of plotlines. Even if a person can care about *a* life story, will the person care about *every* story of that life? Moreover, suppose that death before one of those stories has reached its conclusion (assuming, what might be uncommon, that one is working toward some more or less well-defined conclusion to a particular life story; this does not seem to describe me) could reasonably be said to harm the story—to make the story less interesting, say, or less inviting (as if there had

---

[5] "It is possible to be concerned about how the story of that life will turn out. It seems reasonable, therefore, to be concerned about the possibility of death cutting off that life before its envisaged conclusion" (Warren, *Facing Death*, 121–22).

[6] "Well-Being and Time", 341. See also his "Narrative Explanation".

[7] For some spirited criticisms of the notion that persons are defined or properly described by life narratives, see Galen Strawson, "Against Narrativity".

been a choice[8]). Even with that supposition, harm to a story of a person does not necessarily harm the person whose story it is. Consider, for example, a person who works with good prospects of success at some grand project—a business empire, say, or some important social reconstruction. Imagine that the person suddenly dies. The project, we might then say, remains in an unfinished state, and perhaps even falls to ruin, and so it might not be unreasonable to say that it (or the story that includes it) has been harmed. But how has the person (now an experson) been harmed? Some narratives of the person's life, as people would tell them, would not fail to include the postmortem collapse of the person's life work, and so such stories might seem tragic. But in the absence of compelling argument, whatever tragedy there might be in the ruined project cannot touch the person, who is no more.[9]

There is another, but closely related, notion of "premature" that might be tried. A death might be said to be premature if it occurs before the life (not a story of the life, but the life itself) is somehow "complete". Striker's analogy is an opera-goer.

> The eighteen year old who wants to continue living is like someone who has watched the first act of an opera and is justifiably annoyed if the performance breaks off at this point. He is angry, not because he had thought he was going to spend three hours instead of only one, but because he wanted to see the entire opera, not just a part of it. On the other hand, the person who worries about being mortal might be compared to someone who wished the opera would never end. ["Commentary on Mitsis", 325][10]

Let us investigate the possibility of "premature death" as meaning "incomplete life", because, even though both terms are vague, they are used by Striker (and by some Rescuers) as characterizing the same issue. In order for the Rescuers to show that

---

[8] "Deciding when to die [. . .] is rather like deciding when and how to end a story" (Velleman, "Well-Being and Time", 346).

[9] One might try to claim that in fact there is a tragedy. The tragedy is that the person's story, while he is still living, is going to be, after his death, a tragedy: Even if postmortem events can not affect him (i.e., in life), later events can affect the meaning of earlier events in the life story; so the fact that before his death his life story was going to have a tragic ending means that before his death he was living an unenviable narrative (even if he did not know it). This is not unlike the view of George Pitcher ("The Misfortunes of the Dead") and Joel Feinberg ("Harm to Others"), who claim that such a person was living in a "backwards shadow" of misfortune. But if it is claimed that the antemortem person is misfortunate because of what is going to happen postmortem, then what is going to happen postmortem (even assuming that "what is going to happen" can be considered to be some kind of fact) would have to be something bad for him, and to claim that the postmortem event is going to be bad for him would be to assume the very thing that the Epicurean view denies. But this issue takes us off in another direction. I gave it some closer attention in my "Death and Other Nothings".

[10] See also Annas, *The Morality of Happiness*, 346.

Epicureanism can withstand the challenge raised by the issue of premature death, they try to strengthen his position by showing that there are Epicurean texts that describe a sense of "complete life" such that although death before the complete life is reached would be premature, one can nevertheless achieve the complete life (even at an early age), such that once one has achieved it, death at any time thereafter can no longer be premature. But clearly death can terminate a life that would otherwise have continued to be a good life, perhaps for a long time, so the notion of completeness that is needed cannot rely only on duration; it is not mere length of life that is important. Nor, similarly, is it "a normal life span", nor "a life narrative", even if such terms seem to point toward some notion of completeness.

We might get closer to an idea of "complete life" by searching Epicurean texts for answers to questions such as: What good thing, or what part of a life or aspect of life, could there be such that having achieved it, life would be complete, and there would be no need to prolong life in order to achieve more of it? What kind of good would be such that having obtained it, death would not be a threat? What kind of good could be such that having achieved it, one would not rationally fear death? Those questions represent the challenge raised by the prospect of the badness of a premature death, and Rescuers have suggested that the resources for a satisfactory response are already available in Epicurean texts if we read them carefully. Let us consider a few of them.

> Unlimited time and limited time contain equal pleasure, if one measures its limits by reasoning. [PD 19]
>
> The flesh took the limits of pleasure to be unlimited, and [only] an unlimited time would have provided it. But the intellect, reasoning out the goal and limit of the flesh and dissolving the fears of eternity, provided us with the perfect way of life and had no further need of unlimited time. But it [the intellect] did not flee pleasure, and even when circumstances caused an exit from life it did not die as though it were lacking any aspect of the best life. [PD 20]
>
> And just as he [the wise person] does not unconditionally choose the largest amount of food but the most pleasant food, so he savours not the longest time but the most pleasant. [Let Men 126]

We will consider these passages, and others, anon. But first it is crucial for the Rescue attempts that we understand a distinction. Epicurus tells us that the goal of the best life is pleasure. But we must be careful with this term. Here is Epicurus:

> So when we say that pleasure is the goal we do not mean the pleasures of the profligate or the pleasures of consumption, as some believe, either from ignorance and disagreement or from deliberate misinterpretation, but rather the

lack of pain in the body and disturbance in the soul. For it is not drinking bouts and continuous partying and enjoying boys and women, or consuming fish and the other dainties of an extravagant table, which produce the pleasant life, but sober calculation which searches out the reasons for every choice and avoidance and drives out the opinions which are the source of the greatest turmoil for men's souls. [*Let Men* 131–32]

Diogenes Laërtius reports that these two notions of pleasure have the names "katastematic pleasure" and "kinetic pleasure":

> He [Epicurus] disagrees with the Cyrenaics on the question of pleasure. For they do not admit katastematic pleasure, but only kinetic pleasure, and he admits both types in both the body and the soul [. . .]. 'For freedom from disturbance and freedom from suffering are katastematic pleasures; and joy and delight are viewed as kinetic and active'. [*Lives* 10.136]
>
> They [the Cyrenaics] hold that the removal of the feeling of pain is not pleasure, as Epicurus said it was, and that absence of pleasure is not pain. For both are kinetic, while neither absence of pain nor absence of pleasure is a motion, since absence of pain is like the condition [*katastasis*] of somebody who is asleep. [*Lives* 2.89]
>
> Happiness is conceived of in two ways: the highest happiness, which is that of god and does not admit of further intensification, and that which <is determined by> the addition and subtraction of pleasures. [*Lives* 10.121a]

It is instructive to see how Cicero objects to such claims:

> But if one thinks that happiness is produced by pleasure, how can he consistently deny that pleasure is increased by duration? If it is not, pain is not either. Or if pain is worse the longer it lasts, is not pleasure rendered more desirable by continuance? [*De fin* II.87]

Cicero has evidently not here taken into account the Epicurean distinction between the two kinds of pleasure.[11] Kinetic pleasures are such that they wax and wane, come and go. Katastematic pleasure, on the other hand, is not momentary; it is rather a "static" and satisfactory condition of living without pain, and it is said to be "complete" at all moments of its experience. Katastematic pleasure

---

[11] Cicero is well aware of the distinction, but he is bothered (and says so at great length) by what he takes to be an inappropriate and misleading use of either the Latin *voluptas* or the Greek *hēdonē* for the so-called katastematic variety; see, for example, *De Fin* II *passim*, and especially this: "He [Epicurus] calls a thing pleasure that no one ever called by that name before; he confounds two things that are distinct. [. . .] Now that is language that does not call for a philosopher to answer it,—it ought to be put down by the police" (II.30).

(hinted at, but not named, in *PD* 3, 18, 19, 20, 21, and elsewhere) cannot be more satisfactory than it already is; prolonging one's life cannot increase completeness.[12] Such a pleasurable living can be described as *aponia* (a condition free of physical pain) and *ataraxia* (a condition free of mental turmoil—a condition of contentment or tranquillity). Since mental pains and pleasures are said to be more important than physical pains and pleasures, the perfect life is achieved when one has *ataraxia*.

This distinction between katastematic and kinetic pleasure implies that if a person seeks kinetic pleasure, then when the pleasure decreases or disappears (as it always does), the person will seek to increase it, or to renew it, or to find new kinetic pleasures. But this means that death will prevent the person from repeating it or from having more (or more intense) kinetic pleasures, and it would be no wonder that death would be thought to be some sort of misfortune. So when Epicurus tells us that the complete or perfect life is a life of pleasure, he cannot mean kinetic pleasure but rather katastematic pleasure. Once one has achieved *ataraxia*, a life of katastematic pleasure, one has achieved the complete life, and going on longer will not make such a life more complete.

The Rescuers say that we can see how this is implied in *PD* 20. I have marked out and labeled it into three sections, and I will comment on each below.

> [A] The flesh took the limits of pleasure to be unlimited, and [only] an unlimited time would have provided it.
>
> [B] But the intellect, reasoning out the goal and limit of the flesh and dissolving the fears of eternity, provided us with the perfect way of life and had no further need of unlimited time.
>
> [C] But it [the intellect] did not flee pleasure, and even when circumstances caused an exit from life it did not die as though it were lacking any aspect of the best life.

Comments on section A: Our natural desires for kinetic pleasures (food, drink, sex, power, and many other things that we find attractive) are insatiable. The fine banquet we enjoy tonight will give way for a desire for food and drink tomorrow. We have, as Hobbes noted, "a perpetual and restlesse desire of Power

---

[12] A common analogy is to health as an all-or-nothing property. When one is healthy, one does not seek to prolong one's life in order to attain more health. Both Furley ("Nothing to Us?", 81–82) and Rosenbaum ("Epicurus on Pleasure and the Complete Life", 26–27) use this metaphor. Rosenbaum also recommends that "complete living" is more apt than "complete life", because the latter implies a kind of time dependency that the former does not (37).

after power" (and, he might have added, also for food, sex, drink, and so on).[13] These desires are for kinetic pleasures, and there is no way that a life devoted to trying to fulfill such desires can ever be finally satisfied.

Section B: When we understand which of our desires need to be satisfied (to avoid pain) and which do not (cf. *Let Men* 127, *PD* 3, 8, 18), we will realize that we do not need to keep desiring more and more ("our mouths forever agape", as Lucretius puts it in *De Rerum Natura* 3.1084), in order to be content. *Let Men* 128 expresses this idea, albeit with an uncertain use of "pleasure":

> The health of the body and the freedom of the soul from disturbance [. . .] is the goal of a blessed life. [. . .] As soon as we achieve this state every storm in the soul is dispelled, since the animal is not in a position to go after some need nor to seek something else to complete the good of the body and the soul. For we are in need of pleasure only when we are in pain because of the absence of pleasure, and when we are not in pain, then we no longer need pleasure.

In part C we learn that the wise person does not shun kinetic pleasures (there is nothing wrong with such pleasures as long as they do not give rise to pain later on: *Let Men* 129–30, *PD* 8), nor, when he faces death, does he think that anything was lacking in his life, because he has already achieved the complete life.

The Rescuers hope to make out an argument that if we achieve this "perfect way of life" with "no further need of unlimited time", then our having only finite time will not be grounds for anxiety, because the complete life cannot be made more complete by going on longer, nor can death cut short what was already complete; death cannot make it the case that we did not have all that we could have had. This would not be so if the goal of the "blessed life" were the amassing of kinetic pleasures. A person who strives for kinetic pleasures thinks that his death will be bad for him because there are always more kinetic pleasures to be had (and so he will want to not die), whereas if a person has reached katastematic pleasure, then he has achieved the goal; his life is complete (or perfect) and it will not matter whether he lives longer or not. This can be seen especially in the case of the Epicurean Sage, whose life is characterized by katastematic pleasure; it is not threatened with the loss of any good by a shorter life (i.e., by death when

---

[13] "Continual Success in obtaining those things which a man from time to time desireth, that is to say, continual prospering, is that men call FELICITY; I mean the Felicity of this life. For there is no such thing as perpetual Tranquillity of mind, while we live here; because Life itself is but Motion, and can never be without Desire" (*Leviathan*, chapter 6).

his life could have gone on longer); nothing can be added to make that life even better than it already is (Cf. VS 42[14], PD 19).

Let this be a synopsis of the Rescue argument that Epicurus does indeed deal with the issue of premature death:

1. Some people fear untimely death because they hope to get more goods (or pleasures) by living longer.
2. So the ordinary fear of premature death is the result of treating pleasures as kinetic.
3. But Epicurus says that what is truly good and complete (katastematic pleasure) does not depend on duration, and so it is wrong to think that a longer life (of true pleasure) can be made more satisfactory.
4. Hence, there could not be an untimely death for one who has achieved a life of katastematic pleasure.
5. So if we achieved a complete life (a "perfect way of life"), we would not fear a premature death.

3 Critique of Rescue arguments

Rescue arguments, however scholarly and well-intentioned they may be, are misguided.

3.1 Weak evidence

The first problem is that the textual evidence is weak. Even one of the Rescuers, having tried to make katastematic pleasure the ground for completeness, and then to make completeness the ground for not fearing death, warns us that "the most significant Epicurean discussions of the completeness of a life, however, are to be found not in any context which is explicitly concerned simply with the fear of death".[15] We may add that in the Epicurean texts, discussions of pleasure (of any sort) are never found to form a basis for arguments about not fearing

---

[14] VS = *Vatican Sayings*, a collection of short maxims discovered in the Vatican in the late 1800s. Most of them are of unknown origin, but many could be from Epicurean authors. (A few of them are in fact identical to *PD*s.)

[15] Warren, *Facing Death*, 126. Moreover, Epicureans' claims about a complete life "is perhaps the least plausible of the Epicurean arguments, not simply because it relies heavily on other aspects of Epicurean theory [. . .], but because it relies heavily on counterintuitive and highly debatable elements of the Epicurean theory, in particular the claim that pleasure cannot be increased beyond the absence of all pain" (217).

death (or about death's irrelevance). If the Rescue attempts were correct in teasing out the details of such a central issue, we would expect to find not only completeness but also pleasure (especially when characterized as katastematic) having a prominent foundational role in the Epicurean arguments against the reasonableness of the fear of death. But we do not find any clear connection in the required way. Pleasure is conspicuous by its absence, not only in Epicurus's central argument about death in *Let Men* 124–25 (where Menoeceus is advised to attend to the elements that *make for*, but are not the *result of*, the good life, among which is the thought that death is nothing to us) but also in Lucretius's lengthy arguments in *De Rerum Natura* (3.417–829) that the soul is mortal, along with the companion claim that death is not to be feared: "Therefore death is nothing to us, of no concern whatsoever, once it is appreciated that the mind has a mortal nature" (3.830). Neither Epicurus nor Lucretius says anything like "death can be understood as being nothing to us once we have katastematic pleasure".

In Epicurus's writings, getting rid of the fear of death (in any form) is an aid in attaining contentment, not a result of contentment:

> Hence, a correct knowledge of the fact that death is nothing to us makes the mortality of life a matter for contentment, not by adding a limitless time [to life] but by removing the longing for immortality. For there is nothing fearful in life for one who has grasped that there is nothing fearful in the absence of life. [*Let Men* 125]

What produces the pleasant life is "sober calculation which searches out the reasons for every choice and avoidance and drives out the opinions which are the source of the greatest turmoil for men's souls" (132), and one of the opinions that reasoning is to drive out is that death is bad. And at 133 the absence of the fear of death is mentioned as one of the ingredients of the good life: "For who do you believe is better than a man who [. . .] is always fearless about death, has reasoned out the natural goal of life and understands that the limit of good things is easy to achieve completely [. . .]?"

Cicero nowhere suggests that Epicurus claims that achieving the perfect life allows one to be rid of a fear of death (premature or otherwise). Although not a reliable presenter of Epicurean views, Cicero can be expected to have mentioned such an important doctrine somewhere. The closest he comes is *De fin* I.40–41, where he has us imagine a person living in a condition that could not be "more excellent or more desirable". "One so situated must possess in the first place a strength of mind that is proof against all fear of death or of pain; he will know that death means complete unconsciousness, and that pain is generally light if long and short if strong [. . .]. Let such a man moreover have no dread of supernatural power [. . .]." All this is almost a restatement of the *tetrapharmakos*,[16] and notice why the man is said to not fear death: because he knows that death is "complete unconsciousness", not because now his life is perfect.

Perhaps some possible candidates for Rescue interpretations might be the final sentence of *PD* 20, or the speech of Nature in Book 3 of Lucretius's *De Rerum Natura*, or some sections of Philodemus's *On Death*. But even in those cases the Rescue interpretations are unconvincing, as I will discuss in the next section.

3.2 Questionable interpretations

A second problem with the Rescue attempts is that some of the textual evidence is misinterpreted. Let us return to *PD* 19 and *PD* 20. They may seem at first glance to have something to do with length of life (and hence with death as the terminus of life's length). But that is not their point. To take *PD* 19 and 20 as implying something about death (or length of life) is to misunderstand Epicurus's views on both pleasure and death. *PD* 19 and 20 tell us something about how and how not to live. They can be summarized this way: "If you strive for kinetic pleasures—if you attend to the pleasures of the flesh—then you will never find satisfaction, even if you went on like that forever. On the other hand, if you attend to katastematic pleasures, then contentment is not hard to find." These claims are not difficult to understand, and notice that they say nothing directly about death.

PD 19's claim that infinite time and finite time contain equal pleasure (if one judges them by reason) has perplexed some scholars. I interpret it this way: Pain is, or contains, or calls up, a motive away from itself, as though it were bent on self-destruction. The absence of pain is said to be a kind of pleasure; let us call it "satisfaction", because a condition of satisfaction has no motive to be rid of itself, although there can be gentle desires for variations. For example, a summer afternoon sipping lemonade on the veranda and talking with friends might give way to the desire for a light supper before joining a friend for a movie. The next day might be spent reading and writing, or painting, or hiking. To the extent that one finds one's activities satisfying, one has no motive to work great changes. If

---

[16] The "four-fold cure" for the main ills of an unhappy life (said to be expressed in the *Principal Doctrines*) may be simplified to: Do not fear the gods, do not fear death, what is good is easy to get, and what is bad is easy to endure.

one is satisfied (and has reasonable expectations of continuing this way and not dropping into anxiety or depression or other turmoil), then one can say that one is leading a good—a pleasant, an enjoyable—life, and one can consider one's life perfect or completely happy.

This already pleasant life is to be contrasted with a thrill-seeking, or at least a pleasure-seeking lifestyle wherein the absence of some "positive" pleasure (as we might say) moves one to seek more, or other, or more intense pleasures, as though without them one would be bored, at a loss, perhaps full of anxiety for another "fix".

Earlier I said that *PD* 20 might be thought to be a good candidate for a Rescue interpretation, so let us revisit it. Again, I have made a division for the sake of discussion.

> [A] The flesh took the limits of pleasure to be unlimited, and [only] an unlimited time would have provided it.
>
> [B] But the intellect, reasoning out the goal and limit of the flesh and dissolving the fears of eternity, provided us with the perfect way of life and had no further need of unlimited time.
>
> [C] But it [the intellect] did not flee pleasure, and even when circumstances caused an exit from life it did not die as though it were lacking any aspect of the best life.

Comments on part A: We cannot be satisfied if our lives are characterized by seeking kinetic pleasures, because we will never reach satisfaction that way. The Rescuers go a step further and suggest that this way of life can produce a fear of death, because the end of life will be premature in the sense that we will not be able to continue having more and more kinetic pleasures. But this implication is misguided. The issue of death does not enter here explicitly (as we would expect it to, if the Rescuers were correct in their interpretation, since the issue is so important), and need not enter in here by implication. We are being told how not to live; the quest for kinetic pleasure is never-ending. That is a simple, straightforward Epicurean claim, and it is used as contrast to the proper way to live that is given in the next part.

In part B we learn that the intellect—that is, philosophy (and prudence)—can do two things: (1) It can understand how to deal with our desires; and (2) It can understand that death is not to be feared. The result is that life can be complete (or perfect). As to (1), we can find more details in *Let Men* 127, where we learn something about desires. Some desires, Epicurus says there, are natural and some are groundless. Of the natural, some are necessary, and others are merely natural.

Of the necessary desires, the satisfaction of some is necessary for happiness, and the satisfaction of others is necessary for getting rid of pain in the body, and the satisfaction of still others is necessary if we are to live.[17] "The unwavering contemplation of these enables one to refer every choice and avoidance to the health of the body and the freedom of the soul from disturbance, since this is the goal of a blessed life" (*Let Men* 128).

A preceding section of *Let Men* can be consulted as to (2), where we learn that "death is nothing to us" (see Chapters 1 and 2). But notice that neither in *Let Men* nor in *PD* 20[B] is there any claim that (2) is grounded in, or is supported by, (1). Philosophy can teach us about katastematic pleasure—satisfaction arising from the removal of pain, especially the removal of turmoil in the mind. When we have learned our lessons, we will have abandoned a never-ending quest of trying to amass kinetic pleasure. Again, this tells us how to live, and there is no need to think that there is, by implication, a claim that having katastematic pleasure is the foundation for understanding that death is nothing to be concerned about.[18]

Part C tells us that the wise person does not shun kinetic pleasure (when there is no risk of consequent pain: *Let Men* 129), nor, when he faces death, does he think that anything was lacking in his life, because he has already achieved the complete life. The Rescuers say that the implication is that the wise person does not fear death because he knows that, having achieved the perfect life, death cannot deprive him of what he could have had. But I read it differently, and in a way that is more consistent with Epicureans' explicit statements about pleasure, about the complete life, and about death. The mention in C of perishing is merely a claim that the wise person has already rid himself of the fear of death, and so the perfect life is attainable; it does not claim that the wise person understands katastematic pleasure and *therefore* does not fear death. As for the possibility of death's being a deprivation (of a complete life or of anything else), we will look at that in Section 3.3 "The deprivation view" and then again in Chapter 5.

Sometimes Lucretius's *De Rerum Natura*, near the end of Book 3, is cited as being a useful ally for the Rescue interpretation. But let us see how here, too, there is a mistaken reading. After having criticized the tendency to think that

---

[17] See also *PD* 29. The scholion to *PD* 29 reads: "Epicurus thinks that those which liberate us from pains are natural and necessary, for example drinking in the case of thirst; natural and not necessary are those which merely provide variations of pleasure but do not remove the feeling of pain, for example expensive foods; neither natural nor necessary are, for example, crowns and the erection of statues." Annas has a good discussion in *The Morality of Happiness*, chapter 7.

[18] We are given the same lesson in *PD* 21: "He who has learned the limits of life knows that it is easy to provide that which removes the feeling of pain owing to want and make one's whole life perfect. So there is no need for things which involve struggle." Notice that the explicit conclusion is not "So there is no need to fear death."

death is a deprivation (3.894–903), Lucretius presents us with a common event ("this is the way among men"): Men are drinking during (or after) a banquet, and at one point they lament that life is short and that after death a person won't even be able to recall these pleasures. Lucretius remarks: "As if after death their chief trouble will be to be miserably consumed and parched by a burning thirst, or a craving possess them for some other thing!" Of course, no such thing can happen in death; Lucretius is telling us that people mistake what annihilation means. The banqueters think of death as they think of life, as though in death they will be missing out in the way they would in life if they did not have access to the pleasures that they seek. "In fact", Lucretius continues, "no one feels the want of himself and his life when both mind and body alike are quiet in sleep; for all we care that sleep might be everlasting, and no craving touches us at all. [...] Death therefore must be thought of much less moment to us, if there can be anything less than what we see to be nothing" (3.921–927).

And then, at 931, Lucretius has Nature speak "to one of us". Since this comes on the heels of the scene with the banqueters, and since the banqueters exemplify "the way among men" (namely, that we are by nature attracted to kinetic pleasures such as food and drink), we may suppose that any one of us might be the target of Nature's rebuke. (I have marked the sections with letters D, E, and F.)

> [D] What ails you, O mortal, to indulge overmuch in sickly lamentations? Why do you groan aloud and weep at death? For if your former life now past has been to your liking, if it is not true that all your blessings have been gathered as it were into a riddled jar, and have run through and been lost without gratification, why not, like a banqueter fed full of life, withdraw with contentment and rest in peace, you fool?

> [E] But if all that you have enjoyed has been spilt out and lost, and if you have a grudge at life, why seek to add more, only to be miserably lost again and to perish wholly without gratification? Why not rather make an end of life and trouble? For there is nothing else I can devise and invent to please you: everything is always the same. If your body is not already withering with years and your limbs worn out and languid, yet everything remains the same, even if you shall go on to outlive all generations, and even more if you should be destined never to die.

And if some older man complains that he will die, Nature might say

> [F] All life's prizes you have enjoyed and now you wither. But because you always crave what you have not, and contemn what you have, life has slipped by for you incomplete and ungratifying, and death stands by your head unexpected, before you can retire glutted and full of the feast.

Lucretius tells us that Nature "urges against us a just charge" and "sets forth a true case" (3.954).

Tobias Reinhardt ("The Speech of Nature") says that Nature is presenting a "rhetorical dilemma". The first horn (part D) describes "the attitude towards death Nature regards as desirable" (296), and the second horn (part E) is "clearly the attitude she regards as undesirable" (297).

> The speech [. . .] primarily addresses the fear of death *qua* curtailment of pleasures. [. . .] What is crucial is that the speech is first and foremost concerned with the type of fear of death which the Epicurean sage would counter with his theory of [katastematic] pleasure, a theory that is not covered in D.R.N. in detail and which consequently the reader cannot be expected to accept. [298]

> We are urged to be grateful for what we have received, for appreciating that our soul is sufficiently filled (like a vessel) with pleasant memories to make us part with life contentedly. [302]

"Apparently", says Reinhardt, "Nature suggests to us to adopt, provided we have enjoyed our lives, an attitude of contented freedom from worries which resemble katastematic pleasure, and Lucretius has tried to encapsulate this idea in a non-Epicurean metaphor" (296). This Rescue interpretation is that Nature is warning the person that kinetic pleasures leave one's life "incomplete", the implication being that if one seeks (and obtains) not kinetic pleasure but katastematic pleasure, then life would not be incomplete, but would rather be complete, and therefore one would be able to "depart from the feast of life filled to repletion", that is, satisfied and without fear.

But I understand the passage differently. Nature is addressing a person at a drinking session who thinks that pleasures are to be gathered and perhaps totaled up, who spends his life trying to get all those things conventionally thought to be good: food and drink in this case; and, because the drinkers are festooned, we may assume that the affair is a bit lavish.[19] Nature says to him (and to us) something like this:

> Look, the way you're going about this can have one of two results. Either you have amassed enough of those good things, and you are at the point of not wanting more, and your quest has ended; you're like a banqueter stuffed full. Isn't that what your life has been devoted to? And in that case what is there to

---

[19] "They have laid themselves down at table and hold goblets in their hands and shade their brows with garlands" (912–13).

complain about? Or else you are going to go on in this way forever, trying to amass temporary pleasures (and really, all I can give you are the same ones, over and over), in which case you will never be satisfied, so you might just as well end it all now.

Nature makes a similar rebuke at F, saying, in effect, "You've been trying to pack in all pleasures, yet you've always wanted more, and now you are old enough (and near enough to death) to have already seen that you never will finish your life-as-a-banquet."

We tend to "indulge overmuch" in kinetic pleasures (just as we "indulge overmuch" in "sickly lamentations"), because by nature we are drawn to one pleasure after another; that's the way of the flesh. Nature "makes a true case" not by telling us about katastematic pleasure (because in fact she says nothing, and knows nothing, of the kind) but by pointing out what it means to live for the sake of (kinetic) pleasure. If we follow Nature, we have only the two options: either we really are contented because we're stuffed full of pleasures or else we'll always want more and so we'll never be satisfied. Notice that Nature is not contrasting a right and a wrong way to live. It is the speech of *nature*, not the speech of *reason*. If we reason about the issue (with Epicurus, of course), we will see that neither of Nature's options describes the ideal way to live.[20]

James Warren, making a point similar to Reinhardt's, concludes: "It becomes clear why the full and satisfied diner can be described in such positive terms. This is a representation of katastematic pleasure, a state in which all desires are fulfilled and anxieties removed" (*Facing Death*, 138). But this cannot be right. The description of the drinker/banqueter is inappropriate to characterize the Epicurean, who does not engage in drinking bouts.[21] A good life, for the Epicurean, is not like a banquet, taking one sensuous delight after another. That way of living cannot succeed in reaching stable satisfaction. It can be expected, on the contrary, to be an unfulfilling life. The Epicurean does not stuff himself with sensuous pleasure with the hope that he will eventually have

---

[20] And later on (3.1003–1010) it is not Nature, but rather Lucretius himself, who warns us "to be always feeding an ungrateful mind, yet never able to fill and satisfy it with good things—as the seasons of the year do for us when they come round bringing their fruits and manifold charms, yet we are never filled with the fruits of life—this I think, is meant by the tale of damsels in the flower of their age pouring water into a riddled urn, which, for all their trying, can never be filled."

[21] Reinhardt calls the banquet "a non-Epicurean metaphor" ("The Speech of Nature", 296), but surely that is a good reason for questioning his interpretation. The passage from *DRN* ought to recall *Let Men.* 132: "For it is not drinking bouts and continuous partying and enjoying boys and women, or consuming fish and the other dainties of an extravagant table, which produce the pleasant life, but sober calculation which searches out the reasons for every choice and avoidance and drives out the opinions which are the source of the greatest turmoil for men's souls."

satisfied all his possible desires. It simply cannot be done, but you won't learn that by following nature. Rather, you need philosophy and prudence, which, whatever else they may be, are disciplined responses to, and refinements of, natural tendencies.

We can see this contrast in *PD* 20 as well. At *PD* 20[A] we are told that nature's appetite is unlimited, and then at *PD* 20[B] we see, contrasted with nature's way, the way of the intellect—of reason—which recognizes that you cannot reach the limit of something limitless. So when we are told that amassing (kinetic) pleasures would require an infinite amount of time, the intellect can see that such a project is silly, not because you know that someday you will die, but because you will not find satisfaction that way even if you were immortal. The issue is not "You will not have satisfaction before you die"; the "before you die" is irrelevant. The issue is "You won't find satisfaction *that* way". It may be trivially true that you can't achieve satisfaction without spending some amount of time at it. But the issue is *how* to achieve satisfaction. Epicurus is not saying this sort of thing: You need time to build a house, but use that time wisely, or else you will come to the end of the time allotted, and you will not have finished your house. He is saying, rather, that of course you need time to build your house, but if you proceed in the wrong way (by amassing drops of water, for example), then it won't matter how long you have to build it, you still won't finish it. He could add "even if you worked at it for eternity", but such an addition would be for rhetorical emphasis and ought not to be thought to raise issues of temporal limits.

What Epicurus is getting at by referring to time has nothing to do (directly) with death. His comments would work just as well if addressed to an audience of immortals. An immortal being might be unhappy, because he believes that happiness has to do with the pleasures of the flesh, and so there is always more to be had. Happiness, on that view, would be an ever-receding horizon; on such a view there could not be completeness. But, Epicurus says, happiness as tranquillity is obtainable if we follow reason.

A Rescue interpretation might try to gain some support from Philodemus of Gadara, a contemporary of Lucretius. Part of his fourth book of *On Death* is available to us only in the carbonized remains of a papyrus scroll discovered in the late eighteenth century in a villa in Herculaneum that had been buried by Vesuvius's eruption about a hundred years after Philodemus's death. Philodemus says at the beginning of Book IV (with reminders here and there as the discussion proceeds) that if death is a deprivation, it cannot be the usual kind.

> The unconsciousness that goes with being dead is nothing to do with us, [. . .] deprivation of good things, being accompanied by unconsciousness, is painless and not such as in life. [1.2][22]

As an example of how people tend to conflate death-deprivation with in-life deprivation, consider his remarks about the fear of not being remembered after death:

> to experience suffering at the prospect of not being remembered by anyone at all seems natural: for it is sometimes the consequence of a life (that is) friendless and has nothing good. [35.34]

But

> we have a need of consequential concomitants not for their own sake, but (for the sake of) the acceptable life on which they naturally supervene: thus if that (life) is brought about, we shall pay no heed to what is nothing to do with us. [. . .] But they seem to consider it painful to be unremembered after their lives, when they do not exist, turning their thoughts to (the idea of) being unheeded by men in life. [36.12]

Philodemus's responses to various fears of death incorporate a typical Epicurean therapy that deals, in part, with false beliefs. Voula Tsouna gives us an example:

> Let us take a person's fear that he will die childless. He fears death in that case because he judges that dying without issue is a very bad thing and it is appropriate for him to feel despair on that account. Part of the philosophical therapy, then, is to refute these beliefs: convince the patient that having no children is not an evil and, consequently, there are no good grounds for his distress. ["Rationality", 84]

This is indeed the approach that Philodemus takes. But he goes a step further and reminds the patient that it won't make any difference in any case:

> whether relatives have been left behind or not, and whether the things that we mentioned before are performed by them or by some strangers or by no one whatever, it will be no more to do with us than in the time of Phoroneus's contemporaries. [23.36–24.4][23]

---

[22] I refer to the scroll's text by column number followed, in most cases, by line number. I use W. Benjamin Henry's translation (*Philodemus*, On Death). Readers must bear in mind that much of the scroll is missing or severely damaged so that often only incomplete sentences (and sometimes only isolated words or letters) are available.

[23] In Greek mythology, Phoroneus was a primordial king.

So Philodemus's therapy is to respond to each particular fear by questioning the beliefs involved and then by following up with a reminder of the central issue of death with which Book IV begins, saying something such as "but it won't matter to us anyway once we're dead". This is the way Philodemus handles most, if not all (the text is too corrupt to be sure), of the various fears about death: the prospect of death such that one's enemies will gloat over them (20.4), death without having had children (22), being buried in a foreign land (25.37), dying in bed instead of in battle (28), having or lacking postmortem glory (28.32), having a humble funeral (30), death at sea (32), being forgotten after death (35), and others. Each of those sections includes an "it won't matter anyway" coda.

The reminder of the nothingness of death occurs also in his discussion of a sage's death:

> A person has become wise and lived on for a certain extent of time; and (now that) the journey (is) in progress (that is) in accordance with its equality and sameness of form, it is appropriate for (this good) to persist to infinity, if it were possible. But if a line should be drawn under it,[24] there does not come about a taking away of the happiness that has come into being, but a prevention of the continued enjoyment of it; but there is no perception even of the fact that it no longer exists. [19.3–19.11]

And notice that there is no indication here that such a death would escape misfortune on account of the wise person's having achieved the highest good, nor that a death before that time would be something to be feared. We are told that once one has achieved the best life, it might as well continue without end. Why would that be? Philodemus does not say, but we can say it for him: There is no downside to extending happiness forever; given the best life possible, there is no motive to yearn for something higher, better, further; that is, this is satisfaction. But if the wise person's life does reach an end, then two things can be said. First, "there does not come about a taking away of the happiness that has come into being", because (obviously and trivially) there cannot come about a taking away of anything that has already occurred. More usefully we can say that the nonexistent person will not be in a condition without happiness. That is to say, ordinarily to have one's happiness taken away is to end up unhappy, but a dead person is not an unhappy person, and so it would be wrong to say that his happiness had been taken away. (More on this in Chapter 5.) And second, the person will not be aware of being dead and no longer in a condition of

---

[24] That is, if death occurs. Philodemus's clever metaphor of the paragraph line is discussed in Armstrong, "All Things to All Men", 51f.

happiness; a dead person cannot be dissatisfied (cf. 19.32: "and he will be pained not at all at being removed from out of those that exist"). This is another instance of Philodemus's constant reminder that even if death is thought to be some kind of deprivation, it is "not such as in life".

Although the Epicureans say that a wise person will not fear death, Philodemus introduces something new. Tsouna explains it as

> a special category of emotions that even the wise man has, which he calls "bites" or "pangs" [*degma*].[25] These are the natural and healthy counterparts of harmful passions like anger and the fear of death. They involve both ways of experiencing and beliefs, but in this case the beliefs are true and the painful feelings are usually mild and of short duration. Concerning the fear of death, Philodemus repeatedly contrasts "bites" of distress with deep grief (λύπη) and treats them as distinct but conceptually related kinds of πάθη. [. . .] However, in so far as "bites" involve beliefs, they can be weakened and may even disappear [. . .] because they can be influenced by argument, as other emotions can. [Tsouna, "Rationality", 86–87]

So, for example, Philodemus says:

> Now leaving behind parents or children or a wife or certain others of those close to us, if they will be in dire straits on account of our death or will even lack necessities, has of course a most natural sting [*phusikotaton degmon*], and this alone, or more than anything else, stirs up emissions of tears in the sensible man. [25.2–25.10]

The term "prick" (*nuttein*) is used similarly:

> But when (death occurs) in a foreign country, [the suffering] is natural even for intellectuals, and especially if they leave parents or other relatives in their fatherland: but only so much as to prick them—not so much as to confer a pain. [25.37–26.7]

And here, too, Philodemus reminds us that "even this death *qua* death is not to do with us, inasmuch as so far from (perceiving) that our remains are lying in a foreign country, we shall perceive nothing" (26.10).

The notion of *degma*—"bite" or "sting" or "prick"—that a person might feel in contemplating a premature death is not much help for the Rescuers.

> Let us then for our part say, specifically concerning the case of one who is snatched away when capable of progressing in philosophy, that it is natural for such a person to be stung. [17.32; cf. 14.2]

---

[25] See 17.32, 25.37–26.6.

As far as I can make out, such "natural bites" are expected results of our ordinary habits, so that if one is facing death, one might naturally and uncritically think "I won't be able to X", where "X" is just about anything at all: "I won't be able to finish important projects", "I won't be around to see my grandchildren grow up", "I won't be able to compete in the next Olympics." Even a wise person might experience such a momentary disappointment or "sting". But upon reflection, it ought to be seen that not being able to X because of death is, as Philodemus says in 1.2, unlike not being able to X in life (cf. DRN 3.885–887).

Might Philodemus help rescue the Rescuers with the following?

> But the sensible man, having received that which can secure the whole of what is sufficient for a happy life, immediately then for the rest (of his life) goes about laid out for burial, and he profits by one day as (he would) by eternity, and when (the day) is being taken away, he neither <considers the things happening (to him)> surprising nor goes along (with them) as one falling somewhat short of the best life, but going forward and receiving in a remarkable manner the addition provided by time, as one who has met with a paradoxical piece of good luck, he is grateful to circumstances even for this. [38.14–38.25]

Part of this is not unlike PD 20, which I have already discussed and found to be of little help for Rescuers. But why does Philodemus say that having achieved the good life, one "goes about laid out for burial"? That might seem to be saying that one need no longer to fear death. But that is not quite right. The wise man walks about like someone already set out for burial not because *now*, on account of having achieved the perfect life, he knows that death is nothing to him, but rather because he has achieved the perfect life in part by having realized that death is nothing to him. The sensible man can be opposed to the fool who is caught by surprise when "suddenly, hidden, there approaches, taking away great hopes, necessity" (38.13) and becomes paralyzed by fear and denial. As Tsouna says, "Fools are dragged out of life in mental and emotional disarray [. . .], because they have refused to accept the reality of death and consequently have been devastated by its advent" (Tsouna, "Rationality", 112).

There is one more possibility that Rescuers might wish to use:

> [And when it is possible] in a finite time both to win and to enjoy the greatest (one) of them [good things], as [he[26]] demonstrated, one who goes by the appellation "young" will not in addition, [when he has] this, require even infinity, never mind the life of an old man: but while still a lad, he will obtain

---

[26] Pythocles, at the age of about eighteen.

these [good] things in abundance, so as to go away gladdened, and as one who could be said to have lived more than those who had no enjoyment in [all] the years they lived [through]. [13.3–13.10]

Once it [a soul] has tasted the [goods] (that proceed) from philosophy, then it is entirely out of the question that it should [not] grasp a wonderful good, so that he departs full of exultation. [18.5; cf. 13.10]

Again, the first part ought to remind us of *PD* 20. The phrase "go away gladdened" I take to mean happy even up to the time of death, that is, to have been truly happy, which would of course include not being afraid of death. But there is no implication that the absence of the fear of death is brought about by having achieved happiness.

3.3 The deprivation view

Although the Epicurean notion of a complete (or perfect) life is not recognizably what Gisela Striker has in mind (however vague it might be) when she says that Epicurus does not address the issue of premature death (or incomplete life),[27] we can agree that a complete life cannot be fashioned in an instant; it takes time and study to appreciate and to put into practice a simple life of contentment. One has to rid oneself of fears of the gods; one must learn to restrict desires to the natural and necessary ones, and so on. So even if having a complete life could remove the possibility of death's being premature, what is to be said about a death that occurs before a complete life is achieved? Rescuers will say that in such a case death is premature. That implication is the desired one, because they want to show that, *pace* Striker and others, Epicureanism is sensitive enough to recognize the misfortune of premature death.

But if such a premature death is not nothing to us, then Epicurus's claim that "death is nothing to us" has not been rescued at all; in fact, it has been severely injured, because Rescued Epicureanism would imply that most people's fear of death is warranted after all, because death for almost everyone is premature, and therefore a misfortune, because very rarely does anyone even try to attain anything like an Epicurean complete life, much less succeed at it.

I think the Rescue attempts have gone down the wrong road, having taken a bad step at the beginning. Let us ask of a student of Epicureanism who has not

---

[27] Kirk Sanders, speaking specifically of Philodemus, says that "Philodemus' own analysis of prematurity also turns on a notion of completeness, albeit one markedly different from that envisioned by Striker and other critics of Epicureanism" ("Philodemus and the Fear of Premature Death", 222).

yet attained the perfect life, "What are the consequences for you of not attaining the perfect life for several years to come?" The answer is obvious: During those intervening years he will be less than content, he will have a troubled mind, etc. These are exactly the features that Epicurean therapy is designed to help with. Now let us ask a slightly different question: "What are the consequences for you of not achieving the perfect life *before death in several years*?" The answer to the previous question is appropriate as an answer this second question as well.

Of course, there are some different logical implications of the two situations. In the first, after the several years have passed and the student has finally achieved happiness, he will then have a contented life (until death at some later time), whereas in the second, after several years have passed he will die without having lived those years of contentment. But in both cases he will first have several years of non-contented life. If the student thinks that the second would be worse than the first (or the first better than the second),[28] then we can see that the real issue for him is not (or not simply) the "perfect way of life". It is, rather, the issue of deprivation, which evidently can arise in the case of a life in pursuit of kinetic pleasures as well as in the case of a life devoted to katastematic pleasure; the student in the second situation is concerned that he will die and therefore lose (or be deprived of) some years of contentment that he could have had.

And what can Epicurus say to the student? There is nothing at all about the complete or perfect life that will make a difference for those several years before dying (or, in the first situation, before attaining the complete life), and so a rehearsal of the nature of the complete life will be of no help in allaying the student's concern. Moreover, it would be a mistake to suppose that a person who has not yet attained the perfect life could reasonably wish to avoid a premature death (i.e., death before a complete life has been achieved), because that would mean that it would be reasonable to want to take steps to prolong life so as to eventually attain the perfect life. The advice to prolong life would usually be odd even when a goal is other than a particular kind of life. Suppose someone wants to visit Paris, and we ask, "Do you mean that you wish to avoid premature death—do you wish to prolong your life—so that you can visit Paris?" I imagine the puzzled reply to be something like: "Well, I suppose so. But . . . I mean . . . I'd like to go maybe next June. Why are you mentioning death? Do you know something that I don't?"

---

[28] Mitsis speculates: "Perhaps those who have not yet achieved complete happiness still have reason to fear death and to regard the duration of life as important" ("Epicurus on Death and the Duration of Life", 322 n 38).

If a person desires to live the good life, what is being desired? It seems improbable that the person will say "I desire the good life *before I die*". The "before I die" is, for most people, I should think, not part of their thought. A person (usually) wants to live "the good life" by earning a lot of money and flying around in a private jet, or getting married and raising a fine family in a large house without a mortgage, or living self-reliantly in rural New England.[29] She wants her living to be a good kind of living (by her lights). The issue of the termination of living usually does not arise unless some philosopher gets in the way.[30]

Let us summarize the issue as the Rescuers see it:

1. It takes time to achieve a complete life.
2. Death before having achieved a complete life is premature.
3. Premature death is bad for the one who died.
4. Therefore, death before having achieved the complete life is bad for the one who died.

The first proposition is an acceptable Epicurean claim. The second makes use of notions of "complete life" and "premature" that we have seen before. Although the terms are both vague and ambiguous, we could accept the claim as an attempt by the Rescuers to stipulate a meaning for "premature". In any case, where does the third come from? What could support such a claim? Even if the first premise is abandoned—if somehow a complete life (of katastematic pleasure) were ordinarily available instantly at the commencement of one's being—the Rescue position would have to maintain that if that perfect life were for some reason not granted at birth, then there could be a premature death, because the perfect life would come later (or not at all), and in the meantime death might occur. And such a death would be bad, because premature death is bad.

---

[29] See, for example, Scott Nearing and Helen Nearing, *Living the Good Life*. Thoreau, on the other hand, who also wanted to live self-reliantly in New England, did allow death to enter such thoughts: "I went to the woods because I wished to live deliberately, to front only the essential facts of life, and see if I could not learn what it had to teach, and not, when I came to die, discover that I had not lived" (*Walden*, 172). Thoreau could have left out that attempt at drama; he could have made the issue more simple by saying "learn what it had to teach and not discover that I had not been living". Such a discovery is what he did not want at any time—next month, or next year, or in ten years. Even if he anticipated that he would live for a long, long time, he would not want to discover at any time that he had not been truly living.

[30] Prolonging one's life in order to do or to have something is like deciding first to not die. The Epicurean *tetrapharmakos* is a kind of recipe for a complete life, but what Epicurus would not put into the recipe is "First, don't die". No more would Epicurus be concerned to say anything in such a context about not dying than would Julia Childs when she gives you advice about making Reine de Saba. She does not say, "First, don't die. Next, melt four ounces of semi-sweet chocolate in two ounces of rum." Death, the prospect of death, going on longer, and so on, are topics in a different category.

But why? How could *any* premature death be bad (on *any* definition of prematurity)? The only answer that makes sense here is the deprivation view. The underlying claim, accepted by Rescuers and attackers alike (but usually not made explicit by the Rescuers), is that death *qua* deprivation is bad; that is, prematurity is bad because prematurity implies deprivation, and deprivation is bad. My point is that the Rescuers go wrong at the outset by granting legitimacy to the idea that death could be a deprivation (without which there would be no motive to try to use a notion of "complete life" in order to show how some death-as-deprivations could be avoided). Any version of the death-as-deprivation view has very serious problems that, so far as I can see, cannot be overcome, as I will discuss in Chapter 5. And if I am right about that, then Rescuers have actually made Epicurus's thanatology out to be weaker than it is. It is interesting to note that both Lucretius and Philodemus make the point that death is not a deprivation.

3.4 Paradox

The fourth reason for saying that Rescue attempts go wrong is that they can result in paradox. Rescuers say that it is by having a life of katastematic pleasure that one comes to know that one's death cannot be (or can no longer be) premature. But clearly, one's life cannot be a life of katastematic pleasure if one has important fears, one of which is the fear of premature death. So one needs katastematic pleasure in order to be rid of the fear of death, yet one needs to be rid of the fear of death in order to have katastematic pleasure.

> We can see that in order to cope with fear of death in all its varieties, one already has to be an Epicurean sage. One needs to have fully accepted the Epicurean theory of pleasure and must be able to bring it to bear on the way in which one lives. [Reinhardt, "The Speech of Nature", 292][31]

Kirk Sanders recommends a way to avoid the paradox, but I think it only partially succeeds. A fear is rational, he says, provided that its object is both harmful and imminent. Even assuming that premature death is harmful, most people (especially young people, but perhaps excepting very old or very sick people) have no good reason to believe that their death is imminent. "It would therefore be exceptional rather than ordinary for any person making progress

---

[31] See also Warren, *Facing Death*, 156–57.

toward *ataraxia* with the aid of Epicurean philosophy to have reason to fear a premature death", so in the non-exceptional cases, the paradox need not arise.³²

The problem with Sanders's solution is twofold. (1) Some fears seem not to have as their object something imminent. I can fear spiders, or confined spaces, or flying, not only when in the presence of a spider, or trapped in a cave, or on board an airplane. Such fears will act so as to keep me from approaching possible spider locations, from entering tight spaces, and from flying. If it is objected that I will stay away from such situations not because I presently fear them, but rather because I know that if I were in such situations I would then experience fear, then there is an ambiguity in the concept of fear—an occurrent as opposed to a dispositional sense, perhaps. But I see no good reason to be confined to only one sense. And if I can be concerned about, or feel anxiety about, or fear (even if only dispositionally), a premature death that is not imminent, then the paradox can arise. But (2) even if Sanders is right that only imminent death is to be reasonably feared, the paradox will still arise in the case of any students of Epicureanism who do have reason to believe that they have only a short time to live, however rare such students might be.³³ So if you are not yet an Epicurean sage, and you are near death, it would be impossible to have peace of mind. That would make death not "nothing to us", but rather something very important. I would rather not interpret Epicurus in a way that yields that conclusion, because I do not find Epicurean texts making anything like such a claim. Moreover, my position in this book is that the nature of annihilation means that any kind of death—premature or otherwise—should be "nothing to us".

A better way to avoid the paradox is simply to reject the idea that Epicurus's thanatology relies on the idea of katastematic pleasure or any notion of "complete life". One important question that Epicurus addresses is, "How should I be living?" Part of the answer is to attend to katastematic pleasure. When it comes to Epicurus's recommending katastematic pleasure over kinetic pleasure (or contentedness over cupidity, or simple foods over luxuries, or philosophy over superstition, and so on), the issue is how to live—what to do with and in one's life. Epicurus's advice on such matters has nothing to do with death (except

---

³² "Philodemus and the Fear of Premature Death", 231.
³³ Referring to Philodemus's remark (*On Death* 38) that the sage goes about his business "already buried", Warren says that "the single day becomes for him eternity, not in the sense that he lives his life 'slowly', but, presumably, because he has recognized that a single day offers him the chance of absolute fulfillment" (*Facing Death*, 242). But the claim that "a single day offers him the chance of absolute fulfillment" makes it seem that if he needed *two* days, then death after the first day *would* be bad for him.

the advice to rid oneself of various unnecessary fears, one of which is the fear of death).

Another important question is, "How can I rid myself of the fear of death?" The answer is to attend to the metaphysics of death. A person is a complex material object which, when death comes, is destroyed (i.e., whatever is left over is not an experiencing thing and does not behave in ways typical of living persons—if it can be said to behave in any way at all). After the person has been annihilated, there is no "the person" to regret the annihilation, to wish it were otherwise, to experience a loss, or to have any experiences at all. Such considerations have nothing to do with pleasure, whether kinetic or katastematic.

Those two questions are crucially different, and so are their answers, and in trying to support Epicurus, the Rescuers have pushed the two issues together into an unfortunate confusion. It is true that a person who seeks kinetic pleasures might view death as a deprivation of further chances to have such pleasures. But if katastematic, instead of kinetic, pleasure were a person's goal, and if he wanted to avoid death in order to finally experience that kind of pleasure, then he would be just as confused about the issue as he would be if he wished to prolong life in order to have more kinetic pleasure. When it comes to the issue of death, what he needs instruction in is not pleasure but rather annihilation. To paraphrase Epicurus (*Let Men* 125), when the issue of happiness is there, the issue of death is not; and when the issue of death is there, the issue of happiness is not.

4 Conclusion and anticipation

The most important failing of Rescue arguments is the mistaken assumption that Epicurus's thanatology needs to be rescued at all. On the contrary, one can rid oneself of the fear of death *in any sense* by a proper understanding of Epicurus's argument that "death is nothing to us", even if one knows nothing of katastematic pleasure or a simple life of contentment.

I am not claiming that death cannot be premature in some way or other: before finishing important projects; before completing expected stages of a "normal" life; before this, before that. But even if it were the case that all deaths were premature, it would not matter. The proper response to the suggestion that Epicureanism cannot account for the misfortune of premature death is not to look for a special notion of "complete life", but rather to point out that the claim that premature death can be bad relies on the notion of death as some kind of deprivation, and then to show how the notion of deprivation cannot apply in the singular case of annihilation. I hope that the discussion in this chapter made the first step a plausible one. I fancy that the previous two chapters provided a good foundation for the second step, but we must now look more closely at the notion of deprivation and some attempts to use it in anti-Epicurean ways. That will be the topic of Chapter 5, after a short preparatory on the nature of counterfactuals in Chapter 4.

4

Counterfactual Comments

Prelude

What if there were no counterfactuals?

1 Causal explanation

Consider the following from an NTSB[1] accident report involving a Cessna 182C (a 4-seat, single engine light plane) in Reno, Nevada, in January 2010.

> The pilot reported that during cruise flight, he felt a "significant shake" in the airplane and noticed that the engine was losing power. He initiated a precautionary landing to a nearby road. During the descent, the engine failed completely, and despite the pilot's attempts to restart, the propeller would not rotate. Subsequently, the pilot landed on an unoccupied road. During the landing roll the airplane encountered a ditch and nosed over, which resulted in structural damage to the fuselage, vertical stabilizer, rudder and both wings. Examination of the engine revealed that the number one and two connecting rods separated from the engine crankshaft and exhibited thermal and mechanical damage, consistent with oil starvation. The forward, intermediate, and rear main bearings exhibited signatures consistent with oil starvation. Fragments of the connecting rod bearings were located within the oil sump along with portions of what appeared to be paper towel material. The oil pickup tube was intact and undamaged. The paper-towel-like material was also observed around the oil pickup tube screen and inlet port which restricted the oil flow within the engine. No additional anomalies were noted with the engine. The pilot reported that the engine had accumulated a total time in service of 3,039 hours, with 993 since last overhaul. [National Transportation Safety Board Aviation Accident Final Report[2]]

---

[1] The National Transportation Safety Board is an agency of the US government that collects and analyzes data from accidents in aviation and other kinds of transportation.
[2] Complete bibliographic information on this and all other sources in this book is provided in the Bibliography.

What was the problem that was investigated? It was damage to the aircraft. (There were also minor injuries to the pilot and passenger.) The report seems to be telling us that paper towel-like material in the sump blocked the oil pickup tube, starving the connecting rod bearings of oil, causing the bearings to fail, causing two of the connecting rods to fail, causing the engine to stop (and not restart), causing the plane to glide without power, forcing a landing (under the pilot's control) on a road with a ditch that caused the plane to nose over, resulting in airframe damage. In the NTSB report (and in my summary version) we are given only several parts of the entire incident, leaving plenty of lacunae. But this is to be expected, for not everything can be made explicit, and we are confident that at least some of the finer details can be supplied if called for.[3] Thus, for example, the NTSB report says that "the airplane encountered a ditch and nosed over, which resulted in structural damage". Even though we are not told how the ditch caused a nose-over, it is unlikely that anyone even a little familiar with airplanes would be at a loss to fill in some plausible details. Let's do so. We know something about how a small plane with a nose wheel (which is what the 182 is equipped with) rolls on the ground, and so the nose gear, going down into the ditch, brought the nose of the plane with it, abruptly stopping the fast-moving plane, causing the tail to be thrown up and over so that the plane came to rest upside down. Here we encounter still another lacuna in the explanatory sequence: The nose-over is said to have resulted in structural damage, but the *how* is left unstated. And here again we could easily supply some plausible details: The nose-over brought the vertical stabilizer and the wings into forceful contact with the ground; the aluminum skin and skeleton of the plane were thereby caused to change shape. Such details would have been too obvious to the report's authors and readers to have needed mentioning. Similarly, the investigators were not interested in pursuing why there was a ditch in the road, and we would probably be surprised if they had pursued it. The report also mentions why the plane landed on the road: the pilot guided it there. But another lacuna appears: Why did the pilot guide it there? Because, of course, the continued powered flight of the airplane was interrupted. We are not told, but we can easily imagine, why the pilot chose a road instead of, say, a lake or a sycamore copse. All these details, and countless others, are left unstated, because the practical requirements of the report are satisfied by mentioning the larger events.

---

[3] "Lacunae" might therefore be slightly misleading, as though there were already obvious gaps or omissions. I mean rather to say that between items or events that are explicit, still more detail could be added. But I do not know a term for that. Perhaps "latent lacunae" or "lurking lacunae" would have worked.

Although potential lacunae within the explanatory narrative are to be expected, an unacceptably large gap would be revealed in a very simple version of the account. It would not do to say "The probable cause of the structural damage to the airplane was the lack of oil in the engine". There would be too much missing in such a claim, because almost all piston aircraft engines are without oil once or several times a year when they undergo oil changes, and yet no structural damage occurs at those times; there is no reliable link between mere lack of oil and subsequent structural damage. If all we have is point A and distant point Z, we may wonder how causality travels from one to the other. But if we have seen a connection so often in a certain kind of context that we are not surprised (perhaps having experienced something like Mill's methods at work), then it might not be necessary to indicate intermediary points B, C, and so on, even if, were we to attend to the matter, we would know that such points could in principle be made explicit.

Not only are there expected potential lacunae within the NTSB report of the probable causal sequence of events, we can notice that the sequence ends with the damaged plane on the road. What happened next? Is the plane still on the road? What did the pilot have for breakfast the next day? There are countless ways that the narrative could have continued, but if we pursued them we would find that each step would take us further into a deep ditch of useless details. We do not expect such questions to be part of the report, because there seems to be no practical point in making them explicit, even if we are convinced that at least some of them could be investigated and answered.

There is also an issue near the beginning of the reported sequence: How did the paper towel material get into the oil sump of the engine in the first place? The answer could be useful to know in order to prevent future occurrences of the same kind. Perhaps, for example, it was the pilot's own doing when, having checked the oil level before flight (as pilots should), he wiped the oil dipstick with a paper towel, and scraps of the material tore off and were pushed with the dipstick into the sump. This possibility seems rather remote, but in any case it would have its own causal ancestors, and if we began to wonder about them, we would soon find that we had fallen backward into a pit of irrelevancies. For example, what was the causal provenance of the chemicals (e.g., the bleaching agents) and the machines (e.g., the pulpers and the rollers) used in the manufacture of the towels? Where did the ore come from that was used in making the rollers? And so on *ad tedium*.

The point of these rather unprofound remarks is to remind us that even a careful causal explanation does not bring into view everything that could be brought into view. A narrative focuses our attention on various events; it begins *in medias res*, skips over a practical infinity of details (as "don't cares") just before and just after each intermediate event, and finally ends also *in medias res*. What happened before the beginning of the story is shrouded by a fog of "don't cares", such that there seems to be no urge to follow the pedigree back and back and back. And the account ends in another fog of "don't cares" such that we see no practical advantage to go sleuthing still further along.

2 The fog of were

Counterfactuals gather some facts, change one or several of them, and then appeal to accepted regularities to describe other things or events, which might be the same or might be different from other accepted facts. "Had there been no paper towel material in the sump, the plane would not have been forced down and damaged." Our acceptance of that explanation with its counterfactual can be weakened by noting (or introducing) unexpected details. If someone says "the strobe lights on the wing tips had been recently replaced; had they not been replaced, the crash would not have happened", we will ask for more information in order to find a regularity that connects the strobe lights to the crash. The counterfactual implicitly uses some regularity, and if we do not have access to it, then we will not find the counterfactual plausible.

When accepted regularities are easily recognized as consorting with the counterfactual, we can allow ourselves the convenience of saying that the counterfactual is true, but that only means that the connection raises no obvious problems for our satisfactory use of the regularities in the present case. Once the alternative-to-fact in the antecedent is imagined, other things and events clamor for association. But between any two named things or events, some story can be constructed making use of known or easily hypothesized regularities, so that the more obvious the connection, the more plausible the counterfactual conditional, and the more hidden the connection, the more implausible the counterfactual. These are epistemic constraints. When there are no obvious patterns to apply, or when there are too many issues to sort out and apply, we are puzzled. "If Socrates had been a dog (instead of a human), Plato's philosophy would have been very cynical", illustrates the former. Here is an example of the latter:

> Consider Athens as it actually was, with its wonderful culture supported by slaves. Compare this with Athens as it might have been: with the same free citizens, and the same culture, but with the work of all slaves done by machines. [Derek Parfit, "Future Generations: Further Problems", 121]

But is it not necessary for a culture to be quite different if it supports machines to replace slaves (machines, one might add, of a level of sophistication far beyond what we have even today)? Would it not be a culture very different from ancient Athens in terms of mathematics, physics, materials science, politics, religion, agriculture, medicine, art, philosophy, and literature? Would the culture not give a great deal of attention to machines, their creation, and their maintenance? Would not new machines be introduced regularly? Would not the citizens be careful to not allow other cultures to steal their technologies? Would they not have enormous military advantages, such that they would be carrying on their wars (there were many wars then) in a different way? Mustn't one ask where these machines came from? Would we not have to imagine changes in Athens's history such that these many (and probably many types of) machines became available? Could Athens have progressed in one day from oxen to robots? If so, then the culture must have been filled throughout with talk of new miracles, laid over with a fear of sudden things, and perhaps visited with an epidemic of great anxiety. And if we do not imagine a rapid transformation, then we must imagine Athens's history (and no doubt the histories of surrounding cultures) to have been, for a very long time, vastly different from what it was.

All counterfactuals imagine of something or of some state of affairs that it has properties or relations other than its actual properties or relations. "The gloppy paper towel material blocked the oil pickup tube, but what if it had not been gloppy but rigid and porous?" Obviously this counterfactual, in interrogatory form, is speculating, of the paper towel, that it had properties that it did not have. But "if there had been no paper towel material in the sump, then the bearings would not have been starved of oil" does not image the paper towel as being other than it was. Rather, this counterfactual imagines, of the oil sump that actually contained the paper towel, that it did not contain paper towel material. Do we thereby imagine the nonexistence of the paper towel? I suppose one could express it that way, but it may be misleading to do so. One finds absences against a background of presences. The absence of the paper towel would make sense—it would become something to grasp, to have meaning—when there is a contrast or change. I can imagine the paper towel *but without being gloppy*. I can imagine the oil sump *but without the paper towel*. I can imagine the Cessna *but without the engine failure*. And in order to imagine the Cessna as never having existed, I will imagine some change in the factory in Wichita.

It is tempting to think that a fully detailed account of anything would, in principle, lead back to the Beginning of Everything, and so a counterfactual causal sequence would form an alternative "possible world", a term that Leibniz took seriously. Might he have been right that this is the best of all possible worlds? One is tempted to answer in the negative, or at least with a "maybe not". We can easily imagine some *local* area being better than it is (using any standard you wish), but the world being all interconnected, a change here will require a change there. However we are to measure better and worse when it comes to worlds, could it be that any change from the actuality would make for an overall worse world? How could we finite minds know whether an alternative world was worse, better, or neither? Leibniz, of course, did not trace out the evaluative consequences; he relied on a meta-argument invoking the absolute goodness of a perfect being. Our nontheistic approach makes the question an empirical issue, but of the sort that could not be settled if we were required to have complete information about the alternative world. We cannot have such information, yet we cannot give up the use of counterfactuals.

This tells us two things: (1) The problem of evil—the apparent existence of evil as being incompatible with divine goodness—is not a problem at all for a view that takes divine goodness to be the unassailable reality, so that evil becomes mere appearance. Such a view need not bother trying to give an account of *how* an alternative world would be worse; it is an endless task to explain everything in particular. A candid theistic response to the problem of evil is to say at the outset what must eventually be said at some point, namely, "It is a mystery that finite minds cannot unpuzzle."

(2) The second thing we learn is that counterfactuals never do give us alternative worlds at all, but only (and quite satisfactorily) alternative local areas.[4] To imagine that something did or did not happen, contrary to what we believe did happen, is to imagine a few local changes more or less isolated from the rest of the world; or else, if "isolated" is too strong a term, then we imagine some changes connected to the rest of the world by relations of "don't care". How is a local area separated from the rest of the world such that changes here do not have to be followed out to the beginnings and endings of the world? It is not so much a divine mystery as it is a matter of "that's not the point".[5]

In some possible world semantics the counterfactual "if C were true, then D would be true" is non-vacuously true if a possible world in which both C and D

[4] This view is similar to the more rigorous discussion by Chas Daniels and James Freeman ("An Analysis of the Subjunctive Conditional"), but they rely on the notion of possible worlds.

[5] "When we think of a subjunctive conditional we ask only for a small departure fork from actuality and do not dig into how it might have come about" (Jonathan Bennett, *A Philosophical Guide to Conditionals*, 226). I do not think that we—or the plain, non-theorist—posit or suppose any kind of fork at all. Rather, we attend to the counterfact, and perhaps to a few earlier differences (as get-readies for the counterfact) without imagining a fork, especially not a fork in need of any accounting, and *especially* not a fork whose only accounting would have to be the non-accounting account of a miracle. Similarly, when engaged with other kinds of fiction (usually more elaborate stories), we do not ask for, or seek, or feel any need for, describing a "fork" of any sort; rather, as with causal accounts, we begin *in medias res*.

are true is *more like* the actual world than is any possible world in which C is true but D is not true.⁶ But can we know that one possible world is *more like* the actual world than is any other possible world? It would seem to require omniscience in order to fill in all the potential lacunae of the description of even a small part of even a single possible world.⁷ What we finite minds actually do in judging counterfactuals is reflect on the regularities we are familiar with and say that the truth of C usually implies the truth of D, which is to say that the counterfactual "if C were true, then D would be true" is *plausible*. Consider C and D as events.

A1: If C had happened, D would have happened.

We must look not merely to C and D to understand and approve (or disapprove) of A1. A1 is similar to

A2: If C happens, D happens.

Except in formal relations, how is something like A2 ever confidently asserted? On the basis of experience, of course. A2 expresses a pattern. A1 is then A2 plus an implied claim that C did not occur. (A1 might, but need not, also be taken as claiming—it certainly *suggests*—that D did not happen.)

But our approval of a pattern may rely on a context of patterns, many of which are assumed unawares. "If Charles had not been drinking so much at the party, he would not have hit that deer when driving home." Such an explanation would probably satisfy us, but if we were required to give a fuller account, we could trot out a few familiar connections and say that when a driver is in a clear-headed state it is easy to avoid deer (by looking ahead, or by faster reaction times), and (here we play a game by denying regularities that we think no one would accept anyway) deer are not attracted to drunk drivers, and a person's drinking does not cause paved roads to shift their course so as to run through more deer-infested areas.

B1: What would happen if I (were to) press this button?

B2: What happens if I press this button?

B2 expects there to be a regularity which could also be used to respond to B1. That is, B1 is understood as an instance of B2, and B2 could include "usually" or "probably". So also for B3:

B3: What would have happened had I pressed this button?

---

[6] David Lewis, *Counterfactuals*.
[7] "What makes us omniscient? Have we a record of omniscience?" (Robert S. McNamara, in Errol Morris, dir., *The Fog of War*).

Consider the assumed regularities in this pair of counterfactuals:

C1: If Caesar had been in command in Korea, he would have used the atom bomb.

C2: If Caesar had been in command in Korea, he would not have used the atom bomb; he would have used catapults.

Seahwa Kim and Cei Maslen say of the above (which are Quine's examples): "Both statements can be reasonably asserted. Yet, the first statement implies that the second is false and vice versa. A statement cannot be both true and false, so each must express at least two different propositions depending on factors other than the background facts" ("Counterfactuals as Short Stories", 91).

Granted that for most of us those counterfactuals seem reasonable, yet there is no need to suppose that they have incompatible truth values—or indeed any truth values at all. Why not more simply say that both are plausible? We could agree that "if Caesar had used the atom bomb (and not catapults), then it would not be true that he used catapults (and not the atom bomb)" is true, perhaps logically (formally) so. And perhaps that is what is driving the feeling that the two originals must have opposite truth values. Nevertheless, both of these counterfactuals are plausible together; they simply make use of different regularities: the first appeals to Caesar's ruthless use of available weapons; the second appeals to weapons available to Caesar.

The fog surrounding a subjunctive conditional in any account or story (a conditional is like a wee story) is usually not noticed, because the point of the conditional or story is within the clearing—the neighborhood, the space—surrounded by fog, and to notice or attend to the fog is effectively to change the subject. One could, of course, try to peer into the fog to see more and more of the details. And one could suppose that causal chains going off this way and that into the fog could, in principle, be traced out (backward and forward) *ad lib*. But again, that would represent a change of subject, for it is not the purpose of most accounts to give more than some core details and peripheral principles.

> '*If kangaroos had no tails, they would topple over*' seems to me to mean something like this: in any possible state of affairs in which kangaroos have no tails, and which resembles our actual state of affairs as much as kangaroos having no tails permits it to, kangaroos topple over. [Lewis, *Counterfactuals*, 1]

The provision that an alternative state of affairs "resembles our actual state of affairs as much as kangaroos having no tails permits it to" involves a great deal of hand-waving. If "state of affairs" is taken to mean "possible world", we are returned to the problem already mentioned: We use counterfactuals all the time, but we cannot say that they describe everything in some possible world. Moreover, the term "permits" seems itself to rely on counterfactuals, and in any case the word calls up a variety of regularities that we might use in order to add details not mentioned. If kangaroos had no tails, maybe they would be unable to balance, and so (given our experiences with imbalance and toppling) they would topple over as a result. That claim might be investigated empirically by amputating some kangaroos' tails and seeing how the animals fare. Or the counterfactual might be understood as being part of a joke: Imagine a mob of kangaroos sitting around, suddenly losing their tails. Why, they'd all topple over, and wouldn't that be funny. That, too, would rely on tails as balancers. Or maybe tailless kangaroos would be able to balance by maintaining a forward lean, but from time to time they might intentionally fall backward just for the thrill; or maybe they would be members of a new species of tailless marsupials that fool human predators by suddenly toppling over backward and playing dead as if shot.

In such speculations there would be empirical patterns along which we would have to backtrack with decreasing degrees of confidence such that very soon, if not immediately, we would feel obliged to say "never mind the details; let's just suppose . . .", because waiting for a final accounting would mean waiting until we had traced generalities, patterns, and causal sequences back to the beginning of everything.

In explanatory contexts, which of course include counterfactuals, we cannot make all background material explicit. Rather, we offer certain patterns as explanations, without tracing the patterns or histories of things and events back very far or extending them very wide or deep, even if we feel that we could go further if we wanted to. The result is that the explanatory web has no clear edges. That any explanatory field, however successful it may be for either factuals or counterfactuals, is foggier the further out we go, indicates that we need not demand an account which cannot be more detailed than it already is. Often we simply ignore issues of pedigree. It may be enough to think that Nixon might have pressed the button and launched some missiles (Kit Fine's example[8]); there seems to be no pressing need to include a causal history of Nixon and his ancestors, or the precise source of the copper that was refined and used in the circuit, etc. The fog covers all that.

[8] Kit Fine, "Critical Notice: *Counterfactuals*", 452.

And even if we want to speculate about antecedents, we very soon have to resort to more hand-waving. What would it have taken for Nixon to have pressed the button? Boris Kment considers (without endorsing) something "small and inconspicuous", such as "some extra neurons fire in Nixon's brain".[9] But think of how very much is ignored in what seems to be a little step that attempts to point only to one event (or to some few events) which we might take to be part of a larger pattern. Those extra neurons' firings would have required chemical concentrations at synapses; the chemicals would have to have come from somewhere. Would it have been something Nixon would have eaten? Would he have reached for the buttered toast instead of the blueberry muffin? And so on and on throughout an apparently in-principle unending series. But very quickly we let our mental gaze go fuzzy, because we don't care; we already have the important stuff, and the rest of the universe will just have to take care of itself.[10]

If the use of counterfactuals were reducible to, or alternatively expressible in terms of, non-inconsistent indicatives only (which seems to be what some possible world theorists are trying to do), then it would be possible for us to do away with counterfactual expressions altogether.

So now we can ask: "What if there were no counterfactuals?"

I think that counterfactual expressions cannot (or cannot always) be translated into consistent indicatives; that we use inconsistencies all the time without insisting (or even wishing to insist) on those inconsistencies; and that higher intelligence cannot be carried on without them.

We harbor inconsistent beliefs all the time; it is necessary to do so in order to have the kind of imaginations that we have. For example, we have empathy, which is believing that you are the other person (while also believing that of course you are not the other person). And we have engagement with fiction, wherein you believe you are the fictional character or in the fictional situation (while also believing that you are not).[11]

Only rich, sophisticated languages and minds that can maneuver in such languages can handle counterfactual thinking. When a child (of four or five years) begins to understand points of view not his own, he is, in a way, learning to accept what would otherwise be false. That is to say, the child knows that p is

---

[9] Boris Kment, "Counterfactuals and Explanation", 266.
[10] Similar considerations apply to a work of fiction, where the author leaves out (although not necessarily intentionally) all the details of how and when—or even whether—Hamlet urinated. Mark Sainsbury mentions "the incompleteness essential to fiction" (*Fiction and Fictionalism*, 77). But incompleteness is essential to any account, fictional or non-.
[11] I discuss these issues at length in my "Really Believing in Fiction".

true, but is now able to appreciate that, from another point of view, *p* appears to be false. "I can see *x*", he might say (or think), "and so *x* is visible." Yet he can now imagine that from another's point of view it is not true that *x* is visible.

A typical experiment goes something like this: A child watches a puppet show wherein a cute puppet puts a candy bar in a dresser drawer and then goes out to play. A mischievous puppet is seen to come in, move the candy bar from the dresser drawer to a cabinet, and then leave. The cute puppet then comes back from play. Now the child, who has been watching all this, is asked where the cute puppet will look for the candy bar. Children younger than about four years old tend to say that the puppet will look for the candy bar in the cabinet, where it in fact is. Older children begin reliably reporting that the puppet will look for the candy bar where he had earlier put it (and not where it was secretly moved to). That is, older children seem to appreciate that the puppet will have a false belief.[12]

Some writers say that such experiments provide evidence that older children are developing a "theory of mind"—that they are entertaining second-order beliefs (beliefs about others' beliefs).[13] I wonder if a slightly different description could prove useful. The child might take the question put to him as what we would describe as a counterfactual: "If you were in the cute puppet's position, where would you look for the candy bar?" This is not a question about beliefs about others' beliefs, but rather a question about oneself.[14] And if I am correct in taking counterfactuals to be essentially learned from inductions, then older children simply make more sophisticated inductions (based on their experiences) than younger children; older children have more experience with error and ambiguity. (Younger children even have trouble appreciating multiple names for a given thing.[15]) There might be good empirical support for that view if children's progress in induction can be shown to track their progress in differential perspective taking.[16]

Moreover, perhaps there is a way of thinking of factual propositions as being understood with the help of counterfactuals. "The cat is on the mat" can make sense only if "cat", "mat", etc. are understood, and an appreciation of the

---

[12] H. Wimmer and J. Perner, "Beliefs about Beliefs".
[13] M. Chandler, "Doubt and Developing Theories of Mind", 394.
[14] Reasoning with counterfactuals usually begins to develop at about the age of six. See Eva Rafetseder, Maria Schwitalla, and Josef Perner, "Counterfactual Reasoning: From Childhood to Adulthood".
[15] E. V. Clark, "Lexical Meaning"; W. E. Merriman, L. L. Bowman, and B. MacWhinney, "The Mutual Exclusivity Bias in Children's Word Learning".
[16] But the issue of induction might not be crucial. Some recent studies have indicated that children younger than four are able to pass *nonverbal* versions of the false-belief task. See Paula Rubio-Fernández and Bart Geurts, "How to Pass the False-Belief Task Before Your Fourth Birthday".

meaning of these terms is partly conditioned by their alternatives. A mat is not simply a floor covering, but rather something that covers a floor that would be bare without the mat. To understand a mat is to understand—or to imagine or hypothesize—what might have been the case without it. To want a mat is to want what is not yet. To appreciate the mat is to appreciate the changes from what was, which is also what might now have been.

There are two important features to this brief description of counterfactuals. They are learned from inductions—or anyway they rely on familiar (or sometimes hypothesized) regularities. And they never appear in thought as though they were complete descriptions of some alternative world. Rather, they are like all other ordinary explanations and expectations: They go forward a little way into a fog, and they can be traced back only a little way, into a fog. Since there is fog at both ends, no conflict with actual events, or with other expected events, is usually noticed. We appreciate fiction in the same way; we simply do not try to push through the fog; nor do we usually want to.

3 Two kinds of counterfactuals

In the next chapter I will investigate the now-popular claim that death is bad because it deprives a person of what she could or would or should have had. Such a claim of deprivation makes use of counterfactuals. After a person's death, we can of course speak of her using counterfactuals, but it will be helpful to distinguish two kinds of counterfactuals that will eventually play a role in the discussion.

An *in esse* (IE) counterfactual takes a point of view from a time during which the object exists, and it proposes an alternative to one or more of the object's then-present properties or relations. Something, I, exists up to time t and then continues to exist after t. During the post-t time, I has some properties, but it is imagined to have, during that post-t time, some properties different from those it actually has. We express this by saying that I could have been otherwise. For example, an ibex forages for a while and then stops and rests. We can imagine that the still-existing ibex could have continued to forage instead of resting. The "instead" in an IE counterfactual involves some contemporaneous alternative to one or more of I's actual properties.

A *post esse* (PE) counterfactual is understood from a point of view of a time after the object ceased to exist. Something, P, existed up to time t but then went out of existence. We can imagine that during the post-t time, P still exists and (therefore) has various properties and relations (many of which could be the ones it had while it existed). A parrot lasted for a while and then ended. But we can imagine that the parrot could have continued longer, and in that longer time it (the merely imagined parrot) would have had some experiences and interactions with its environment. That is, had it continued to exist, it might have continued to have many of the same properties that it had before, and it might have had some different properties. We often express this in the same way that we express an IE counterfactual, namely, that P could have been otherwise. Yet the counterfactual is significantly different. In PE counterfactuals, P only counterfactually has any properties at all, because now there is only a counterfactual P.[17]

The cessation of the existence of P made it the case that P is now nonactual (i.e., counterfactual, imagined-to-be-existing). We can express this (in most cases without risking misunderstanding) by saying that P stopped existing although it could have continued instead. In many cases—perhaps in most cases—it is not necessary to insist that PE counterfactuals be expressed in a way different from the way in which IE counterfactuals are expressed. But strictly speaking, in the case of PE counterfactuals the "instead" has to do not with P (which no longer exists, and therefore no longer has properties, and therefore can no longer have alternative properties) but rather with the still-existing situation (in a local area, surrounded by a fog of "don't cares") that previously included P but that actually no longer does; the surviving things and processes do not include P but could have. Carefully speaking, then, we might say not that the parrot could have lasted longer than it did, but rather that there could have continued to exist the parrot, or better still (but even more awkwardly) that the present situation which is parrotless could have had a different property instead, namely, being parrotted; it could have continued to have included the (now counterfactual) parrot. In such a case it is the actual situation, and not the nonexistent P, which is described using IE counterfactuals.[18]

In the next chapter we will investigate the issue of whether death can be a deprivation, and we will see that in a case where there is no longer a P to be deprived of anything, it is the actual situation (the situation which previously included P) which is deprived (if there is any deprivation at all); it is now deprived of P.

[17] Of course, there might for a while continue to exist the body of a (dead) parrot, and that body will continue to have properties (such as mass) and relations (such as spatial location). It may help to imagine that the parrot was vaporized by a nuclear explosion. In any case, there is no longer a living parrot.
[18] "Polly died" is probably best understood as "at one time the world contained Polly, and at a subsequent time the world did not." We can say that something happened to Polly such that eventually (even very soon) there was no more Polly, but if we prefer to be picky, we might say not that it was death that happened to Polly, but rather that it was Polly's death that happened to the world.

5

Death and Deprivation

Prelude

The school term has just ended. In a basement hallway of the ancient Liberal Arts building old fluorescent bulbs flicker weakly. From a shadowy corner emerges the cloaked and hooded figure of Professor Reaper. He smiles knowingly, eyes narrowing as he stops a passing student. "I have some bad news for you." The smile broadens and his eyes narrow even further as he leans forward and repeatedly jabs a bony finger at the student. "You. Failed. My. Course. On. Death."

"What?" The student squints at the face under the dark hood, then quickly steps back. "Wait. I know you. I dropped your course after the first day."

The professor straightens up and shrugs. "Nevertheless, you failed the course. The grade has been posted, and there's no changing it."

"How can I fail a course if I didn't even take it?"

"Oh, tsk tsk! I'll give you a lesson in arithmetic for free. There were four exams in the course, each worth twenty-five percent of the final grade. Each exam had twenty-five questions, each of which was worth one point. Are you with me so far?"

"But—."

"So the score on any given exam was simply the number of questions that were answered correctly on that exam. Except for that extra credit question on the final exam about counterfactuals. You didn't respond to that question, I noticed."

"Now, would I be likely to answer any of your stupid questions if I didn't even take the course?"

"Hey, don't get smart with me! Anyway, if you had responded, I could have given you some points."

"That's irrelevant, because *I did not take that course!*"

"As if that mattered! Tell me, did you answer correctly any questions on the first exam? That was the one on nothing."

"I was not in the course after the first day, so how could I have taken that exam?"

"I'll take that as a 'No'. You answered no questions correctly, so you got zero on that exam. And the same for the other three exams. Now, do you know how to add four numbers together to get their sum?"

"Of course, but—."

"Of course. So you can add zero plus zero plus zero plus zero. And what is the sum?"

"I did not take that course!"

"Come, come. It's a simple question. There's nothing to it. What is the sum of four zeros?"

"Zero. But—."

"Correct! Zero! *Nulla!* A big fat goose egg! Nada! Zilch! That means you failed the course. Does that really mean nothing to you?"

"If I had taken that course—which I didn't, but if I had—I would have aced all the exams. I'm a good student. My grade point average is nearly 4.0."

"*Was* nearly 4.0. Sure, you *might* have done well, had you stayed in the class. But that only makes things worse. As a matter of fact you failed the course. And as a matter of counterfact, you could have done better. So you must see how terrible a misfortune it is for you, being deprived of a better score and all. You now regret dropping the course, don't you?"

"Look, old man", says the student, backing away, "I don't know who you think you are, but—."

"Why, I am the teacher! I am the bringer of light! But who do you think *you* are? In my book, you are nothing!"

(*Evanescit scholasticus*)

1 Death can be bad

Death can be an evil. Ordinarily, evil involves suffering of some sort and in some way; evil (or badness) in any of its forms, mild or terrible, usually has to do with what people have experienced or might come to experience. Dying can sometimes be painful, but being dead cannot possibly involve suffering, nor even the risk of suffering. How then can death be evil? According to popular wisdom (in much ordinary talk and in many philosophical theories) death is bad not because being dead is painful in any sense, but because it interrupts a life, causing or representing a loss for the one who died.[1] This view of the badness of death comes in slightly different forms. Sometimes the term "loss" is used;

---

[1] Such a view is therefore an example of what Stephen Rosenbaum calls "abstract bad", as opposed to "concrete bad". See his "Appraising Death in Human Life" and "Concepts of Value and Ideas about Death". (Complete bibliographic information on this and all other sources in this book is provided in the Bibliography.)

sometimes death is said to be bad when it is premature. Both notions are at work in this passage from Martha Nussbaum:

> Death will be most terrible when it is, in conventional terms, premature; for then the value of many preparatory activities—activities involving training oneself so as to be able to act in some valued way in the future—will be completely lost, in that they will never lead on to the fruition that gives them their entire point.[2]

Whether death is said to be bad because it is a loss, or an interruption of ongoing projects, or merely not getting possible future goods of any sort at all, the key point is that death is thought to cause some kind of deprivation. Death makes it the case that the person did not have good things which she otherwise could or would or should have had. I will accordingly use the terms "deprivation view", "deprivation account", or "death-as-deprivation" to signal this central theme. (Nussbaum uses the term "interruption argument". Still, it is a deprivation view of the evil of death, because it is the deprivation which is supposed to account for whatever badness an interruption is thought to have.[3])

Might death be thought to be bad not because it is a deprivation but because of the possibility of postmortem harm? A person's reputation might be tarnished posthumously; a person's life's work might fall apart after death; a person's will or deathbed wish might not be honored after death. I will not address these issues directly, except to mention three points: (1) I believe there are compelling reasons against the notion of postmortem harms of any sort, but I will not present those reasons here (although some of them may be inferred from my discussion of deprivation later on).[4] (2) Even assuming that some postmortem events can be postmortem harms, they seem to me to be no different from similar harms in one's life. When one is alive, one's reputation might be ruined, one's major projects might fall apart, or one's wishes might not be honored. If such things could be harms after death, then it would appear that it would not be on account of death; that is, in such cases it is not death which is the evil, but the slander or the ruination of work or the breaking of promises. (3) Some such postmortem harms (again, assuming that they are harms at all) might properly be classified

---

[2] Martha C. Nussbaum, *The Therapy of Desire*, 209. A similar expression of the idea was used by Michael Lockwood, "Singer on Killing and the Preference for Life", 167, and by Mary Mothersill, "Death". See also Jeff McMahan, "Death and the Value of Life", 262.
[3] The deprivation view is not a recent invention. Among the ancients, Plutarch ("That Epicurus Actually Makes a Pleasant Life Impossible", 1106–7) was enthusiastic in his use of it to ridicule the Epicurean claim that "death is nothing to us".
[4] Some problems of making sense of postmortem harm are discussed in James Stacey Taylor, *Death, Posthumous Harm, and Bioethics*, esp. chapters 1, 2, and 3. Also see my "Death and Other Nothings", 219–23.

as harms of deprivation: the deprivation of a good reputation, the deprivation of the fruition of one's projects, or the deprivation of fulfilled promises. (And it might be argued that one's death also deprived one of the opportunity to repair such damage.) To the extent that such things can be thought of as deprivations, to that extent death might be thought to cause—or at least to participate in—such deprivations, and if so, then the deprivation account of the evil of death would be so much the stronger for trying to offer a unified account.

The purpose of this chapter is to show that if we inquire more closely into the notion of deprivation, we will see that it cannot apply to a person in the singular case of death. To call death a deprivation for the one who died is to push the concept of deprivation well beyond any plausible justification. First I will look at the notion of deprivation as it is normally used to characterize parts of our lives, and I will show that it cannot apply to death. Then I will examine and reject proposals that attempt to employ special senses of deprivation. I will also argue that the deprivation theory does not take into account an important difference between counterfactuals about dead persons and counterfactuals about living persons.

Nevertheless, death can be an evil; that is the starting point. But if death does not involve suffering for the one who died, and if death cannot be a deprivation for the one who died, then in what way can death be bad? The answer will be easy to see, once we look in the right place.

2 Ordinary deprivation

Robbery can take away some good things one had. Racial discrimination in access to adequate schools can prevent one from getting good things one did not have but should have had. Such cases can be described as deprivations, in part because one ends up not having good things which one otherwise could or should or would have had. But there is more to deprivation than that. I propose that a person is deprived (in the ordinary sense) if and only if the following five requirements are met.

> D1: There must be a plausible counterfactual situation[5] which the person would have been in . . .

---

[5] One might wish to claim that there are no counterfactual situations, but only counterfactual statements. I am not opposed to that warning, but in what follows I will allow myself a little convenience and sometimes speak of things, properties, and relations as counterfactual, even if "counteractual" or "nonactual" might have been more proper.

D2: . . . at the time of the deprived condition were it not for some event (or event-package).

D3: A comparison between the actual situation and the imagined (i.e., counterfactual) situation yields an evaluation that the former is worse for the person than the latter would have been, and the latter would have been better for the person than the former is.

D4: The person's actual situation merits some distress (even if the person does not experience distress) on account of that comparison.

D5: The person is in some situation or other. (This is presupposed in D2 through D4.)

Each of the five conditions deserves discussion.

D1: There must be some plausible alternative. If an alleged alternative is impossible, then the claim of deprivation is silly. I could never be a square circle, and so I could never be deprived of being one. That is, being a square circle is not a "could have been" for me. If the alleged alternative is possible but unlikely, then the claim of deprivation is far-fetched. It is possible that a complete stranger might have given me a handful of diamonds, but I certainly do not think I am deprived by not having received such a gift. In usual, noncontentious cases of deprivation, the counterfactual is thought to be likely or expected ("expected" in the rather broad sense of being in accordance with some accepted principle—causal, ethical or otherwise). A forest fire comes my way and destroys my house. The winds could have shifted, causing the fire to miss my house, and so I am deprived of the good things my house would have provided me had it not been destroyed.[6]

D2: The counterfactual alternative must be imagined to be contemporaneous with the actual situation. I cannot now be deprived by *future* possibilities, no matter how likely such futures are thought to be. If there will probably be a deprivation, then it is a future (and hence a possible but not yet an actual) deprivation. I might of course anticipate it and worry about it, but I will be worrying about a possible future deprivation. If I plot the path of a forest fire and see that my house will probably be consumed, then I will hope that the winds

---

[6] How do we judge which alternatives are likely? For present purposes, it is not necessary to investigate that question, and we can leave the issue to be settled in each case by common experiences. Still, it is interesting to speculate that in a more thorough inquiry into counterfactuals, we would discover this principle: Given any brief description of any situation, and any brief description of any alternative, there is some way to fill out the details such that the alternative is a likely one (see Chapter 4). There is a companion thesis: The more the details of a situation are specified, the fewer are the likely alternatives. This was Spinoza's view.

will shift. But I won't actually be deprived of the good things my house could have provided for me until and unless my house is actually destroyed. If *past* conditions affected me at an earlier time, such that a likely alternative at that time would have been better for me (see D3), then I might say that I was deprived at that earlier time. It is of course true that a past event—even an event that occurred before I existed—can have created a deprivation for me even now. But that past event would be the distant cause of the deprivation and would not itself be the present situation of deprivation.

D3: The comparison between the actual situation and some alternative must show that the alternative would have been better than the present situation actually is. The usual sense of deprivation requires that I be denied some good that I had or could have had or should have had. Such a good could have been an intrinsic good (on some views, this could be pleasure or the absence of pain), or it could have been some instrumentally good thing or condition (which perhaps would have led to some intrinsic good).

D4: I follow a point made at length by Kai Draper: a deprivation is accounted bad—something that merits disappointment or distress or anger or sadness or some other negative emotion.[7] A could-have-been is not enough to guarantee that an actual state of affairs is a deprivation *and hence bad* even if the actuality is not as good as some counterfactual would have been. Suppose a person is in some intrinsically good situation but an even better situation was possible. This is not necessarily a cause for distress, anxiety or disappointment; it need not be bad for her, in any recognizable sense of "bad".[8] Otherwise, winning an Olympic Silver Medal would be bad for her if she could have won a Gold. Even winning a Gold would be bad for her, if she could have won two. On that view, since every alternative has its own branching alternatives, nearly all conditions would be bad for her just in case she lacked perfection. On the contrary, if a deprivation is to be bad, then, like any tale of woe, it is eventually woe that must be pointed out.

D5: In ordinary cases of deprivation a person cannot actually be deprived unless the person is in some situation or other. To put this another way, only actual people are actually deprived. A fictional character, such as Shakespeare's Romeo, was never, is not now, and never will be, actually deprived. (Perhaps Romeo can be fictionally deprived. In that case, conditions D1–D5 must be imagined to obtain: Romeo must be imagined to be in some actual situation, and there must be imagined to be some plausible counterfactual alternative at the

---

[7] Kai Draper, "Disappointment, Sadness, and Death".
[8] A similar point is made by Stephen E. Rosenbaum in his review of Fred Feldman's *Confrontations with the Reaper*, 234.

time of his imagined actual situation, and so on.) Is it possible that unborn (or, if you wish, unconceived) persons could be deprived (that is, deprived now, when they do not exist)? Well, perhaps they, like Romeo, might be imagined to be actual, as though they were waiting impatiently in the wings of the theater of life, and if they are not called onto the stage, then they are deprived of their chance to participate. But that is not to say that the unborn are actually deprived, but only to imagine that they would be deprived if they were somehow already actual. I do not see how the idea of an actual person who does not yet exist can be made coherent. (Nor would it help to refer to a present, actual person, and wonder if she would have been deprived if she had not come into existence. Prior to her existence, she was not in any situation at all, and had she not come into existence, she would have remained nonactual—that is to say, there would have been no she to have been deprived.) What of expersons—persons who at one time were actual, but who no longer exist? That case will be discussed in the next section.

Condition D5 is central, in Epicurean writings, to the claim that "death is nothing to us". Harry S. Silverstein appropriately labels it the "'no subject' difficulty",[9] and it is not unlike what Jeff McMahan calls "the Existence Requirement".[10]

3 Death cannot be an ordinary deprivation

A fundamental objection to the death-as-deprivation theory is that death cannot be a deprivation in the usual sense; it can be only a "deprivation"—a figurative sense in which the word ought to be shrouded in death-quotes in order to give warning that it does not apply in its living sense. Even though the case of death is like ordinary cases of deprivation whenever condition D1 (that there be a plausible alternative) is satisfied (i.e., the person might have experienced good things had the life been longer), death is nevertheless radically unlike ordinary cases of deprivation, because condition D5 (that a person *be* in some situation) is not satisfied, and therefore both D2 and D3 (that the contemporaneous alternative to the person's actual situation be comparatively better) are not satisfied. That is to say, in the singular case of death, we can speak of a would-have-been, but not of a contemporaneous actually-is. The absence of actual conditions for something means that that something simply does not exist. In

---

[9] "The Evil of Death". While I do not agree with Silverstein's attempt to respond to the Epicurean challenge (see the next chapter), his article is an excellent presentation of some of the key issues. See also Phillip Mitsis, "Happiness and Death in Epicurean Ethics".
[10] "Death and the Value of Life".

the absence of the actually-is, there is no one for whom the would-have-been is an alternative, and so there is no deprivation. Neither the unborn nor the dead can be deprived in any usual sense. There is no actuality for them, and so there is no actuality to compare a counterfactual to.

According to William Grey,

> Intuitively, the death of Frank Ramsey at the age of twenty-six is more regrettable than the death of Bertrand Russell at the age of ninety-eight. Ramsey, clearly, was deprived of more *praemia vitae* than Russell.[11]

But this must be incorrect, for the simple reason that neither the death of Ramsey nor the death of Russell deprived them (in the usual sense) of anything, even though it is plausible to say that had they lived longer, they would have had more *praemia vitae* (and we usually expect a twenty-six-year-old to live more additional years than a ninety-eight-year-old).

It is instructive to note that if the deaths of those philosophers are regrettable, it is certainly not those philosophers themselves who can do the regretting (a point I will return to anon). It is also instructive to note that on the subsequent page Grey writes:

> Consider the untimely death of Frank Ramsey. His loss of *praemia vitae* deprived the antemortem Ramsey (and the world of philosophy) of the many possible continuations of that brilliant life. [364]

And now we have a clear case of deprivation that we did not have in the former quote. But this clear case of deprivation is whispered in parentheses—an afterthought, a by-the-way. It is "the world of philosophy"—that is, you and I and all other survivors—who are said to be deprived of Ramsey and his likely further accomplishments.

This raises a serious problem for the death-deprivation theory. If, according to the theory, Ramsey's death deprived Ramsey of some goods, and if those goods included us (as friends and colleagues, say), then Ramsey was deprived of us. In the clear case of deprivation mentioned earlier, Ramsey was part of our *praemia vita*, and so Ramsey's death deprived us of Ramsey. But if there are two deprivations, going in opposite directions, as it were, then why is our deprivation of Ramsey a significantly different kind of thing from Ramsey's deprivation of us? We can lament Ramsey's death, wish it were otherwise, grieve, and be now worse off for not having Ramsey around, whereas the dead Ramsey cannot

---

[11] William Grey, "Epicurus and the Harm of Death", 363. Similar sentiments are expressed by other death-as-deprivation theorists.

possibly lament his loss of us, wish it were otherwise, grieve, and be now worse off for not having us around. Perhaps Grey recognizes the problem, because he tries to find an actual person for the deprivation to attach to, and he chooses the person *before* death. No doubt Ramsey was actual before he died, but how can it be the "antemortem Ramsey" (i.e., the Ramsey who was before he wasn't) who was deprived of us, whereas it cannot be the antemortem-Ramsey-we (i.e., the we who were before Ramsey wasn't) who were deprived of Ramsey? Necessarily, we were not deprived of Ramsey until Ramsey died, and so it is the postmortem-Ramsey-we who are deprived of Ramsey. But then the deprivation theory ought to say that it is the postmortem-Ramsey-Ramsey who is deprived of us. Yet there can be no such Ramsey. (This is the "no subject" difficulty again.)

Consider an epistemological parallel to the ontological requirements of deprivation. If we know only that Zoë did not visit the zoo, then we cannot conclude that she is deprived. It does not matter if such a visit would have been profitable or entertaining or educational. Let it be plausible that there could have been far more good things than bad things as a result of such a visit. Even then we do not know whether she is deprived, because we do not know whether that counterfactual situation would have been better for her than her actual situation is (nor whether her actual situation merits some distress on account of that comparison).

Condition D3 requires that an actuality be compared to a counteractuality. Absent the actuality, there can be, at best, only a counterfactual deprivation. Zoë comes to a fork in the road. She can choose path A or path B. Which one would be better for her? Not "Which one *is* better for her?" except as we interpret the "is" as a kind of apparent inevitability that hides a conditional. Path A, say, is better for her in the sense that *if* she chooses it, she will be better off (than if she chooses the other path). But that is an important "if". Suppose Zoë gives up her deliberations and walks away from the situation of choice; she is no longer a traveler facing a choice between two paths. Then we ought to refer only counterfactually, and in a past tense, to those two previous choice possibilities. Path A would have been better for her than path B would have been; if she had chosen path B, she would not have benefited as she would have, had she chosen path A. But that describes, at best, a counterfactual deprivation. If there is any actual deprivation after Zoë has left the situation of choice, then it would require that she continue to exist (although no longer as a traveler at the fork in the road), and would require, too, that she be worse off for not having whatever benefits she would have received, if she had continued as a traveler and chosen path A.

Suppose that instead of leaving the situation of choice, Zoë died before taking either path. Then even if we know that she could have taken path A, that counterfactual cannot be compared to her actually going a different way, since, by hypothesis, she did not actually take either road. Rather, counterfactually taking one road can be compared only to her counterfactually taking the other road. The most we can say, then, is what we first said earlier when Zoë abandoned her travels, namely, she would have been better off, had she taken one road, than she would have been, had she taken a different road. Actually (and not counteractually) being better off or worse off has to do with which path is actually taken, compared to what would have been the case had the other path been taken. But that kind of comparison cannot be made if no path is taken. Now, her death is not one path from the fork and life another. Rather, her death is the eternal not taking any path. In the case of Zoë's death, the actuality has vanished, and so any comparison can involve only two counterfactuals, not a counterfactual and an actuality, and so there is no actual deprivation (in any usual sense).

Still another issue: If death is thought to be the deprivation of good things, then there will be a puzzle in the case of some things considered good. A man steps into the road and flags us down and says that his wife has been deprived of insulin since yesterday. "Where is she?" we ask. "We'll take her to the hospital. Or we can rush you to the pharmacy for more insulin." The man waves the offer aside. "Oh, I have plenty of insulin. See? Vials and vials of it. The problem is that she died yesterday. Had she lived, she would have received her injections. As it is, death deprived her of all this insulin, and so she is worse off because she does not have the insulin she would have had."

Zoë broke her arm and needed to have it set in order to relieve her pain (and promote future good). If something prevented her from getting proper medical attention, then she was deprived (and she no doubt suffered). But suppose that on her way to the doctor, she died. It would be, at best, misleading to say that now dead she is deprived of proper medical attention for her broken arm.[12]

These examples also show that another reason that death cannot be an ordinary deprivation is that an alleged death-deprivation cannot have a present tense as ordinary deprivations do. If Zoë was deprived of proper attention to her broken arm, then there was a time during which it was appropriate to say "Zoë is deprived of adequate medical attention". But the alleged deprivation of

---

[12] These examples follow a pattern discussed by Stephen Rosenbaum, "Appraising Death in Human Life", 162–63.

death has no present tense. If Zoë died before visiting the doctor, then there is no time—then or thenafter—during which we can say that she is deprived of medical correction, because, unlike ordinary events, a person's death cannot put the person into a situation or condition of any sort. So anyone who wants to claim that Zoë *was* deprived on account of death, must address the fact that at no time can it be true that she *is* deprived on account of death.[13]

That feature of the alleged deprivation of death might easily be overlooked if the issue is expressed, as many writers do, in a "tenseless" (or "timeless") way: "Death *is* bad for the one who *dies* because death *deprives* the one who *dies* of the good things she could have had." The result of using tenseless verbs, which look just like present tense verbs, can be a vague but misleading feeling that the victim and the counterfactual alternative are contemporaneous (i.e., that condition D2 somehow is satisfied). Consider this argument:

1. S's actual life had *a* units of happiness (balance of pleasure over pain, say).
2. Had S died later, S's life would have had *b* units of happiness.
3. So if *b* is greater than *a*, then S's death deprived S of the good things S would have had, had S died later.

"*a*" represents some number or other, and so does "*b*". Arithmetical relations are supposed to be "timeless", and so "is greater than" makes use of "is" in a timeless sense. But in the context of the argument, "*a*" represents a number pertaining to some past actuality, whereas "*b*" represents a number pertaining to a later counteractuality. When a timeless "is" is used, the pedigrees of those two numbers is hidden, and so it might go unnoticed that the timeless "is" does not actually pick out a *contemporaneous* actuality-counteractuality pair (and hence cannot describe an actual deprivation).[14]

"Death prevents us from doing things we want to do, and experiencing things we want to experience."[15] This can be misleading not only because of its use of tenseless verbs but also because it is "us"—*we* are to imagine having died. But then we seem to also imagine what we are missing out on *at that time*, as though D2 were satisfied. If we put the matter in the third person (and in a tensed manner), our tendencies shift a little. Maybe there will be something in

---

[13] In Section 5 below I will examine some attempts to address that fact.
[14] Here is another improper mix of a tensed copula and a tenseless copula: "Abraham Lincoln's height (at its greatest) was 193 cm. Louis XIV's height (at its greatest) was 162 cm. Since 193 *is* greater than 162, it follows that Lincoln *is* taller than Louis XIV." Not only is that conclusion wrong (because we have background information that the times of the adult lives of those persons did not overlap), it has also led to some head-scratching regarding relations: "*When* was Lincoln taller than Louis XIV?", or "*When* did the 'taller than' relation hold between Lincoln and Louis XIV?"
[15] Ben Bradley, "When is Death Bad for the One Who Dies?", 4.

Zoë's future which will prevent her from doing things which she *now* wants to do in the future; but will she still want to do them tomorrow, next week, next year? If she changes her mind and vacates her earlier desire, then her subsequent not doing what she previously wanted to do is not concurrent with her (previous and now vacated) desire. The case of death is similar. If Zoë died, her death made it the case that she did not do what she previously wanted to do, but never is it the case that death's "prevention" and the desires are concurrent. We cannot put the matter in the progressive sense: "Zoë's death (that is, when she no longer exists) is preventing her from doing what she wants to do." We cannot put it that way, for the obvious reason that after her annihilation there is no Zoë who desires anything, or who can be prevented from either desiring or doing anything. That fact is not the evil of death for Zoë, but rather the singular irrelevance of death for her.

Here is a more involved story that may help us to better understand how death cannot be an ordinary deprivation. Baby-Zoë is in a crib. Across the room in the bookcase there sits a volume of Epicurus's writings, and no doubt if Zoë grows into adulthood, she will be able to read and enjoy that book. But the Evil World Government now enacts a law requiring the destruction of all of Epicurus's works, as a consequence of which the volume of Epicurus in Baby-Zoë's room is soon removed and destroyed. Suppose that someone now claims, "Taking the book away deprived the baby of the good of reading Epicurus, because if the book had not been destroyed, then the baby would have grown into an adult who would have found much satisfaction in reading Epicurus." Notice the form which this alleged deprivation takes: it is a future deprivation (or, more precisely, a prediction of a future deprivation). But clearly it is not the baby who *is* presently deprived (because she cannot read and enjoy Epicurus in any case), but rather the later adult who *will be* (or might be) deprived. Given a point of view from the future, when she has finally become an adult with no Epicurus to read, we can say that the earlier destruction of the book (when Zoë was a baby) was not a deprivation for her then; rather, it was the cause of the present deprivation for her now, as an adult.

But suppose that as Zoë reaches adulthood and is mature enough to read Epicurus, the Evil World Government is overthrown and a volume of Epicurus's works is discovered to have been preserved; it is reprinted and again made available. Then there is now no deprivation for Adult-Zoë after all, although earlier it seemed that there was going to be.

A person is not deprived of Epicurus's writings if she is capable of reading and enjoying Epicurus and Epicurus's works are available to her. Since Epicurus's works are available when Adult-Zoë is capable of using them, the earlier destruction of the book did not cause a deprivation for her. Whether a given event causes a deprivation depends on whether a situation of deprivation exists as a result.

So far, then, I hope to have shown what no one would disagree with: Zoë was not deprived as a baby, but *might* be later on *if* Epicurus's works are not available when she can read and enjoy them.

But now change the story slightly. Suppose that shortly after the Epicurus book is removed from her room, Baby-Zoë dies in the crib. We have already decided that she was not deprived when she was a baby. And now, on account of her death, she will not ever after be in a situation of deprivation, regardless of whether Epicurus's works are available later on. She *was* not deprived when she was a living baby in the crib; nor *is* she deprived as an adult, since she never became an adult. In such a case one can speak only of a counterfactual deprivation: Zoë would have been deprived, had she grown up without Epicurus's works to read.[16]

After Baby-Zoë's death it can be said that she never had the chance to read Epicurus. True. But that does not describe a deprivation *for her*. During her short life it was not true that she was deprived of Epicurus, although it was true that she could not read and enjoy Epicurus (because, to repeat, she was a mere baby). And now, after death, there is no longer a Zoë to be deprived (or to be not deprived) of anything. Especially inappropriate would be this, uttered at any time after Baby-Zoë's death: "Zoë is deprived, because she does not now have a chance to read Epicurus."

Condition D5 requires the actuality of the person deprived, and D2 requires a contemporaneous counteractuality. The firm grounding which these conditions have is simply that, as far as I can see, all non-death instances of deprivation require them. Take either D2 or D5 away, and there is no deprivation. There are as yet no grounds for supposing that death is a special case—a case where

---

[16] To put this another way, we may ask: If there was a deprivation, what caused it? The answer is obvious (because it was given in the story), namely, the destruction of the book. But why, we may ask, was that the cause of a *deprivation* and hence, presumably, bad? Why was it not the cause of something very good, or neutral? Because, we say, Epicurus is good to read, so an adult who does not have access to Epicurus is deprived of that good. Quite right. But then the destruction of the book is bad if later on the person does not have the opportunity to read Epicurus, and not because it takes that opportunity away from the baby, for the baby already does not have that opportunity; the baby cannot read and enjoy Epicurus, even when there presently exist works of Epicurus. If, by means of some unexpected brain development, the *baby* were able to read Epicurus, then the destruction of the book at that time would cause a condition of deprivation for that remarkable infant. What matters, then, in considering cases of deprivation, is that the person does not now have what she could (or should) have had.

necessarily neither D2 nor D5 (nor, therefore, D3) can be satisfied yet a deprivation, which is a contingent matter, exists anyway.

It may be useful to pause here to examine some comments by Thomas Nagel, who wishes to produce an example of an in-life deprivation in order to show how death can be a similar kind of deprivation.

> [It is] worth exploring the position that most good and ill fortune has as its subject a person identified by his history and his possibilities, rather than merely by his categorical state of the moment—and that while this subject can be exactly located in a sequence of places and times, the same is not necessarily true of the goods and ills that befall him.
>
> [...] Suppose an intelligent person receives a brain injury that reduces him to the mental condition of a contented infant. ["Death", 65]

Nagel is correct that deprivation has to do with history and possibilities, and in his example we are confronted with a condition that has both. A history—a past tense—alone will not do to identify any harm (unless we can identify past instances of harm), yet death completes the history of the person and prevents all future possibilities for the person. It is natural to unwittingly assume that there still remain possibilities of some sort for the person, because most of our experiences seem to be like that. When we drive into a cul-de-sac, we run out of possibilities for driving further along the road, but we certainly do not run out of possibilities tout court, for we can always back up and try a different road. We can, as it were, revisit our history and create some more possibilities. But death is not like that; there is no backing up, no undoing, and no second chance.

> If, instead of concentrating exclusively on the over-sized baby before us, we consider the person he was, and the person he *could* be now, then his reduction to this state and the cancellation of his natural adult development constitute a perfectly intelligible catastrophe. ["Death", 66]

Yes, but this will not do as an adequate analog for death, because in judging the brain injury to be a catastrophe for the person, we must take note of what he now *is*. Here is a brain-damaged person before us. Previously he was developing in a certain way, and suddenly most of the important expectations about him were shattered. Now we must replace them with other expectations about him (which can be a difficult thing to do), and we might desperately hope for some cure for his condition. But in the case of death, there is no longer a person before us (even though we may be in the presence of a corpse), and so there are no longer any grounds for any expectations or any hope at all about him (although our habits continue for a while).[17] All future possibilities for the person have vanished precisely because it is a case of death. In the case of the brain-damaged person (who continues to exist as a person) we can speculate about what the person could have been and also what he might now subsequently become. These kinds of speculations can apply to any living person, brain-damaged or not. But in the case of death we are reduced to speculating *only* about what the person (not the corpse, but the person) could have been. This limitation characterizes death.

As another reason for denying that death can be any sort of ordinary deprivation, consider a parallel case that is just like a deprivation except that what has been denied to the person is not something good, but rather something bad. In such a case we do not usually use "deprive"; perhaps "spare" will do. If the deprivation theory claims that death deprived Zoë of the good things she could have had, then the theory should also claim that death spared her the bad things she could have had. That is supposed to be the blessing of euthanasia (and sometimes of suicide), and it may seem at first to be a point in favor of the deprivation account: If Zoë was suffering terribly, then if she died, she no longer suffers.[18] Yes, after her death, it is no longer true that she suffers, but she is no more relieved of suffering than she is relieved of nearsightedness or the burden of jury duty. Similarly, Zoë can be cured of a disease only if she then exists in a cured condition. One would be thought mad if one claimed to have invented a cure for a disease by having created a new means of killing victims of the disease.

You take your car to Reaper's Auto Repair, complaining that the engine is running roughly. The mechanic examines the engine for a while. "This problem is a killer", he says, shaking his head. Then his eyes narrow. "Wait. I can make it the case that the engine does not run roughly." He tosses a few sticks of dynamite into the engine compartment, and the car is blown to bits. Sure enough, the engine no longer runs roughly. The mechanic has not repaired your car; he has instead given you a practical demonstration of an important fallacy, to be explained next.

---

[17] Nagel himself says something similar elsewhere: "Unconsciousness includes the continued possibility of experience, and therefore doesn't obliterate the here and now [and, he ought to add, the future] as death does" (*The View From Nowhere*, 226).

[18] "Death [...] has its obvious drawbacks, but also its benefits; for the dead are at least free from pain, grief, despair, and other unpleasant sensations, moods, emotions, and so on" (George Pitcher, "The Misfortunes of the Dead", 159).

4 The Fallacy of Misplaced Contingency

Some properties and relations apply bivalently in a person's life but fail when an attempt is made to straddle the existence-nonexistence divide. It would be misleading (at best) to say that Abraham Lincoln is deaf because he died long ago and so he can hear nothing. Here is a short selection of similar sillies about Lincoln:

- He does not want to be involved in politics.
- He hasn't had a medical check-up in years.
- He no longer has headaches.
- He is not concerned about the plight of slaves.
- He hasn't decided whether to go to the theater next week.

In each case what is said of Lincoln involves the attribution of a contingent property or relation. Those contingencies usually apply bivalently to living persons, and they are accompanied (almost always only implicitly) by counterfactuals. But trouble can result when such properties or their negations are predicated of an experson. A person who became blind is a person who can no longer see but who might have continued to be sighted, whereas a corpse, although it is false that it can see, is not blind; neither being sighted nor being blind is appropriately said of a corpse. For an unemployed person there is a counterfactual alternative at that time, namely, that he has a job. Although it is false that an experson has a job, its name is not to be put on the list of the unemployed. A lovelorn person only contingently has no lover, whereas a corpse has no lover yet cannot be lovelorn. If it were true that after death a person is at peace, then it would be so only in the same sense that a carrot is at peace, and not in the way a satisfied person is at peace: a peaceful person is not in anguish but *could* be; a carrot is not in anguish and *could not* be. A person who has not eaten all day might be hungry and wish it were otherwise, but being hungry is improperly predicated of Abe Lincoln, even if it is true that he has not eaten in over 150 years.

To return to an earlier example, Frank Ramsey died, so we have lost Ramsey; but he has not lost us. Why the asymmetry? The explanation has to do with the natures of loss and annihilation. Loss is a contingency; only those who exist can have (now) lost something, because to have lost something is to *be* but without that something that one used to have (and counterfactually might still have). "Ramsey lost his position as Director of Studies in Mathematics" implies "At one time Ramsey was a Director, and at a later time, *when he was still the sort of thing that could be a Director*, he was not a Director"; being and not being a Director are at that later time contingent features of Ramsey. But since he is dead, then he (or, more precisely, what remains of what used to be him) is not the sort of thing to be a Director; so although it is false that he is a Director, he has not lost his position as Director. Being a Director is no longer a contingent matter for Ramsey (or rather for what remains of what used to be Ramsey).

"This rock cannot see, but it is not blind" is an odd thing to say, but it does not have the paradoxical character that "My father cannot see, but he is not blind" has. In the latter case, we search for some account; perhaps the speaker's father has normal vision but just now has his eyes covered. If that proves to not be correct, then we might search for some other explanation. If we are finally told that the father cannot see because he is dead, then the only thing that needs explaining is why the speaker would bother us with such a low-witted claim.

Usually when it is said that something fails to have a certain property, we suppose the existence of that something and deny of it the predication of that property. "S does not have the property P" is easily understood as "There exists something named S that does not have property P". But "is dead" (and similarly, "does not exist") is not really a property (or the denial of a property) of Abe Lincoln. "Abe Lincoln is dead" can be understood as a convenient shorthand for the rather awkward predication of something not of Lincoln but rather of the world: "The world used to include Abe Lincoln, but now it does not", or "The things and processes of the world no longer have Abe Lincoln to work on, react to, and be affected by".

In the earlier examples, the attribution of a property where it cannot belong is a kind of category mistake; we will name it the *Fallacy of Misplaced Contingency*. Although in this chapter (and in Chapter 7) I point out how the fallacy is committed in the case of expersons, the fallacy is not limited to such cases. Both "S is a father" and "S is not a father" can be said of adult males, but if S is a female, or if S is not an adult, or if S is not a biological organism, then usually neither the predicate "is a father" nor its denial will apply to S, even if "It is false that S is a father" might be taken to be true. If it is obvious that something is not the sort of thing to have a particular property, then it is odd (or at least unexpected) to say so. "This fish does not have a high school education" is odd in that way. Similarly, it would be a surprise to say of a two-year-old that she is unemployed, and that is because she is not taken to be in the category of "employable"—that is, something which might or might not be employed.

There are borderline cases, of course. Leon was mauled by a lion and now lies in a hospital bed in an irreversible coma, kept technically alive by sophisticated machines. He may be little more than a vegetable, and so it seems odd to me (but perhaps it will not seem so odd to some people) to say that Leon has lost his sense of humor. It seems odd, because he now seems to not be the sort of thing which can have a sense of humor; it is no longer a contingent matter for Leon.

J. David Velleman says that there are many stories we can tell about our death.

> Yet even after we adjust our stories to the realities of death, the adjusted stories remain compelling: we really will be relieved of our burdens, even if we won't feel the relief; we really will miss out on the future, even if we won't know what we're missing. [. . .] There's a story in which death prevents us from accompanying our loved ones into the future; it's a sad story, and it's also a true story; being sad about death therefore makes perfect sense. There's a story in which death brings all our trials to an end; it's a happy story, and it's also a true story; being happy about death therefore makes sense. ["Comments", 521]

The term "true story" used here is crucially misleading, because Velleman's comments miss an important part of the Epicurean view. There are *two* true stories in which we cannot accompany our loved ones into the future: one is when we exist, but we are only contingently unable to accompany them (because, for example, we are carted off for a life sentence in prison, or we are shipwrecked on a remote planet); the other is when we necessarily cannot accompany them because there is no "we" to do any accompanying of anyone. And there are *two* true stories in which our trials are brought to an end: one is when we are living, but our trials are contingently over because we manage to live happily ever after; the other is when we necessarily have no trials because there is no "we" to have any trials—or anything else. There are two true stories about the car's engine's no longer running roughly, but only one story is the kind we pay the mechanic for. There are two true stories about no longer having a disease, but only one story is the kind we pay doctors for. There are two true stories in which the ship's captain was not drunk today, and two true stories in which he has no ability to hire a crew, no prospect of earning a salary, no hope of a calm sea, no ability to appreciate music, no friends, no enemies, no food, no hopes, no stories, and no wonder.

Sadness and happiness are appropriate at the prospect of your continuing to exist with either burdens or relief of burdens. But the case of your nonexistence is not a case for *you*, but only for the world without you. If death makes it the case that you no longer have burdens, then that can in a very practical sense relieve your survivors, but not you. If your death makes it the case that you cannot be with your loved ones, then that can sadden your loved ones, but not you. Such final stories can end up happy-making or sad-making only for others. That is a unique feature of annihilation—the singularity of death.

5 Could death be a special kind of deprivation?

Consider Jeff McMahan's comment that "although one does not experience death, it does affect one's experience—by limiting or ending it".[19] But that is misleading. Ordinarily when we say that some event affects a person's experiences we mean that the person's experiences are such that they would have been different had the event not occurred. But death cannot affect experiences in *that* way; death cannot create experiences (for the deceased) which would have been otherwise had death not occurred. That is to say, although death ends all of one's experiences, it cannot change one's experiences.

There is an important difference between experience-as-experienced (an internal view) and experience-as-thing (an external view). Your experiences are, to me, an object of my experience but are not themselves experienced by me (which is only to say that your experiences are not mine). I can talk about them, in the same way I can talk about, and exist beyond, the temporal boundaries of something. That cloud in the sky, for example, formed, floated a while, then dissipated. I can experience the temporal boundaries of the cloud because I can experience things outside those boundaries. I can similarly speak of the spatial boundaries of, say, this table, and I can experience things outside those spatial boundaries. I can *be* outside the temporal and spatial boundaries of something that is not me; but I cannot *be* outside my own temporal and spatial boundaries. When it comes to my death, I can think of the end of my experiences only by imaginatively taking an external point of view, as though from some other experiencer.[20] So even if death could make a difference *to* my experiences, it cannot make a difference *in* my experiences. But I am always *in* my experiences.

I mention McMahan's comment because it is typical of the shift in focus that characterizes some attempts to save the death-as-deprivation theory by, in effect, proposing that there is a sense of deprivation in which the actually-is of condition D5 is replaced with an implied external view of an actually-*was*, such that the would-have-been—the counterfactual condition in D1—is not an *alternative for* an actually-is but rather a counterfactual *extension of* an actually-was. On such a view, death is said to be a deprivation (but it would have to be a unique kind) if the life of the person who died could have been longer and contained good things (or perhaps more good things than bad).

---

[19] "Death and the Value of Life", 234. Christopher Belshaw (*Annihilation*, 87) makes a similar claim.
[20] This was Freud's insight: "It is indeed impossible to imagine our own death; and whenever we attempt to do so we can perceive that we are in fact still present as spectators" ("Thoughts for the Times on War and Death", 289).

We may take it as true that many completed lives—lives which were, but are no longer, actual—could have been longer and contained good things. But it is a mistake to say that therefore there could be some special kind of deprivation (which in turn is necessary, on the death-as-deprivation theory, in order to characterize death as bad in some special sense). It is that mistake that I want to investigate here. I will do so by making use of Fred Feldman's version of the death-deprivation account. It is not necessary to use Feldman's version; I find the same problem with other death-as-deprivation views. I pick Feldman's because it can be presented in a clean, simple way, free of distracting complications. Besides, his account is also well known. It is, moreover, an account that seems initially to be plausible.

On Feldman's version we are to assume that hedonism is true. Or, rather, we are to assume that a very simple variety of hedonism is true, namely, one in which the only thing that is intrinsically good is pleasure, and the only thing that is intrinsically bad is pain. Interpret intrinsic value in any reasonable way; the subtleties need not detain us.[21]

Next, assume that every person's life has a hedonic value; this value is reckoned by subtracting the total of the intrinsically bad things in that life from the total of intrinsically good things in that life. Again, this is a very simple version of hedonism, and we might wonder whether there could be such things as totals of pleasures and pains and whether and how we could ever come to calculate them. And even if we could do that, we might wish to improve upon such a calculus by, for example, taking note not of the totals, or at least not the totals alone, but also the way in which the goods and bads are distributed. Such possible improvements in hedonistic reckoning need not concern us here. Make use of any version you wish; I will use the term "hedonic value" as a shorthand way of referring to any such summary.

Next, examine a plausible counterfactual extension of the dead person's (now past) life—that is, the extra years he might have lived, had he not died when he did—and find its hedonic value (assuming, again, that that is even possible).

Finally, compare the hedonic value of the actual life to the hedonic value of the actual life plus the counterfactual extension. If the latter is higher than the

---

[21] Fred Feldman, *Confrontations with the Reaper*, chapters 8 and 9. Feldman cautions us that he does not endorse the variety of hedonism as presented; he uses it only to make what he takes to be an anti-Epicurean point: even on the basis of a simple version of hedonism, death is a deprivation and is therefore bad. But, just to be careful when assessing Feldman's view, we ought to remember that Epicurus did not endorse such a hedonism either; he (and later on Lucretius) was clear that what is good is not the amassing of pleasures nor achieving a balance of pleasure over pain.

former, then, according to the theory, the person was deprived, and death was bad for that person because of that deprivation.

But something odd has happened in the attempt to make such a comparison. Feldman compares the hedonic values of *entire* lives. But it is not clear that we should do so, if doing so hides something important. And it does. Since the actual life and the actual life plus the counterfactual extension coincide up until the alleged depriving event (death), their hedonic values at that point are equal, and so they can be ignored; the important arithmetical comparison is of the hedonic value of nonexistence with the hedonic value of a counterfactual continuation of life. Now we can see that the application of the concept of deprivation is unwarranted (or is at least suspicious), because the contemporaneity condition of D2 has been violated.[22]

Let me propose an analogy. Instead of examining a counterfactual temporal extension, I will investigate a counterfactual spatial extension such that it is not difficult to understand how its use in a comparison is illegitimate. And then I will suggest that the relevant illegitimate feature of the analog is present in the original, thus making the original an illegitimate comparison too.

Notice first that on the view here under consideration it is not life itself which is supposed to be good, or better than death, but rather the things and events and experiences in life. That is why we are to summarize not length of life but the hedonic value of a life. Similar considerations will apply to the analog; it is not mere extension in space that will be important, but the good things that are available within that spatial extension. Notice also that a counterfactual extension of a (past) life would change nothing in that (past) life; the extension would only allow for more of some things that the actual (past) life had, or would now provide some new things that the actual (past) life did not have. So it is with the spatial analog: We are to imagine a counterfactual spatial extension which would not change what is already there, but which would allow for more of what is already there, or would add some things that are not there.

Let us assume that wax is good for wooden tables and lack of wax is bad for them. This will be a simple "hedonism" for tables as an analog for a simple hedonism for persons. You enter your newly waxed heirloom dining room table in Reaper's Antique Furniture Awards Show. The judge examines your table and shakes his head. "There is nothing wrong with this table as it stands—as far as it goes." His eyes narrow. "Except that it is deprived of wax, because if it were

---

[22] When Feldman's view is used to describe a case of deprivation in the ordinary sense for a *living* person—a person whose life is going one way but could have gone another—then condition D2 is satisfied.

longer", he says as he holds his bony hand in mid-air, just beyond the end of the table, "then it would extend out to *here*, as some tables like yours do, and in that case you would surely have given it more wax. So the end of the table deprives the table of wax. Too bad."

Has your table been properly judged? You complain that you don't understand the judge's reasoning.

"Look", he says, dipping a cloth into a can of paste wax and then moving the cloth around horizontally in a circular motion in the air at the height of the tabletop but beyond the end of the table. "If the table extended out to here, it would receive the goodness of this wax. I don't mean, of course, that if you moved the table from its present location and put it here, then it would receive this wax. I don't mean that. Besides, the table as it actually is has as much wax as it should have. I don't mean to say that the table as it actually is, is deprived of wax. What I mean is, if the table were longer than it actually is, then it would receive some additional goodness of appropriate wax—the wax on this very cloth, for example. The logic of the issue is quite simple. The table does not have as much wax as it plausibly would have, were it longer. Consequently, the table is deprived of that additional wax. Q.E.D."

The judge's apparently unpolished logic can be recounted in terms of a deprivation theory calculus. Add up all the wax (or all the surface area waxed) on the actual table, and subtract any unwaxed areas. Next, add up all the counterfactual wax (or all the surface area which plausibly would have been waxed) on the counterfactual extension, and subtract any counterfactually unwaxed areas. Finally, compare the total for the table as it actually is to the total for the actual table plus the counterfactual extension. If the second is more than the first, then, according to the calculus, there is a deprivation. Yet it is clear that the table is not deprived of wax. Even the judge described the actual table as having as much wax (appropriately applied) as it ought to have. How can that be true and yet also be true that the table is deprived? Let us look more closely.

If not every area of the actual table is waxed, we can say that it would have been better for the table if the table had been more thoroughly waxed. In that case, we are comparing the actuality to an ordinary counterfactual alternative. And if we say that if there were an extension, then waxing it would have been better for the (counterfactually extended) table than not waxing it would have been, then we are comparing two counterfactuals with each other. But the deprivation theory must say this: "It would have been better for the table if the table had a counterfactual extension, because then the table could have received more wax." The judge's error is manifest: it violates the spatial analog of the contemporaneity condition (D2), because if you look outside the boundaries of the table, you will discover that there is no table *there* to have or to not have wax. Deprivation of wax for the table cannot apply where the table does not exist.[23] (Moreover, if the table did extend past its actual boundaries and were satisfactorily waxed in that counterfactual extension, then the judge could say that it was still deprived of wax—the wax it would have were it to extend even further. The upshot would be that the table might be deprived wherever wax was available and the table wasn't.)

It is not difficult to think of many more spatial analogs. Here are two: An orchard exists within a certain geographical boundary; the sun is shining on the orchard; but the sun is also shining on the ground beyond the orchard—where the orchard does not extend (but might have). Is the orchard deprived of sunlight beyond the orchard's boundaries? A person who is deprived of clothes is naked. But is a clothed person naked outside the spatial boundaries of the body?

Let us apply the analog back to the original. Within the temporal boundaries of an actual person—that is, during life—there may be reason to say that the person is deprived of what the person could then have had instead of what the person actually has. In that case, we are comparing the actuality to a counterfactual alternative for that person. If a person's life is imaginatively and counterfactually extended, then we could of course say, of that counterfactual extension, that it would be better that *it* contain pleasure or happiness or flourishing or, in general, good things, than not contain good things; it would be better for the *counterfactually extended* person to experience good things in that counterfactual extension than to suffer in that counterfactual extension. In that case, we are comparing two counterfactuals with each other. But that would not indicate an actual deprivation, and so the death-as-deprivation theory must say this: "It would have been better for the person if the person had a counterfactual life extension, because then the *actual* person (and not a counterfactually-extended person) could have received more good things." But there is no actual person after the person has ceased to exist,

---

[23] If the table is deprived of wax, then there is some spatial location on the table—or within the spatial boundaries of the table—where the table does not have wax. To put it another way (in order to highlight the spatial analog of the contemporaneity condition), if the table is deprived of wax, then there is some spatial location where the table exists without some wax which it could or ought to have. This is not to say that the proposition that the table is deprived of wax is not true outside the spatial boundaries of the table. If the table is in London, and if it is deprived of wax, then it is true in both London and Paris that the table (which is in London) is somewhere deprived of wax. The claim, we might say, is true spacelessly. If we switch from space to time, and if it is true that the table is deprived of wax, then there is some time when the table exists without some wax which it could or ought to have. This is not to say that the claim that the table is deprived of wax is not true outside the temporal boundaries of the table. If the table exists only in the twenty-first century, then perhaps it is true in both the twenty-first and the twenty-second centuries that the table (which exists only in the twenty-first century) is somewhere deprived of wax. The claim, we might say, is true timelessly.

and so none of the things that might show up *then* could be possibilities for a then nonexistent person.[24] (This tangle of counterfactuals will be addressed further in Section 7 when we return to the distinction made in the previous chapter between *in esse* (IE) and *post esse* (PE) counterfactuals.)

6 Postmortem well-being

Part of Feldman's approach involved attending away from the postmortem absence of the actual person and focusing instead on some sort of quantitative hedonic value. Let us look at a similar attempt that recommends using a "well-being level". Assuming that a person's well-being level could be quantified, we might be able to construct an interpretation of ordinary deprivation that begins like Feldman's. If Zoë's present well-being level is lower than what her well-being level would have been had some event or condition been otherwise, then we might say that she is deprived of that counterfactually higher well-being level (or of what would have brought about that higher well-being level). In this way we would be comparing two contemporaneous things, as D2 requires, namely, an actual well-being level and a counterfactual well-being level. According to Ben Bradley a well-being level is based on the values of events for a person, and

> the value of some event for a person depends on the difference it makes to how things go for that person. To determine this, we look at how well things actually go for the person, and compare that with how well they would have gone had that event not happened. [*Well-Being and Death*, 50]

I have no quarrel with that, provided that "how things go for that person" is understood as presuming that there is a "that person" for things to "go for"; it is always a contingent matter that an event or situation does or does not affect a person (who is already assumed to be there). But after the person is annihilated, the contingency has vanished, and we ought to say that in such a case there is no "going for" the person at all. Neither rain nor the absence of rain can "go for"—make a difference to—the people at a picnic when there actually are no longer any people there. Simon Keller says:

> At one level of detail, [...] the question of what can befall you after your death is not a matter of controversy. The disagreement only sets in when we ask whether

---

[24] This complaint against the death-as-deprivation view is consistent with Silverstein's cautions about life-death comparisons ("The Evil of Death").

any of the things that can befall you after death are relevant to your welfare. ["Posthumous Harm", 189]

The mistake is understandable, but significant. There is no *you* after your death, so nothing can befall *you* then. (Or, put another way, something's befalling you has no application postmortem.)

So far, we seem to have made no progress over Feldman's version, because after death there would seem to no longer be a well-being level, because there is no longer a person to have a well-being level.[25]

The solution proposed by Bradley is supposed to be straightforward: "When I am sitting in a chair and having no pleasant or painful experiences, I have a well-being level of zero" (*Well-Being and Death*, 106). Since a nonexistent thing cannot have experiences, it follows that it cannot experience any pleasure (which would be represented by some positive value on a scale for well-being) or pain (which would be indicated by a negative value on a scale for well-being), and so, according to this view, the appropriate value to assign for an experson's well-being would be the same as the value assigned to Bradley when in his chair and experiencing neither pleasure nor pain, namely, zero. This is supposed to allow for a simple comparison of zero (the number representing the actual well-being level of the nonactual person) to the number representing the contemporaneous counterfactual well-being level of the person if the person had not died.

In order to look as much like ordinary deprivation as possible, a death-deprivation theory must theorize *some*thing into that otherwise empty postmortem time—the time that would have been occupied by the person who died if that person had not actually died. But Bradley's recommendation of a well-being level of zero puzzles me, because a well-being level (of any value) is not something that can exist on its own, and there is no longer a person postmortem to have any well-being. It looks like there is an attempt to get something out of nothing. But Bradley thinks that we can reasonably assign a value of zero to a nonexistent person: "I find it hard to see how it could be obvious whether dead people have welfare levels of zero or simply fail to have welfare levels at all" (*Well-Being and Death*, 98). But really, it is not difficult to see; in fact, it ought to be obvious that there is an important difference, because dead people are actually nonexistent people. We can understand "John and Jane have no children; but if they *did* have a child, its welfare level *would be* zero". We might be able to come

---

[25] Incidentally, both this approach and Feldman's seem to be variations on Joel Feinberg's attempt ("Harm to Others") to make something other than the person (and, after death, the experson) be the bearers of good and bad. (Feinberg recruited "interests" for this purpose.) If so, they are susceptible to similar criticisms. See my "Death and Other Nothings".

to such a counterfactual valuation if we knew a great deal about John, Jane, and their circumstances. But what could we reasonably make of "John and Jane have no children; the welfare level of their child *is* actually zero"? Would we not rather say that in such a case well-being is inapplicable or undefined?

Still, Bradley insists that there can be an important difference. The Zero View, he says, "gets the intuitively acceptable results in the case of death", and "The Zero View and the Undefined View get all the same results, except in cases where a person goes out of existence. In those cases, the Zero View gets better results" ("Eternalism", 276). Bradley may be comfortable with what the Zero View implies, but I am not. Bradley himself makes an observation that can be used to begin an explanation for why the Zero View is inapt.

> A dead person is not maximally unhealthy, or at a midpoint between good and bad health; he simply lacks health altogether. But well-being in the sense relevant here is not the same thing as physical and emotional health, even if those things are related in some way to well-being. [*Well-Being and Death*, 99]

Setting aside for a moment the issue of what would be the relevant sense of well-being, we ought to extend Bradley's comment about health to include the observation that a nonexistent person is also not in good health. When Bradley says that a dead person "lacks health altogether", I take him to mean that the concept of health is inapt to characterize a nonexistent person; a nonexistent person can be neither healthy nor unhealthy. If that is what he means, then I agree. We could provide a long, long list of other categories that cannot characterize dead things even though they can apply to living persons. Here are a few such categories (some of which we have seen before in the section on the Fallacy of Misplaced Contingency): sense of humor, friendliness, motivation, belief, employment, knowledge, wisdom, empathy, narcissism, philosophy, intention, desire, esprit de corps, language fluency, anger, frustration, suffering, pleasure, pain, contentedness, pride, altruism, attentiveness, being celibate, being a non-drunk captain of a ship, painting with oils, memories of childhood, politeness, and anticipation. Extend that list ad lib. Now for each of those categories, consider how loss or lack might apply. A person (living, of course) can fail to have a sense of humor, in which case he might be dour; lack friendliness, which could make him surly or withdrawn; lose motivation, which could leave him depressed; not have language fluency, making him a poor communicator; lose belief, so that he doubts; and so on and on through a list of characteristics that describe various losses for persons, but that cannot apply to nonliving things.

What now of well-being? The well-being of a person can be dramatically decreased by losing internal organs, or by being burned, or by being smothered. But it would be silly to say that a corpse has well-being (in any ordinary sense) that can be impaired by autopsy, or by cremation, or by burial. Given the organizing principles that structure our thoughts in such cases, why would well-being be an exception? Bradley must be using the term "well-being" in a special sense, in order to get to a notion of deprivation in some special sense. And indeed he is: "The value of any event for a person at a time is wholly determined by how things go for that person at that time [. . .]" (*Well-Being and Death*, 90). This is not yet the special part, because that claim seems to fit pretty well with the ordinary way we think of values of things and events for persons. (Some ambiguities will have to be disambiguated. For example, some past but no longer present things have value for me in that they created or impaired present conditions of satisfaction for me, so the "at a time" will need attention. Bradley does in fact attend to the issue in *Well-Being and Death*, Chapter 3.) The special part comes when the rest of that sentence appears: "in actual and counterfactual circumstances". Bradley ought to have more carefully said: "The value of any event for a person at a time is wholly determined by how things go for that person at that time *compared to how things would plausibly have gone for him.*" The importance of the emendation appears when we realize that counterfactual things cannot ever "go for" a person, but only "could have gone" for the person. Zoë ate some cake, but she would have enjoyed ice cream more; counterfactually eating ice cream did not go for her at all. That is not a little point. If there actually was no ice cream, then only counterfactually could it have "gone for" her. Similarly, after Zoë is no longer in existence, no counterfactual thing and now also no actual thing can "go for" her; at best, things actual or counterfactual "could have gone" for the counterfactual her. The claim that there is a postmortem "how things go for her" (and hence possibly a value of zero for it) is not yet warranted. So there is still the problem of the subject, nuanced now when we realize that there is a double counterfactual involved.

Bradley gives us what he calls a "positive argument" for the claim that a well-being level of zero is appropriate for a dead thing.

1. Insofar as a person cares about his well-being, it makes sense for him to be indifferent between being killed instantly and dropping into a coma for some time, followed by death.
2. It follows that his level of well-being would be the same in both cases.
3. It then follows, finally, that the notion of well-being applies in the case of death (*Well-Being and Death*, 108f).

But the conclusion Bradley draws is unwarranted. If the person is somehow indifferent (never mind the awkward issue of how futures could be known with the certainty necessary), it might be that he could be indifferent between a state guaranteed to remain at level zero (the coma) and no state at all (death). Would he rather be in a coma, or be a triangle? That is to say, he might find it reasonable to be indifferent to both of two conditions: a condition he will be in with a welfare level guaranteed to mean nothing to him and a condition of the world in which he has no welfare level at all (because he does not exist). To put this still another way, in practical affairs we distinguish between, on the one hand, alternatives about which we are indifferent and, on the other hand, non-choices, where both preference and indifference do not apply. One might be indifferent between apple pie and chocolate cake for dessert, but one cannot be indifferent between apple pie and. Notice that an alternative choice possibility was not given in that last sentence; that is quite different from "apple pie or nothing", because the "nothing" in such a case would mean no dessert but some non-dessert condition—some non-dessert experiences—instead; that is to say, to go on but without dessert.

Might the Zero View say that the well-being level of zero *is* after all an *actual* condition of the nonexistent person (and hence that the nonexistent person *is* deprived of what would have been better)? How could that be? Well, it actually can't. But it sort of can. If it could be maintained that nonexistence could after all be an actual condition that something can have, or be in, even when that something is actually nothing, then if nonexistent things had, or were in, conditions (or situations), and if all conditions had well-being levels, then nonexistent things would have well-being levels. But how would it be reasonable to think that nonexistent things were in any condition or situation? Would not such a claim amount to a self-contradiction? Maybe not, if the notion of "exist" were itself made into something special. If there were a special sense of "exist", then there could be a special sense of "condition", and that could yield a special sense of "well-being", and that could encourage a special sense of "deprive". Not only could that be the logic of the matter, it might even be required on a four-dimensional space-time framework suggested by Harry Silverstein and Ben Bradley. (Bradley prefers the term "eternalism"; see his "Eternalism", 271.) But, as might be expected, there are problems with such a view. For one thing, the notion of "exist" on such a view seems to mean something like a disjunctive compound of our ordinary notions of "did exist", "does exit", and "will exist", and such an all-inclusive amplification plays havoc with our usual notions, as though both living dinosaurs and the sun's becoming a red giant both sort of exist, even though these days you can't find any dinosaurs, and even though the sun is no more giant today than it was yesterday. So if Zoë were deprived (in some special sense) postmortem, it actually could not be Zoë, because there is no Zoë, but rather a sort-of-Zoë that would be sort-of deprived. I will not pursue the issue further here; see the next chapter for a more detailed critique of Silverstein's version in particular.

My basic objection to Bradley's proposal is no surprise. His view commits the Fallacy of Misplaced Contingency, and it does so in two ways. Suppose someone answers "zero" to the question "How many felonies has this bit of bologna been convicted of?" That answer would seem to imply that the bologna is better than a person convicted of multiple murders. The answer to that strange question should be not "zero" (which would seem to be a contingent number that might, under other circumstances, be some positive number, as though bologna *could* be convicted of a felony), but rather "N/A". A similar consideration holds for a nonexistent person. In response to "How well-off is the dead person?" we should demur: "But well-offness does not apply to nonexistent things." And if well-offness does not apply, then of course it cannot be represented by any value at all, including zero. We might invoke the spatial analogy used in the previous section: It would be misleading, at best, to say that at all points beyond the edge of the actual table, the level of wax on the table is zero.[26]

To see the second way the fallacy is committed, let us return to Bradley's claim: "When I am sitting in a chair and having no pleasant or painful experiences, I have a well-being level of zero." But in such a case a level of zero would represent a way of being contented or satisfied, with special emphasis on having no motive to change. Now, it is true that expersons have no (and can have no) motive to change their situations (because they do not exist, and hence have no motives or situations), but it would be silly to say that they are contented or satisfied with their lot.

7 How death can be bad

In the previous chapter a distinction was made between *in esse* counterfactuals, which are understood from a point of view during the object's existence, and

---

[26] It may be that zero is used because non-numeric characterizations would more clearly commit the fallacy. Compare, for example, "the dead person has a well-being level of 0" with "the dead person is not at all happy".

post esse counterfactuals, which are expressed from a point of view after the object existed.

Only IE counterfactuals play a role in cautious descriptions of actual deprivations. Zoë, for example, is attending an inferior school, but she could have been attending a better school (had certain conditions been other than they were or are). But death-as-deprivation-for-the-one-who-died cannot involve an IE counterfactual, because at death the person ceased to be, and so after death the person no longer exists to have alternative properties or to be alternatively related to anything. There is no longer any "instead" *for the one who died.*[27] If Zoë died in infancy before attending any school at all, then she was not deprived of a good school, even though her death made it true that she did not attend a good school. Unfortunately, our ordinary habits incline us to keep our attention on Zoë (as though to keep her in existence), and hence incline us to use IE counterfactuals, and so we are tempted to say that her death deprived her not only of attending a good school but also of continuing to attend any school at all. But if we wanted to say such a thing, then we would have to be willing to go the whole route: her death denied her all other properties as well. But that is simply a way of saying that Zoë no longer exists, which means that all counterfactuals about Zoë—some of which, before her death, were of the IE type—are, because of her death, converted into the PE type. And that means that she was not actually deprived.

It is easy to be misled, because a simple (but incomplete) description of an ordinary deprivation will describe (incompletely) the case of death as well. Here is the beginning of an ordinary claim of deprivation: "Zoë did not get to attend a better school." Other conditions necessary for deprivation, some of which involve IE counterfactuals, are not explicitly given, but assumed. (For example, we assume that Zoë's life is now worse for not getting better schooling.) That simple description also describes the case of death, because there, too, it might be said that Zoë did not get to attend a better school. But there, too, the other aspects of a deprivation are not made explicit. When they are made explicit, as I have done in the preceding sections, the absence of Zoë from the world turns out not to be a deprivation for her after all.

Those writers who have tried to show that death can be a special kind of deprivation for the one who died were not making an obvious or silly mistake. In ordinary cases we are not led astray by loose talk of deprivation or by not

---

[27] The principle that there be an "instead" (which is a kind of amalgam of D1, D2, and D5) for an existing thing in order for there to be a deprivation for it I shall adapt for use in a different context in Chapter 7.

distinguishing between two kinds of counterfactuals. Besides, we already know very well that death can be bad. When a person dies—especially when a person dies when she was expected to have continued to live and to have been the beneficiary of many good things—it is a reasonable assumption that something terrible has happened. That valuation is as obvious as the mere fact of her death. We know very well that death can be bad, and so we sometimes try to describe it as though it were like other cases where something bad happened to a person: she was harmed, her projects were not fulfilled, she was deprived of what she could have had, and so on. Yet a little reflection can convince us that Zoë does not live on in a state of pain or frustration; she is dead but she does not suffer; she is now, as she never was during her life, logically exempt from even the risk of suffering. Nevertheless, we know that death can be bad—that is the starting point—and sometimes it seems that the convenient way to categorize death is as one of the many ordinary bad things that happened to her, only worse.

In denying that death can be any sort of deprivation for the one who died, I am not denying the starting point; I am not denying that we can make good sense of the claim that death can be bad. I share that fundamental evaluation with everyone else. But I am claiming both that the nature of the evil of death has been misunderstood and that the deprivation account is mistaken as an attempt to explain that evil. Both mistakes arise from common ways of evaluating events that happened to Zoë in her life, but that suddenly no longer apply in the singular case of her death. Her death was what made it necessary to switch not only from present tense verbs about her to past tense verbs but also from IE counterfactuals about her to PE counterfactuals. Death is a special case precisely because the person no longer exists. And now I want to claim that it is because the person no longer exists that the death of the person can be so bad.

If I seem to be speaking against myself, let me add to the illusion. My view is this: Death can be bad, and when it is bad, it is because of a deprivation. I have discussed at length what a deprivation is, and why a person's death was not a deprivation for her. Nevertheless, the evil of death involves a deprivation. Moreover, it is not a deprivation in some peculiar or scare-quote sense; it is an ordinary deprivation just like all the others. Death can be evil in the most ordinary of terrible ways: it causes suffering. Let us express this using an appropriate IE counterfactual. *The death of a person is a terrible deprivation because it causes terrible suffering (or, if you prefer, the prevention of a lot of satisfaction) that would not have occurred had the person not died.* It is the aspect of actual or possible suffering—the prime mover in most attributions of evil—which the death-as-deprivation theory does not face up to.

But where then is the suffering? Let us open our eyes to it; let us listen to the cries of grief. Since death cannot be a condition of suffering, directly or indirectly, for the one who died, and cannot be a deprivation for the one who died, then the evil of death cannot in any way be an evil for the one who died. A person's death means that present counterfactuals about that person are now of the PE type. But deprivation requires IE counterfactuals, which apply only to the living. Death, Nagel says, is "an evil that depends on a contrast between the reality and the possible alternatives" ("Death", 66). Indeed. But that observation does not justify the death-deprivation view he wants to hold. Rather, we know that the reality is that the person now no longer exists, and so the contrast that Nagel mentions must involve an alternative for *that* reality, and therefore *for* anyone or anything in *that* reality. As I mentioned above in Section 3, to attempt to work out a deprivation theory for the one who is no longer in that reality is to misuse the comparison. So if Zoë's death is bad, it is an evil of deprivation for those who have *not* died. Zoë's death is not bad for her; it is bad for us—for you and me and all other survivors who made Zoë a part of their lives. We are deprived of Zoë, and that is why we suffer, even though she cannot.

6

A Critique in Four Dimensions

Prelude

It is well known that Descartes had three important dreams one night. What is not as well known is that he might have had a fourth, and I would like to report to you what it might have been.

An angel comes to René and intones, in the best of angelic voices:

You will eventually die, and your life as a whole might not have had the richness of content, in comparison with alternative imaginable lives.

René: What do you mean, "*might* not"?

Angel: After your death, I will compare your actual life with a longer alternative life, and the alternative life might turn out to be full of many more, and more kinds of, good things.

René: What good things?

Angel: I can't actually say.

René: Then why are you telling me all this?

Angel: Don't you want to know? Don't you even care how your life is going?

René: Of course I care how my life is going. But you aren't telling me how my life is going. You are telling me in rather vague terms how my life might have gone after it has gone. What good is that for me?

Angel: Gosh, I just thought you'd want to know, is all.

René: I don't see why, unless you want to give me some kind of hint about how I ought to change my ways in order to make my life be filled with more good things. That way, after my death you will make a different assessment of my life.

Angel: Sorry, can't do that. The judgment will be about an Eternal Truth, and Eternal Truths can't be changed, not even by Him Who Made Them in the First Place. Besides, only after you are dead will I make the judgment that you might have been better off with an alternative life. I haven't made that judgment yet, because I don't have all the details of your life yet, so I can't possibly tell you how you might avoid that judgment, can I?

René: But if you haven't yet made that judgment, doesn't that mean that I might change my life for the better, as a consequence of which you will make a different judgment after I die?

Angel: Haven't you been listening? Do I have to repeat everything I say? It's an Eternal Truth, I tell you, and there's no changing it.

René: But I still don't see what difference it could make to me, now, what judgment you will end up making after I am dead. You say that there is this eternal truth, but you won't have any details until after I'm dead, when it's too late. Why should I care that something might be true to God or an angel if I can never have any knowledge of it?[1] So as far as I can actually be concerned, there is no such eternal truth at all.

Angel: *[Long pause.]* Blasphemy!

1 Silverstein's view

In a number of publications, Harry S. Silverstein argues against the Epicurean view that death cannot be bad for the one who died.[2] The following will serve as an outline of his position.

> S1: The goal is to show that the "problem of the subject" (that the person who died cannot be the subject of a misfortune, because the person no longer exists) can be solved, and so death can be bad for a person in the ordinary way that we think that death can be bad: "His approaching death [when he could have lived longer] would typically be the object of negative feelings precisely because of his awareness of the brevity of his life as a whole, and the consequent sparsity of its content, in comparison with alternative imaginable lives" (ED 116).
>
> S2: The solution involves dealing with two key items: "Values Connect with Feelings" (VCF) and the "temporality assumption".
>
> S3: In the spirit of Epicureanism, VCF is the principle that things or events or states of affairs that have value for persons must "make a difference to, or affect, their recipients"; "there appears to be a conceptual connection of some sort" between something's having a certain value for a person and the

---

[1] Descartes refashioned that sentence and included it in his *Replies to the Second Set of Objections*, 103. (Complete bibliographic information on this and all other sources in this book is provided in the Bibliography.)

[2] ED = "The Evil of Death"; EDR = "The Evil of Death Revisited"; EDD = "'The Evil of Death' Defended: Reply to Burley"; TED = "The Time of the Evil of Death"; EDOMT = "The Evil of Death One More Time: Parallels between Time and Space".

person's having an appropriate experience or feeling (ED 106, EDR 122). A weak but plausible version of VCF claims that death need only be an *object* of (and not a *cause* of) the person's experiences (such as negative attitudes) (ED 107; see also TED 284, EDOMT 84).

S4: The second issue in the problem of the subject is the temporality assumption, according to which something that has value for the person must have a temporal location or extent at least part of which is prior to the person's death (ED 106). Clearly, a person's death does not have a temporal location or extent at least part of which is prior to the person's death. In order to show that Epicurus was wrong, we need to reject this temporality assumption (while retaining the plausible version of VCF).

S5: We can reject the temporality assumption by interpreting "exists" using a 4-dimensional space-time framework (to be explained below) such that "*temporally* distant [. . .] events (states, objects, etc.) can coherently be accorded the same status, with respect to VCF [. . .] as spatially distant events (states, objects, etc.)" (ED 109; see also TED 284; EDR 117; EDD 573). That is, if spatially distant events (etc.) can satisfy VCF, then temporally distant events can too.

S6: That solves the problem of the subject.

Silverstein describes three kinds of "frameworks"; an understanding of them is necessary for what follows. A "zero-degree" (0-D) framework incorporates both "here" and "now" as defaults, so that within that framework to say that x exists (which might be written "exists$_0$"), without spatial or temporal adverbs, means that x exists here and now.[3] A 3-D framework has only "now" as a default, so that to say that x exists$_3$, without qualification, means that x exists now and somewhere or other. Finally, a 4-D framework has neither "here" nor "now" as defaults, so that to say that x exists$_4$, without qualification, means that x exists somewhere or other and at some time or other. Understanding the 4-D framework, he says, can help to reject the temporality assumption, which in turn will solve the problem of the subject.

The claim in S5 is that on a 3-D framework, spatially distant events can satisfy VCF, and so on a 4-D framework, temporally distant events too can satisfy VCF.

---

[3] It might seem peculiar that "exist$_0$" means "exist here and now", for what does that second, unsubscripted instance of "exist" mean—"exist$_0$", or "exist$_3$", or what? We should take it to mean that when qualified (in this case by "here and now"), any, or no, subscript would be the same as any other, because the function of the subscript is to provide the default, or implicit, qualifications, which can be overridden by any explicit qualification. Qualification could also be given by a context that stipulates the framework, so that, for example, "In the 0-degree framework, x exists" is equivalent to both "x exists here and now" and "x exists$_0$". (Out of context, and without a subscript or qualifiers, "exist" would therefore be ambiguous.)

But is it true that on a 3-D framework, spatially distant events can satisfy VCF? If it turns out that there is a problem with that claim, then there will be a problem with the claim that the 4-D framework makes it plausible that temporally distant events can satisfy VCF. And if that turns out to be a problem, then the claim that we can reject the temporality assumption (see again S4) is in trouble, and the problem of the subject will still be a problem for the death-is-bad-for-the-one-who-died view.

What I aim to show is that if we understand *how* spatially distant things and events can be the objects of one's feelings, then we will be able to understand *how* temporally distant events can be the objects of one's feelings. But once we have understood the *how*, we will be able to understand that one's death cannot work like that; one's future death is a special case of a future event that cannot satisfy the *how*. This will undermine Silverstein's attempt to undermine the temporality assumption, and the result will be that the Epicurean view will not have been weakened.

2 Understanding the "how"

So let us look more closely at the claim that on the 3-D framework spatially distant events can satisfy VCF. Silverstein investigates the questions of *where* something can be bad for a person (TED 287, 291; EDOMT 92–95) and *when* something can be bad for a person (TED 289–91; EDOMT 92–95), but he does not inquire very far into the *how* (ED 116; EDD 577–78; TED 287–88), except to say what is mentioned in item S1. But something crucial has been left out of his discussion. If it is said that some thing or event can be bad for a person as the object (or possible object) of the person's negative feelings, we should wonder why the person has (or would have) those particular feelings; we should wonder whether, and how, the person is (or would be) justified in having those particular feelings.

It might seem that Silverstein need not investigate that issue, because his suggested solution to the problem of the subject is to make death a possible object of a person's feelings, and it should not matter *what* those feelings are. Let the person be pleased instead of saddened by the thought of death; either way, there will have to exist a possible object of those feelings, and such an object is not available on the usual 3-D framework, whereas it is available on the 4-D framework. So further investigation into the justification of whatever feelings the person happens to have would be beside the point.

Or so it might seem.

Let's examine a version of one of Silverstein's own examples that he uses multiple times (EDR 123, 130; TED 286; EDOMT 91–93). John's wife Ann has an affair in some distant location (i.e., some place where John is not). The affair is, by usual accounts, a bad thing for John. We can make a simple argument to that effect.

> A1. A person's affair is bad for the person's spouse.
>
> A2. Ann is having an affair.
>
> A3. Ann's spouse is John.
>
> A4. Therefore, Ann's affair is bad for John.

What happens in this example when we use different frameworks? We'll start with what Silverstein calls the zero-dimensional framework (EDR 129; EDOMT 86–87, 90–92), which he cautions is an invented framework that no one normally uses (TED 285). On this framework, both "here" and "now" are built in as defaults, so that the bare claim "Ann is (or is$_0$) having an affair" means that Ann's affair exists (or exists$_0$) here and now. So "Ann is$_0$ having an affair" would be false at times when Ann is not having an affair, and it would be false, even if she is now having an affair, at places other than where the affair is taking place. If, for example, John is in one city and Ann is at that time having an affair in another city, it would be false, where John is, that Ann is$_0$ having an affair. And if Ann had an affair (or will have an affair) where John is, but not at the time John is there, then, too, it would be false that Ann is$_0$ having an affair.

Of course, the 0-D framework is very limiting to us who are accustomed to using the 3-D framework. The 3-D framework, Silverstein says, has the concept "now" built in as a default, but not the concept "here". On the 3-D framework, to say that Ann's affair exists (or exists$_3$) is to say that it exists now, no matter where it happens.

On a 4-D framework, which has neither "now" nor "here" built in, to say that Ann's affair exists (or exists$_4$) is to say that it exists at some time or other (not necessarily now), and at some location or other (not necessarily here).

All that was stage-setting. We are now ready to consider the normative claim made in A1, which says that an affair—an act of intimacy with someone other than the spouse—is bad (evil, misfortunate) for the spouse. Within our familiar 3-D framework, we would ordinarily agree that because Ann's intimacy with someone who isn't John exists now (i.e., exists$_3$), even though it does not take place where John is, it is a bad thing for him. Most people would easily agree that the affair is a bad thing for John even if John does not know about it and is not being affected in any way by it.

Silverstein asks us to recognize how a space-time analogy can be useful in conjunction with his version of VCF. So let's see how this is applied to the case of Ann's affair. We can see that on a 3-D framework, Ann's affair, happening now, but somewhere other than where John is, can be a possible object of, even if not the cause of, John's negative feelings. (In EDR 124 Silverstein gives us a not implausible example of this: John might believe correctly, but on bad evidence, that Ann is having an affair, so that John's belief is causally isolated from Ann's affair.) Now on a 4-D framework, if Ann has an affair at some future time, it could be the object of (although not the cause of) John's present negative feelings; a future affair, even though not happening now, nevertheless exists$_4$, and so it is an intelligible, possible object of John's present feelings. On Silverstein's view, if this works for the case of John's possible feelings for Ann's (future) affair, then it ought to work for the case of John's contemplating his own (future) death. Within the 4-D framework, his future death can be said to exist (i.e., exist$_4$), and so it is indeed an intelligible, possible object of John's present negative feelings.

As I promised earlier, there could be a problem with the normative claim, A1, even on the 3-D framework. If there is, then there will be a problem on the 4-D framework too. To see what the problem is, let's ignore the 4-D framework for the moment and stick with our ordinary view, using the 3-D framework. We would ordinarily agree with A4 that Ann's present affair is bad for John.

But let's look a bit closer; this will take us back to my suggestion that we need to understand the *how*. My question is: Why would we say that Ann's present but distant affair is *bad* for John? Why might we not say instead that Ann's affair is a *good* thing for John? Or why might we not say that Ann's affair makes no difference to John?

Well, we might, of course; it depends. Suppose we tell John about Ann's intimacy with another person and John becomes sad, angry, disappointed, or has some other negative attitude. This is just what we expect. Now suppose we learn about a different married couple, Gerry and Sherry. We know that Sherry is having an affair, but when we inform Gerry about it, he is not sad, angry, or disappointed; rather, he is thrilled, pleased, or relieved; he has, that is, some positive attitude. This comes as a surprise to us. But, again: Why? Why is John sad but Gerry happy?[4]

---

[4] A Gerry-like case is mentioned briefly in EDR 124.

Let's find out. We ask John why he is unhappy about Ann's affair. He replies that Ann's affair indicates a loss of her love and affection for him; she is less likely to be intimate with him, less likely to spend time with him, care for him, confide in him, or act in ways intimates usually act with each other. These are understandable concerns.

Now let us ask Gerry why he seems pleased by the news that his wife Sherry is having an affair. He replies that he had fallen out of love with Sherry some time ago and had wanted to get a divorce, but because of their prenuptial agreement, a no-fault divorce would leave Gerry with nothing, whereas, according to that same prenuptial agreement, if Sherry has an affair, Gerry could sue for divorce and also end up with everything; Sherry would get nothing. Now we can understand Gerry's positive attitude toward his wife's affair.

In the light of these considerations, what should we do with premise A1 ("A person's affair is bad for the person's spouse")? Evidently it is false, or anyway not universally true. John has a negative attitude (and we understand why), but Gerry has a positive attitude (and now we understand why). So far, there is nothing that Silverstein could not agree to. And there seems to be nothing that upsets his solution to the problem of the subject. So where is there fault in Silverstein's position?

3 VCF revisited

It is not difficult to see. The reasons John has for his negative attitude to his wife's affair have to do with how that affair is expected to affect him. And what does he expect? Loss of affection, less intimacy, and so on. And the reasons Gerry has for his positive attitude to his wife's affair have to do with how that affair is expected to affect *him*: he'll be rid of his wife, and he'll be financially better off. This is not to say that expectations are infallible. John might discover that because of the affair, Ann's affection for him actually increases and her attention to him intensifies; he might even come to discover that his wife's intimacy with another man is very erotic for him, and he might encourage his wife to do more of the same. And Gerry might discover that he regrets the loss of his wife and that some fine print in the prenuptial agreement does not give him the financial benefit he was expecting after all.

Whether John's or Gerry's attitudes undergo any change is not the point. The point, rather, is that whatever attitudes they have are attitudes that involve expectations of consequences—specifically, possible consequences that could show up at some time for them (i.e., at some time during their lives as experiencing beings) and at some place for them (viz., wherever they are at the time). To put the matter in a different way (and this may be a bit ironic, given that Silverstein suggested that the 0-D framework is not ordinarily useful), John's and Gerry's feelings are always expectations, or involve expectations, that have to do with some effect on their experiences, and *any experience must be describable on the 0-D framework, because when experiences exist, they are of course experiences of the person where and when the person exists.* Even if the 4-D framework can be used to make sense of a husband's negative feelings about his wife's possible future affair, we should realize that his feelings about such an affair involve possible experiences, such as her coldness toward him, or her unwillingness to confide in him as she used to, or her secretiveness about certain phone calls, and so on.

Now when we apply these considerations to the case of death, we see that the shift to a 4-D framework does not solve anything. Silverstein says that according to his weak but plausible version of VCF, some thing or state of affairs need be only a possible object of the person's feelings, and not the cause thereof. That seems very reasonable to me. When a person has feelings (or when it is possible to have feelings) about something, that something need not exist at that same time or at any earlier time; it might be a future event, and of course a future event cannot be the efficient cause of present feelings. Still, a person presently evaluates a future object or event in some way or other because of the anticipation of how he will evaluate it when it happens, or in anticipation of his evaluation of the effects (consequences), either direct or indirect, that the object will (or would) have when (or if) it happens. But what effects will death have on the person? More precisely, how could the person evaluate the effects of death when it happens? He could not, of course. This is not a contingent matter.

The issue can be put this way: In order for something to be of value to you, it, or its effects, must be involved in a possible change to your experiences. That is, if it occurs, your experiences will be such and such, whereas if it does not occur, your experiences will be something else instead. (This is simply a version of VCF.) But this ordinary way of thinking about value cannot apply in the extraordinary case of death.

This principle is sometimes denied, and the denial comes either (1) via a counterexample or two or (2) via the claim that death *does* affect one's experiences. As for (1), the counterexamples follow the pattern of Silverstein's example of Ann's present but distant affair, and we have seen that upon closer examination, Ann's affair can mean something to John precisely because of its anticipated possible consequences.[5]

As for (2), the claim that death affects one's experiences by ending one's experiences is at best misleading, as I mentioned in the previous chapter. The claim makes sense only in cases (non-death cases) where the person experiences something else instead. Suppose that for some reason John misses out on experiencing the third act of a play; his experiences of the play have been terminated. But then he is having some non-play experiences instead of the ones he had hoped for. To have some experience come to an end can be bad for him if he has some other, less desirable experience instead (instead of the experience he could have had). It is true that when death happens, experiences come to an end. But death cannot *change* experiences—it cannot bring about other experiences instead. And this makes death a special case where our usual appraisals cannot function in the usual way.

I have used Silverstein's notion of a 0-D framework to characterize experience. When something affects one's experiences, it, or its consequences, must be met in a 0-D way. When we say that something affects one's experiences, we mean that one's experiences would have been other than they in fact are (or will be at the time), had it not been for that which affected them. There is always a way they are or will be (i.e., there is or will be a *here and now*), and a way they would have been, or could have been (i.e., a counterfactual *here and now*). This is the aspect of contingency which is necessarily absent in the case where there is no subject to be *here and now*. When John thinks with some negative feeling, such as dread or sadness, of his eventual death, he is thinking in the same way as he is thinking of his wife's affair; he is thinking of the absence of experiences of good things. It does not help to say that he is merely noticing that his death means that there will come a time when he could have had experiences that he will not then have, because what that really amounts to is covertly imagining the experience of (or the experience of the consequences of) missing out on those good experiences—that is to say, having other experiences instead. So although John's missing out on certain kinds of experiences is an apt way of characterizing his feelings about Ann's affair, it is an inapt characterization of his lack of all experiences after death—that is, when there is no longer a subject to have experiences.

So the problem of the subject is$_0$ still alive.

---

[5] Nagel says (in "Death") that betrayal is bad for the one betrayed even if the betrayal is undiscovered. Silverstein's example of Ann's affair is one of many variations of that claim. I criticized such cases at length in my "Death and Other Nothings".

7

Killing

Prelude

A camper, cold and hungry, wants to build a fire. She manages to spark some flint into a small pile of dried moss, which starts to smolder. She blows gently, nursing the little heat. Soon she will add some dried leaves, which will produce a small flame, and then she will add some tiny twigs, then larger twigs, then logs. Eventually her fire will have grown to maturity. But in the event, as she is encouraging the gestating flame, blowing with an anxious tenderness, her cheeks aglow with the promise of things to come, some fellow walks over and stomps on the moss, extinguishing both the potential flames and the camper's hopes. The camper is upset because she has lost something of value to her. She is not upset because the potential fire had a right to light. The moss-stomper is a mean and nasty character; perhaps he is immoral. The bad thing he did was cause annoyance, frustration, and perhaps some misery.

1 The right to life

Rights are supposed to be the kinds of things that can be possessed, enjoyed, exercised, infringed, denied, ignored, protected, and respected. Some can be forfeited, assigned, reassigned, and alienated. There are all sorts of alleged rights, and each is awash in issues such as "What kinds of things have it?", "How did they get it?", "Is it alienable?", "Is it absolute?", "Can it be overridden?" A distinction should be made between legal rights generated by legal systems and moral rights that apply independently of legal systems. My contention is that when it comes to what is perhaps thought to be the most secure moral right of all—the right to life (alternatively, and the way I will sometimes express it, the right to not be killed)—an investigation will show that there is no such right.

There are at least four different meanings to the assertion that S does not have a right to x.[1] "You have no right to eat this apple" might mean that if you are already eating this apple, you may not continue; and if you are not eating the apple, then you may not start doing so. When I say that there is no right to life, it may sound as though I am saying that no one has a right to continue living, and so they ought to stop—that is, kill themselves—and, in the case of persons not yet in existence, they ought not to be brought into existence. But that is not my claim.

A second meaning that could be given to "S does not have a right to x" is that S is not the sort of thing to have any rights at all. For example, if S is an apple, it will probably be maintained that S has no rights of any sort. (This might also hold for insects and other simple animals. The less sophisticated are the nervous systems of a species, the more inclined people are to deny rights to any of its members.) But that, too, is not my claim.

Third, S does not have a right to x if there are no rights at all. Some writers prefer to discard all talk of rights, to be replaced by talk of justice (or moral principles).[2] So instead of saying that S has no right to eat this particular apple, we might say that it would be unjust for S to eat the apple; and instead of saying that S has a right to eat the apple, we might better say that S does no injustice in eating it. Of course, there is disagreement about the wisdom of abandoning rights talk. Richard Brandt says: "It appears that 'rights' talk does have a role different from that of talk of duties, obligations, right and wrong [. . .]" ("The Concept of a Moral Right and Its Function", 43). And Judith Jarvis Thomson says: "I think there does not exist any even remotely plausible theory of the logic of rights. And yet [. . .] I think there does not exist any issue of importance in ethics in which we can avoid or side-step them" ("Rights and Deaths", 149).

I will not take sides on the issue of whether rights talk is a mere convenience, or whether there are any moral rights at all. I will assume that there are rights, because I want to investigate a fourth possible meaning for "S does not have a right to x", to wit: Although S does have rights, there are some alleged rights that S does not have, because in fact there are no such rights for anyone to have. S does not have a right to be a leprechaun, not because S has no rights at all, but rather because S cannot be such a thing. S does not have a right to walk along a

---

[1] Depending on the context, the phrase "right to x" might include a verb: "do x", "be x", "have x", and many others. For the sake of avoiding the awkwardness of long-winded precision, I will often use only one form at a time.

[2] See, for example, R. G. Frey, *Interests and Rights*; R. G. Frey, *Rights, Killing, and Suffering*, chapters 7, 8; and R. G. Frey, "On Why We Would be Better to Jettison Moral Rights". (Complete bibliographic information on this and all other sources in this book is provided in the Bibliography.)

path that crosses each of the seven bridges of Königsberg once and only once, because it cannot be done, although it was a pastime for some people to try to find such a route.[3]

I want to say something along the lines of the fourth interpretation. Even if S has some rights, S has no right to not be killed, simply because there can be no such right. It is important to be cautious here, because, as I will explain later, when I say that you have no right to not be killed, I do not mean to say that no one does wrong by killing you, nor that it is morally allowed that anyone kill you if they choose. Moreover, in the absence of a right to life there could still be rights to food, health care, and many other things. It might seem strange indeed that a person might be owed proper health care but at the same time have no right to life. But that will be one of the consequences of my position.

Is there a common core to all rights? Wesley Hohfeld proposed an analysis of rights that was, and still is, influential (although he focused on legal rights).[4] Hohfeld wished to investigate the notion of right by analyzing it into its constituent elements. It is not worth pursuing his analysis at length here, but some of his ideas will be useful.

Hohfeld defines "privilege" as "freedom from the right or claim of another" (55). So if S has a privilege to do x, then S is not under a duty to refrain from doing x. I prefer the term "liberty" (which Hohfeld also uses), because I think it fits better with modern terminology in moral philosophy, and because I want to use the idea of not-having-a-duty-to-refrain-from in a slightly broader sense than Hohfeld's "privilege" might connote. Imagine an explorer in unowned territory coming upon an apple tree. He is not under a duty to refrain from picking an apple from the tree, and so we might say that he is at liberty to pick it. Now suppose a different apple tree has an owner who picks an apple from his own tree. He is at liberty to pick the apple. But the case of the owner is different from the case of the explorer, because people have a duty (or so I will presume) to not pick the owner's apple without permission, whereas no one has a duty to not pick the apple that the explorer intends to pick, which is to say that no one needs permission to pick that apple.

A *liberty-right* to x is a right one has such that one is not under a duty to refrain from x, and no one has a duty either to provide x to the right-holder or to refrain from acting in such a way that the right-holder cannot have x. One implication is that the satisfaction of some people's liberty-rights can be

---

[3] A proof was provided by Euler in the eighteenth century. A description is available at https://en.wikipedia.org/wiki/Seven_Bridges_of_Königsberg
[4] "Some Fundamental Legal Conceptions as Applied in Judicial Reasoning".

incompatible with the satisfaction of the same liberty-rights of other people. If everyone has a liberty-right to pick and eat an unowned apple from an unowned apple tree, then you do no wrong in eating the apple even though another person had a similar liberty-right to eat it, and even though your eating it makes it the case that now no one else can eat it.

Such an apparent conflict in rights-satisfaction can also show up when one person's liberty-right is for x, and another person's liberty-right is for y such that y makes x impossible. One person might have a liberty-right to pick the apple, but its exercise might be made impossible by another person's exercising the liberty-right to clear the land of all trees in order to plant corn.

I will assume that such a rather barren liberty-right (which is what I take to be Hobbes's "right of nature") is not what people mean when they speak of a right to life. If the right to life were a liberty-right—that is, if all it meant was that a person merely had no duty to not continue living—then it is conceivable that one person would do no wrong in killing another.[5] Although that is close to the conclusion I will come to, I do not want my position to rely on a mischaracterization of the alleged right to life. We need the following, slightly stronger notion. If S has a liberty to do x—is not under a duty to not do x—and if, in addition, other persons are under a duty to not interfere with S's doing x (and in some cases have a duty to help S do x or even to supply x to S), then we will say that S has a *claim-right* to x. (This is what Hohfeld says is the proper meaning of "right".) So if the owner of an apple tree has a claim-right to eat an apple from his own tree, then he has no duty to not eat it, and all other persons are under a duty to not interfere. I want to investigate a claim-right to life, because when people speak of a right to life, they seem to mean that the right puts other persons under a duty to not interfere with the right-holder's exercise of that right.

But a claim-right to life could take one of two forms. A "negative" claim-right to life would be a right to not be killed; it would put all other persons under a duty to not intentionally kill the right-holder (and perhaps also to take appropriate precautions to not negligently kill the right-holder). A "positive" claim-right to life would be a right of the first sort, expanded to include whatever is necessary to continue in existence. Such a right would put some (perhaps determinate) persons under a duty to provide the right-holder with certain necessities such as food, water, and air; but other things might be included, such as culturally expected minimal health care, or various forms of education. The conclusion

---

[5] A similar point is made by Joel Feinberg, "Voluntary Euthanasia and the Inalienable Right to Life", 95.

I am arguing for is that no one has the more fundamental of the two claim-rights: a negative claim-right to life. That is, no one has a right to not be killed.

That conclusion can be drawn out of the Epicurean view of death, along with some plausible auxiliary claims. Let the following be an outline of the argument of Chapter 1. Good and bad have to do ultimately with experiences. Death is annihilation. Expersons cannot have experiences. So not existing can be nothing to persons who do not exist; having died causes no pain, no suffering, no regret, and so on. If having died can cause no problems for persons who no longer exist, then existing persons have no good grounds for worrying about their death in advance. Death, therefore, ought to be "nothing to us". That is a summary of the Epicurean position. I want now to work out a particular consequence of this view when applied to the issue of an alleged negative claim-right to life. I will present two versions of the argument that there is no such right. Doing so may help me hedge my bets; since the two versions are very closely related, I trust that they will help and support each other. After the arguments are presented, I will anticipate and respond to a number of objections and then look briefly at some consequences for moral philosophy.

2 The Essential Potential of an "Instead" Condition (EPIC) Argument

EPIC-1: Some thing or event is contingent if it could be otherwise; it is noncontingent (i.e., necessary) if it could not be otherwise. The distinction is problematic, but the issues need not concern us. It is contingent (or a contingent matter, or a contingent truth) that I have a pen in my hand (and also that I picked up a pen), for I could have chosen the pencil instead. Had I picked up the pencil instead of the pen, I would not now have this pen in my hand.

EPIC-2: Morality necessarily involves contingencies. According to the well-known (but still debated) phrase, "ought" implies "can". There is a companion (but not so well-known) phrase: "ought" implies "not necessarily". So "ought to do x" (and similarly "right to do x") implies both "can do x" and also "can do some non-x instead". This is the issue of choice, which seems to be involved in all moral affairs. One support for this is that moral rules are meant to be guides for our behavior, and so they can require nothing humanly impossible. If in a certain situation it is not possible for you to do x, then it makes no sense to say that you *ought* to do x in that situation, and it is idle to say that you ought to *not* do x in that situation. A sufficient defense against a complaint that you did not do what someone claims you ought to have done is that it was impossible for you to have done it.[6] Of course, the meanings of "possible" and "impossible" are context-dependent. Sometimes "possible" means "logically possible", sometimes "physically possible", and sometimes "practically possible". Something similar can be said of "choice". You might reasonably say that when the thief put a gun to your head and said "Your money or your life", you had no choice but to hand over your wallet. Of course you did have some kind of choice, but most people would say that it was not a practically acceptable one.

There is a problem with "ought" involving both "can" and "not necessarily" when applied to issues of responsibility. A common view is that if one intentionally does some action, then one is morally responsible for its happening because one could have chosen to do otherwise. The requirement that there be an "otherwise" in order that there be responsibility is put to the test in counterexamples of the sort presented by Harry Frankfurt[7] and which have enjoyed a decades-long, still-continuing discussion. We are to imagine some mechanism that could, if activated, interfere with one's intention; it could prevent one's changing one's mind. The claim is that one *can* be responsible for an intentional action, when one had no thought of changing one's mind, and even though, because of the mechanism (which did not have to be activated), one could *not* have changed one's mind (and not done the action)—that is, even though, as it turns out, one could not have done otherwise.[8]

If such counterexamples succeed in the case of moral responsibility, then they bear on the twin issues of rights and duties that I am discussing in this chapter. If one could not have done otherwise than one did and yet one is to be held morally responsible for what one did, then it seems that one might in some

---

[6] Well, it is not as simple as that. Suppose Barrow borrows a book from Lender, but then intentionally destroys the book, thereby putting himself in a position such that his obligation to return the book is now impossible to fulfill. Barrow is morally blameworthy, and it might be claimed that the basis for that blameworthiness is that he still has the duty to return the book, which is now impossible. But there is an easy alternative. In order to save the principle that "ought" implies "can", the duty in the stipulated situation can be understood to be the duty (or to have been transformed into the duty) to do whatever might plausibly come as close to returning the book as Barrow can possibly manage. If the book still exists, Barrow should return it. If it no longer exists, then he might now owe Lender a replacement copy, or some monetary compensation. Or suppose Barrow borrows the book and then loses it; he searches but cannot find it. Later on it somehow appears back in Lender's possession. Does Barrow still have a duty to return the book when strictly speaking in this case he cannot? One can imagine many other problematic cases, so that we ought to recognize that Barrow's responsibility was not precisely to return the borrowed book, although returning the borrowed book would be sufficient to discharge his duty, and would be the usual way of doing so.
[7] "Moral Responsibility and Alternate Possibilities".
[8] Such a case ought to remind us of David Lewis's discussion of the use of "can" in a time-travel example ("The Paradoxes of Time Travel").

circumstances have had a duty to do otherwise than one did even though it was impossible to have done otherwise.

But are Frankfurt-style counterexamples convincing? Doing something immoral might justify interference with the action, but merely having an intention to do a wrong (or merely in some way expressing such an intention, which is the way other people come to have knowledge of a person's intentions) normally does not warrant a restriction of the person's liberties, unless the action in accordance with the intention is imminent. In any case, interference with the intention itself is problematic because we do not know how to reliably interfere with it (and leave the person otherwise intact). We can remonstrate, argue, try to persuade, cajole, withhold rewards, or threaten punishment, but those methods are indirect, useful mainly early on, before the intention is fully engaged; such methods are usually weak when set against an already firm determination to act. A mechanism that could reliably prevent one from having an intention different from the one that was active would be revolutionary, both technically and conceptually. Still, if there is thought to be a possibility of controlling a person's intentions, then perhaps that is all that the thought experiments need.

In such Frankfurt-style counterexamples the concepts of responsibility, duty, and right do not apply quite in the way that they usually do, yet the usual ways seem to linger on to bias our judgments in unusual cases. If, in a Frankfurt-style case, one could not have done otherwise than one did, but nevertheless is said to have had a duty to not do what one did, then the use of the notion of duty in such an unusual case would actually be calling attention to some feature of usual cases, perhaps in order to try to assign some sort of responsibility to the actor. But it would be more congenial to our usual notions to not let them stray far from home. Here is one possibility. One has a duty, say, to not harm innocent persons; but if not harming was in a particular case for some reason impossible, then it might be reasonable to say that what would have ordinarily been identified as a duty to not harm has been transformed. In the case of Barrow (footnote 6) who borrows a book that is then destroyed such that he cannot return what he had borrowed, his duty might be transformed into (or to be understood to be) the duty to provide a substitute, make recompense, and so on. Similarly, if we are convinced that a counterfactual intervener *would have* intervened had one been about to change one's intentions to act harmfully toward an innocent person, with the result that someone was actually harmed, then we might say that one's ordinary duty to not so act was transformed into a responsibility to compensate those harmed, more or less as if one had accidentally caused harm to another.

I do not have an argument that Frankfurt-style counterexamples must fail. Instead, I am taking cover behind a strong caution, namely, that we may be too quick to use our usual tendencies when assigning responsibility in such strange cases. In the usual case one is held responsible not merely because one acted (and because one chose to so act) but also because some alternative was possible (and could have been chosen). A man strikes another in response to the other's letting loose an insult. We can say to the first man both "Violence is not an appropriate response" and "You should just let it pass"; and to the other man we could say both "You ought not to insult people" and "You ought to speak more politely". Such comments carry with them the assumption that both men could have done otherwise than they did. That, anyway, describes cases where the notions of action, choice, and responsibility seem clearly applicable. We are not familiar with real cases where one's will is so tightly constrained that the appearance of choice was there, yet it was not possible to choose to do otherwise. The more we doctor up volition and its surrounding conditions such that the will is enfeebled, the more we are obliged to try to reconfigure our notions of choice, responsibility, and duty so as not to fully resemble their use in ordinary ways. Even though Frankfurt-style counterexamples might pose a real and present danger to our ordinary ways of thinking about responsibility (and duty and right), I will proceed on the assumption that our typical claims about rights are consistent with the notion of alternative possibilities.

EPIC-3: So if there is a right or duty to do x, then it must be possible to do x and possible to do some non-x instead. Otherwise, there would be no choice in the matter, and without choice, morality would not apply.

EPIC-4: Several times in the previous paragraphs I used the word "instead". Let us make something of that. For ease of reference, let us call this the *Instead Requirement* that must be expressed or implied in all moral discourse. We will apply it specifically to rights (and duties) in this way:

> *The Instead Requirement:* If there is a right or duty to be x (or to have x or to do x), then it must be possible to be x and possible to be some non-x instead. The realm of moral valuations is a realm of contingencies, and a world of contingencies is a world of possible "insteads". In cases where there seems to be no meaningful alternative to being or doing x, then the concept of right (or duty) will seem to be either idle or inapplicable.

EPIC-5: So if one has a claim-right to have or be x, then the right rests on contingencies. In particular, it must be possible for that right to be violated by a moral agent who creates some event or state of affairs that puts one into a condition of having or being some non-*x* instead of *x*. Note that it is not the mere condition of not being *x* that violates the right to *x*; an accident of nature could bring about such a condition. If I have a right to speak (perhaps in a particular venue), the loss of my voice by disease is not a violation of that right; but if someone intentionally prevents my speaking so that I must remain silent instead, then my right to speak has been infringed.

EPIC-6: If there were a claim-right to life—a right to not be killed—then being killed would be the violation of that right. (Again, the death would have to be at the hands of, or by the design of, a moral agent.)

EPIC-7: But such an alleged right would be inconsistent with the Instead Requirement. If there were a right to life, then being killed (by a moral agent) would have to put the victim into another condition instead. Instead of *what*? Instead of living, of course. But death does not put a person into an "instead" condition; rather, death annihilates the person, and nonexistence is precisely no condition at all.

EPIC-8: Therefore, there cannot be a right to not be killed.

This argument can be summarily structured as *modus tollens*: If there were a right to life, then death would be an "instead" condition. But there is no "instead" for the one who died. Therefore, etc.

3 The Usual Requirement of Unwanted Situations (URUS) Argument

URUS-1: An analysis of rights, duties, and related concepts sometimes leaves unnoticed the motives for deploying them. But the instrumental value of rights talk is easy to spot. Here are a few useful indicators.

Human rights, James Griffin says, protect people's ability to form and pursue conditions of a worthwhile life:[9]

> There is the sort of agency that makes us bearers of human rights—namely, our capacities for autonomy and liberty—and there is the sort of agency that human

---

[9] Here, and in many discussions of rights, the word "protect" is used. But it is important to note that rights do not protect, and never have protected, anyone. People might be attacked, whether or not they have any rights. The *enforcement* of rights and duties, however, can offer some protection to people. But then what people really want, when they speak of rights as offering protection, is the physical protection against being forced into (or kept in) unwanted situations. Since it is that kind of protection that is desired, it is some kind of perceived or anticipated interference or threat that the assertion of a right is meant to deal with.

rights are meant to protect—that is, not only the possession of these capacities but also their exercise. [*On Human Rights*, 67]

Stephen Darwall raises the issues of complaint and coercion:

[To have a claim-right] includes a second-personal authority to resist, complain, remonstrate, and perhaps use coercive measures of other kinds, including, perhaps, to gain compensation if the right is violated. [*The Second-Person Standpoint*, 18]

So does Richard Brandt:

Historically talk of "rights" has occurred in the context of complaint or revolution or lawsuits. [*Morality, Utilitarianism, and Rights*, 194]

And we must not neglect J. S. Mill:

When we call anything a person's right, we mean that he has a valid claim on society to protect him in the possession of it, either by the force of law or by that of education and opinion. If he has what we consider a sufficient claim, on whatever account, to have something guaranteed to him by society, we say that he has a right to it. [*Utilitarianism*, Chapter V, par. 24]

Mill is talking about social and legal rights, and the basic point applies: rights are asserted when enforcement is desired. So it is in unwanted situations—conditions that already are, or that are anticipated or speculated to be, troublesome—that we are keen to wave the rights flag.[10] It is pointless to insist on a right to x if there is no anticipation of interference with the doing or having of x. Let us say that a claim-right is asserted in, or in anticipation of, aversive conditions that would result from interferences with one's values (interferences with having or doing or being what one values) even if, as might be the case with infants, the right-holder is unaware of the threat. Different rights have different ways of being interfered with, but the result is some kind of actual or presumed aversive condition. An assertion of a right might be met with derision if the aversion involved is implausible. It would be difficult to take seriously someone's fear of becoming a leprechaun. We would tell him he needn't be worried; there are no such things as leprechauns, and so he needn't fear becoming one. So it would be silly to postulate a right to not be made into a leprechaun. What counts as aversive is relative to cultures and to persons (and their intentions). Even ancient

---

[10] As a Member of Parliament in 1867, Mill proposed (unsuccessfully) that "person" instead of "man" be used in a Reform Bill in order to at last give women the right to vote. Clearly this was in response to women's having all along been denied a legal voice.

gods were thought to occasionally find themselves in difficult conditions with respect to each other, so it would have been appropriate to have thought of them as having rights and recognizing justice among themselves. But an omnipotent deity could not face threats, and so it would not properly be said to have claim-rights. In general, the more powerful you are, the less you need the protection of rights.[11]

URUS-2: But protections can be breached. Rights can be infringed, violated, and ignored. Where rights have corresponding obligations, those obligations might not be observed. Such invasions and failures can be the subjects of threats. I do not of course say that rights have only these characteristics, nor that nothing else does. It serves my purpose to point out that whatever else one might wish to say about rights, their exercise is threatenable. To have a right is to stand a risk.

URUS-3: A true threat is the presentation of a real possibility of pain, misery, hardship, deprivation, regret, sadness, embarrassment, frustration, or other obviously unwanted condition.

URUS-4: So the threat of the interference with the exercise of a right would be the threat of being put into some aversive situation. If I have a right to speak at a public meeting, and if someone threatened to beat me up if I spoke, then the aversive condition that was threatened would of course be the pain and suffering of bodily injury (and the frustration of not getting my message across, or the consequent dangers that my speaking might have been intended to avoid or to mitigate).

URUS-5: If there were a claim-right to not be killed, then what would be the corresponding threat? It would of course be the threat of death. The threat of being killed (by a moral agent) would be the threat against a "negative" claim-right to life.

URUS-6: If S had a right to life (the right to continue living—the right to not be killed by a moral agent), then the situation in which S could not exercise that right would have to be aversive to S or at least be *possible* to be aversive to S. Insofar as people think of death as bad and hence the prospect of death a threat, they will probably claim that there is a right to life.

URUS-7. But they would be wrong. The main conclusions of Chapter 1 were that (1) having died cannot possibly be aversive, and (2) if we understand that,

---

[11] Maybe this is consistent with Nietzsche's insight: Slave morality invents rights in hopes of saving themselves from their adversity. But the Masters do not say "We have the right to make rules", because they do not face threats (from the ruled). It is when masters begin to say "We have certain rights as rulers" that aristocracy has become corrupt (*Beyond Good and Evil*, §258).

then we will also understand that the prospect of death should not be aversive either.

URUS-8. So if death is thought to be an unwanted situation, it is so because of a misunderstanding of death.

URUS-9. So death cannot be a true threat.

URUS-10. Therefore, there cannot be a right to not be killed.

This concludes the presentation of the two arguments against a right to life. As promised, EPIC and URUS are close allies. The Instead Requirement is working behind the scenes in the second version: the notion of threat is used, and a threat is a kind of promise to put a person into an "instead" condition.

And now let me anticipate some objections.

4 Objections and replies.

Objection 1: Whaaat?!

Reply to Objection 1: One understanding of that visceral response might be expressed in more informative words thus: "Are you saying that if I have no claim-right to life, then I shouldn't be concerned if someone tries to kill me?" And the answer is that I am not saying that. If someone tries to kill you, you can reasonably be concerned, not because you might cease to be, but rather because you might end up in a very aversive condition; that is to say, you might *not* die, and the attempt on your life might leave you with severe injuries and in great pain, in which case you have a major complaint against the person who caused it all. (Incidentally, this reply hints at what I think is crucial about moral issues, and what is usually missing in attempts to justify a right to life. I mentioned it in Chapter 5, and I will return to it later on.)

Objection 2: One has a right to have one's reasonable wishes about oneself respected. It is reasonable to wish to not be killed. So one has a right to not be killed. As Michael Tooley says,

> "A has a right to X" is roughly synonymous with "A is the sort of thing that is a subject of experiences and other mental states, A is capable of desiring X, and if A does desire X, then others are under a prima facie obligation to refrain from actions that would deprive him of it." ["Abortion and Infanticide", 45]

(We can ignore part of what Tooley is interested in, namely, the issue of whether the formulation applies to fetuses and infants. It is sufficient for the objection here that killing an adult who wishes to continue living is a moral wrong to that person.)

Reply to Objection 2: First of all, a caution. Some of the desires that we have are later vacated as we grow, change, and mature. Some desires are consciously given up when we change our minds about something; others simply fade away. In such cases the fulfillment or nonfulfillment of past desires (or, rather, the presence or absence of what used to be the subjects of bygone desires) is no longer an issue for the person. Death is like having vacated of all of one's desires, because an experson is not the sort of thing that can have any desires at all. In addition, as mentioned in Chapter 5, no person is deprived of anything by being killed, and so no person is deprived of the fulfillment of any desire by being killed.

I agree that people have desires such that it can be wrong to interfere with their satisfaction. But when interference with desires is wrong, it is wrong not because it is an interference with desires, full stop. Rather, it is wrong on account of what it brings about or could plausibly bring about: frustration, lost opportunities, hardship, and so on. But then no wrong is done to a person by interfering with desires if there can be no ensuing suffering of that person. Killing a person (painlessly and without warning) is a way of guaranteeing that the person will *not* suffer as a result.

If it were the interference with the desire which is wrong, absent consequent suffering, then we would need a reason for saying so. That is, the causation of suffering is a good reason to judge something to be morally wrong (or at least morally suspicious), whereas the mere interference with a wish seems not to have that sort of basic force, and consequently we would need some further argument. This is more clearly seen in those (perhaps relatively rare) cases where we interfere with someone's wishes because it is an emergency, and we figure that some kind of interference will prevent suffering, after which they thank us for the interference.

Some people voluntarily put themselves into situations wherein they are at risk of having some of their desires thwarted; indeed, it would be unreasonable to expect otherwise. People play games and engage in contests of all sorts. People willingly (even eagerly) engage in romantic courtships. In some such activities the risk of failure is not only prominent, but it is *essentially* part of the appeal. This may be especially true in affairs of the heart, wherein not merely the risk, but sometimes the actuality of some wrenching of desires is at the very core and background of many subsequent pleasures.

Once one has understood the Epicurean account, it is no longer reasonable to wish to not be killed. Yes, a wish to not be killed is an ordinary wish, a usual wish, a wish that almost everyone has. But we can know better. The fear of witches was a real fear for some people, but we know better, and so we would now think it silly to assert, protect, or add to our legal or moral systems a right to not be hexed by witches. This is of course not to say that it is morally innocent to play on such fears. A bank robber waving a toy gun intentionally gives rise to fears appropriate to a situation in which the gun is real. We do not condemn him for creating a possibility that the toy gun could have killed someone, but we can blame him for the anxiety he caused. Still, the claim that one has a right to have one's reasonable wishes respected is based on the consequences (actual, anticipated, probable, or, in some cases, even barely possible) of having one's wishes defeated; the result can be frustration or suffering or some other form of aversion. But such a result *cannot* occur in the case of annihilation.

A wish to not die is often taken to be a preference to remain alive rather than to be dead. But such a preference runs afoul of the Instead Requirement. One can reasonably wish to be or to not be in a certain condition only if it is possible to be and possible to not be in such a condition. Suppose that you are in a certain condition or situation and you want to be in another one instead; or you are in a condition or situation and you prefer to remain there instead of changing. So you have a choice or preference to be in one situation rather than to be in another (and this other might be thought of only as what the present one is not). That usually makes sense. But such a wish or preference does not apply in the case of annihilation, because one cannot be in any condition after having ceased to be. There is no "instead" for the one who died.

Objection 3: Human lives are (or involve) projects. Consider Robert Young's comment that

> what makes killing another human being wrong on occasions is its character as an irrevocable, maximally unjust prevention of the realization either of the victim's life-purposes or of such life-purposes as the victim may reasonably have been expected to resume or come to have. ["What is Wrong with Killing People?", 519]

Just as one can fear the loss of an arm, one can fear the loss of the ability to have and carry through one's projects. Death is such a loss. Therefore it is reasonable to fear death; therefore, death is a true threat after all. This is the special harm—the double insult—of death: not only does death frustrate all your plans and projects, but you cannot have any new ones. And since death can be such a threat, there can be a right that stands against that threat. And that can be called a right to life.

Reply to Objection 3: Why should the interference with a person's projects, or the loss of something valuable, ever give rise to a moral issue such that rights talk would seem appropriate? The obvious answer is: because interference and loss can lead to, or can reasonably be supposed to lead to, adversity. (This is only prima facie, or presumptive, of course. A fuller understanding of a particular project and its context, and what other moral vectors are at work, might result in the moral acceptability of some interferences.)

It is true that people reasonably fear many sorts of losses. But one does not fear the loss of x (where x is an arm or anything else) unless one anticipates that one might want the x after it has been lost—that one will try to regain it, regret its absence, seek a replacement, look for compensation, be unable to continue other projects, and so on. People do not fear the loss of a cancerous tumor or the loss of nearsightedness. In the case of an arm, or eyesight, or anything usually thought to be of value to a person, it is expected that its loss or interference could reasonably be feared. But death (the "loss" of life, as it is sometimes said in unguarded moments) is unique. Death is the annihilation of the person and hence all of the person's desires, intentions, and motivations to have any x or to have and fulfill any projects, and it also makes impossible one's aversion to any ensuing states of affairs. Consequently, one cannot reasonably anticipate that after one's own death one will regret having died; nor will one try to regain life or seek compensation. (Note also that the destruction of the person does not do what losses do, namely, leave the person without x.)

The objection is a version of the deprivation view of the purported evil of death. I criticized that view in Chapter 5, but allow me to say a few more words on the subject. Ordinarily—that is, in life—to interfere with a person's life-purposes is probably to put the person into a worse situation; let us say that it causes various kinds of adversity. Unless we are very careful, we carry the habit of looking out for our (and others') life-purposes over to the issue of death, because we do not attend to the fact that death is not like all other situations wherein life-purposes are interfered with or threatened. Death is the singular case where consequent suffering (of the person whose life-purposes were interfered with) is absent—not contingently absent, but necessarily so.

Positions similar to Objection 3 are common. I have picked one almost at random. George P. Cave gives us a thoughtful description of animals as *Dasein*—a concernful absorption in the world. But Cave's final comment, when he then uses his discussion of *Dasein* to come to the issue of a right to life, is a simple version of the deprivation view:

> The killing of most, if not all animals—whether painlessly or not—is a clear instance of thwarting their concernful absorption in their own possibilities.

> Hence, animals have a moral interest in not being killed. Since they *care* about their existence, they suffer evil if they are deprived of the opportunity of actualizing their possibilities. ["Animals, Heidegger, and the Right to Life", 254]

Cave's final sentence I take to mean "Animals suffer evil if they are killed". The word "suffer" usually refers to pain or hardship of some sort. And "suffer evil" means the same, for "evil" characterizes the cause as that which is repellant—that which is to be avoided or escaped precisely because of (or because of the risk of) the experience of misery, pain, anguish, and so on. But death cannot be so characterized, because having died cannot possibly bring about suffering, nor even the risk suffering, for a dead animal.

Objection 4: Being killed is the worst kind of disrespect. And does not the moral law require us to respect humanity and hence persons?

Reply to Objection 4: One of the principal ingredients in respect for *persons* (if not for the abstraction of humanity) is non-interference with their choices, unless there is good evidence (sometimes this must be presumptive) that an emergency is afoot, which may often be the case for important decisions made by incompetents (children, for example, or adults, even in the prime of their faculties, when they are ignorant of important facts). A person who is apparently competent in the usual sorts of decisions which we expect adults to make, and who, after recognizing the dangers of skiing, nevertheless chooses to ski, ought not to be interfered with. But the same person, distracted by some event and stepping off the curb into the path of an on-coming car, may be interfered with, on the assumption that the person is (temporarily) incompetent at making this particular footstep. (Besides, it would also be a matter of saving the driver of the car from possible injury, and preventing damage to the vehicle.)

Being disrespected is like loss or deprivation. Death is not a loss or deprivation, but many injuries are. Lying to or about you, cheating you, treating you with contempt, and so on, are ways of disrespecting you, and such disrespect is bad if you could be harmed, disadvantaged, set back, pained, or impaired as a result. But your death can bring about no such thing.[12]

Objection 5: Gerald H. Paske says that moral agents (such as most humans) have more inherent value than moral patients (such as nonhuman animals). His argument relies on an earlier claim that a moral agent can experience some kinds of goods that come from being a rational being. For example,

---

[12] Some people claim that if you were maligned, disparaged, or betrayed "behind your back", such that you suffer no ill consequences, it would nevertheless be bad for you. I examine and reject such claims in "Death and Other Nothings".

it is plausible to claim that slavery is wrong even if the slave is hedonically better off than he would be if he were free. If so, it must be because freedom from slavery is a good which is independent of the hedonic situation. It is a good which is based in "human" or "rational" dignity; a type of dignity which applies only to rational beings. ["Why Animals Have No Right to Life", 506]

What we learn from these considerations is that interference with autonomy is a salient moral evil to the person. Being killed is a blatant interference with autonomy. Therefore, killing a person is a wrong done to the person. Therefore there is a duty to not kill. Therefore, a person has a claim-right to not be killed.

Reply to Objection 5: Granted that rational beings are capable of some kinds of goods that moral patients cannot experience. Perhaps for some animals, being caged might be hedonically just as good as being wild. But when the animal is a moral agent, being owned is (or can be—is certainly expected to be) a source of misery and distress. Paske recognizes this, and he points out that there is something wrong with slavery even if the slaves are "contented": they lack dignity (autonomous freedom). Well, suppose a slave has lost some dignity. Might we now ask: So what? If the slave is happy and has no motive to escape slavery, does not accept an offer to escape when provided with one, makes no preparations for leaving, does not fantasize leaving, etc., then what shall we say? We probably would say that the slave would nevertheless be better off as a non-slave—that the slave would have (or might very well have) more satisfaction, or at least fewer impediments to satisfaction, as a non-slave, even if the slave does not realize it. (What else could reasonably be meant? You shall be forced to have dignity whether you like it or not?) Even if some slaves were better off (in any way you please to measure it) as slaves, we would still denounce slavery, because of what we conceive slavery to be, namely, keeping people in a situation even if they judge that a different situation would be more desirable; and we expect that slaves will disvalue their situation, which is why slave owners put barriers to their leaving. If slavery, on some particular occasion, did not produce positive suffering, or at least a hindrance to betterment, then it would nevertheless be the imposition of a very clear risk, just as shooting a gun randomly into a crowd is the imposition of a very clear risk, even if on a particular occasion it does not cause harm to anyone. It would be against all, or almost all, of our experience to suppose that a person might be happier as a slave. Most humans know this (it would be silly to suppose that they do not), which accounts for part of their misery if they are made slaves, or even if they are threatened with slavery. The real issue, then, is not the mere loss of autonomous freedom but rather what that loss means—what it is expected to result in, in terms of adversity.

Finally, interfering with a person's choices while leaving the person alive can of course leave the person with less autonomy. But an experson, although necessarily without any autonomy at all, is not a slave, nor is it a person with less autonomy than before. It is not even a person who used to have autonomy. Whatever it now is, it is not a person, and so it is not something to which the concept of autonomy applies. (See the discussion of the Fallacy of Misplaced Contingency in Chapter 5.)

Objection 6: Alan Goldman offers a distinction between positive and negative rights, insisting that having any positive right implies having the (negative) right to life: "As soon as any positive rights are granted [. . .], the right to life would have to be granted as well" ("Abortion and the Right to Life", 405). This means that the right to life is basic, so that if people (or animals) do not have a right to life, then they cannot have any other rights, and it would seem to follow that no one has any rights at all. But there are positive rights. Therefore, there is a right to life. As Goldman says,

> That being granted a right to life is a necessary condition for being granted other rights seems initially plausible from the fact that it seems to make no sense to grant S a right to x and then maintain that we avoid violating that right either by granting x to S or by killing S instead. Killing S does not seem a way of honoring his other rights. Being alive is a necessary condition for having desires satisfied (except perhaps suicidal desires), and unless killing S allows us to honor his other rights, having a right to life is necessary to having other rights. ["Abortion and the Right to life", 404][13]

And,

> It makes little or no sense to say, for example, that cows have rights to grass or grain, if they lack rights not to be killed. [405]

Reply to Objection 6: That last quote goes too quickly. Perhaps a cow in a slaughterhouse could have some rights (e.g., a right to humane treatment) even though its death is imminent. Similarly, even though prisoners on death row are to be deliberately killed, they could have many rights (to food, legal counsel, religious instruction, and medical care; I mean to suggest possible moral rights, and not merely legal ones). In any case, there is no inconsistency in claiming that killing is allowable (for reasons of self-defense, or for food, or for many other

---

[13] See also Philip Devine: "If a creature has no right not to be killed, it cannot have any other serious rights in contexts where its interests and those of persons are in conflict. Such a conflict could always be resolved by killing the troublesome creature" (*The Ethics of Homicide*, 47).

reasons, or perhaps for no reason at all), yet maintaining at the same time that torturing or otherwise purposely (or even negligently) causing misery in the process is forbidden.

As for the longer quotation from Goldman, there are two closely related claims there. (1) It makes no sense to say that we can avoid violating S's positive right to *x* by killing S. (2) Killing S is not a way of honoring S's positive rights.

But (1) is incorrect. To violate S's positive right is to *prevent* S from exercising that right, as might happen if, for example, S has a right to a formal education, yet we bar the entrance to the school, thereby leaving S without a formal education (at least temporarily). But killing S does not leave S without a formal education. Killing S does not put S into a condition where the exercise of a right is not possible, because a dead animal is not the sort of thing either to exercise or to be unable to exercise a right.

As for (2), it is true that killing S is not a way of honoring S's rights, but neither is it a way of violating them. As in the case of (1), let us be careful to avoid false bivalence. S's death (whether by our hands, or by accident, or by disease) means that S no longer exists, and so there are no longer any rights which S has, either to honor or to violate. We may have a duty to feed a new-born baby, but if the baby dies, then we no longer have that duty. We do not of course fulfill the duty by killing the baby. But neither do we thereby fail to fulfill the duty, because failing to fulfill the duty is possible only when it is possible to fulfill the duty, and that is possible only when the baby is alive.

Why does a new-born have a positive right to food? Why are we under an obligation to see to it that it has food? Why, for example, are we not simply under an obligation not to take food from the new-born? The reason is simple: Under normal conditions the new-born will not get food on its own, and as a consequence it will suffer and not flourish.[14]

What is required of us in order to "honor" an infant's positive right to food? We need not feed it when it has already been fed and is no longer hungry. So there are conditions which must be satisfied in order to then fulfill our duty with respect to such a positive right. We do not have an obligation to keep it alive

---

[14] One then wonders about the distinction between positive and negative claim-rights mentioned earlier. Both are based on the notion of a worse condition. Negative claim-rights have to do with not creating the worse condition, and positive claim-rights have to do with not letting the worse condition come about—of acting so as to prevent the worse condition that would come about unless one acts. This distinction therefore hangs on a vexed distinction between positive and negative actions. But even if that distinction were not problematic, it would not help to show that there is a right (negative or positive) to life, because the change from a living being to a dead thing is not the change to a worse condition—a condition of being worse off (or even a condition of imminent worse-offness).

in order to allow the conditions to arise in which we would then have a duty to honor its positive rights under those very conditions; specifically, we do not have a duty to keep the infant alive so that it will eventually become hungry, all in order that we can finally honor a duty to feed it. Would we honor its rights by feeding it a little milk, in order that it would soon be hungry again so that we could feed it a little more, thereby perpetuating the conditions under which we must act in order to fulfill our positive obligation? If we could give it an injection such that it would never again need food, would we still be under a positive obligation to feed it? No; we have an obligation to feed it only because or when it needs food (because otherwise it will suffer not only on account of pain but also on account of not developing as we wish it to). But if it is dead, then it cannot possibly need food, and it cannot possibly suffer, and so any obligation *to it* to feed it has vanished.[15]

Suppose the argument is put forward in this way:

1. One can exercise no rights unless one is alive.
2. So all rights are conditional on a right to life.
3. It is undeniable that we have some rights.
4. Hence, we have a right to life.

The argument's soundness depends in part on premise 2. Where does that premise come from? Certainly not directly from 1. A reasonable inference from 1 might be: All rights which someone (or something) has are conditional on being alive. I am in favor of that substitution, but the result is that the argument is not valid. An additional principle must be provided, such as: The conditions necessary for exercising a right constitute a right. But that is an implausible principle. If I have a right to have murder charges against me judged by an impartial court, do I have a right to be charged with murder and that there be persons who do in fact charge me? In case the charges are true, do I have a right to have murdered?

Objection 7: Judith Jarvis Thomson expresses what is perhaps a virtually universal view: "The primary control we must place on the acceptability of an account of rights is that it should turn out in that account to be a truth that all persons have a right to life" ("A Defense of Abortion", 56). Killing is the paradigm case of a wrong to a person. Killing an innocent person is wrong if anything is (and killing many people is many wrongs), so if there is no right to life, then there are no prohibitions against anything. So isn't your view so misaligned

---

[15] I emphasize "*to it*", because we might have duties to other people to tend to the infant.

with our settled beliefs that it amounts to a *reductio* of Epicureanism? Frederik Kaufman warns us that

> if Epicureanism is true, the implications run much wider and deeper than bioethics. Any human activity that in any way presupposes the badness of death will be groundless—killing or being killed in war will be morally inconsequential, saving people from death will be without merit and execution could not count as punishment. ["Comments on [James Stacey Taylor's] *Death, Posthumous Harm and Bioethics*", 636]

Reply to Objection 7: Kaufman makes a common mistake. He ought to have said that the Epicurean view implies that any human activity that in any way presupposes the badness of death *to the one who died* will be groundless. And that is correct. But killing can be bad (and morally wrong) even if it is not bad to or for the one who was killed. Both killing and saving people from death have important consequences for living people.

Yes, the numbers might sometimes count. If I painlessly kill someone, I do not invade his rights, but I may cause others to suffer, especially that person's loved ones. If, instead of killing one person, I kill five, then (presumably) I cause the suffering of the loved ones of five people, and (presumably) there will be more who suffer. Similar considerations apply to letting die. If the numbers matter, it is not the number of people who die, but rather the number of people who are subjected to distress, pain, misery, trauma, anguish, and so on. As for Thomson's comment, see the Reply to Objection 6.

Objection 8: If suffering is the fundamental issue—if the evil of death is to be found in the pain of the living—then not only homicide but also suicide, assisted suicide, and euthanasia should be judged on the basis of the adversity caused to others. But then it would seem to follow that a person can rightfully be prevented from dying (even if he wants to die), or even be prevented from engaging in life-risking activities, because his death might cause hardship for others. But then what becomes of autonomy? In such cases, how can we advocate both for autonomy and against causing suffering?

Reply to Objection 8: The response is similar to the answer we could give for anything that a person does that might cause trouble for others. The answer is: That depends. When the issue is seen as one of policy, then we may take it as good policy to allow people autonomy in what are usually considered self-regarding choices, even if some of those choices involve the risk of causing problems for others, because the alternative policy (permit a person to do nothing unless there is a guarantee that no one will be disturbed in any way) is worse, both because it is impractical and because it ignores the disadvantages to the actors who are prevented from acting according to their own choices. If a person is allowed to follow his own star and risk his life mountain climbing, his subsequent death on the rocks may cause his loved ones to suffer. Still, they may realize—they ought to have realized—that being attached to another human being is also risky, because persons are the sort of being for whom autonomy is a major nourishment. Parents eventually allow their children to leave the nest, at first only for occasional sorties into a dangerous world. Children must be allowed and even encouraged to do so if they are to learn to survive and prosper. But lessons carry risks. There is no preventing all risks without preventing growth and learning. Acknowledging the autonomy of persons is usually the best way to deal with human beings as long as it does not interfere with the autonomy of others, even if, on occasion, it proves to be risky. A mountain climber, risking death, does not on that account interfere with his loved ones' autonomy, even if what he does carries a risk of causing them some anxiety. A young woman who does not continue to develop her talents as a cellist, and who would rather manage a fast-food restaurant, may cause her loved ones some distress; but she does not interfere with anyone's autonomy, and so it is good policy that she be allowed to follow her own conception of happiness.

It may be objected that aside from killing, there could be cases wherein one's autonomy is not respected, thereby doing a wrong, but without thereby causing any suffering whatsoever. True, but in such a case it would be an issue of the risk of causing suffering. Even if it is discovered in retrospect that the risk had been acceptably negligible, and that no adversity was caused, we could still maintain that respecting autonomy is a useful policy and not an inviolable rule, because the *usual* cases are cases wherein if you interfere with people's freedom, you cause them some hardship, frustration, or misery. The connection between interference with freedom and consequent dissatisfaction is so well established in our lives that it is a good policy to suppose that most interferences with freedoms might cause suffering, unless it can be clearly shown otherwise in particular cases.

Objection 9: The view you are putting forward seems very callous.

Reply to Objection 9: This objection is close to an ad hominem, but it is worth pursuing anyway. And now it is my turn to say "Whaaat?!" My view is not callous at all; in fact, it is just the opposite. My view insists on attending to the fundamental moral issue that is often given insufficient moral weight, namely, suffering or, in general, adversity.

One kind of "humanitarian" approach to the treatment of animals has it that animals might be farmed, killed, and eaten, but in any case treated in such a way that they are not caused to suffer (or if pain is given, it is in pursuit of some further good, such as avoiding even greater pain). I want to say something like that in the case of humans as well. Farm them, kill them, even eat them if you wish, but you must do so without cruelty—without causing those persons (or anyone else) to suffer, including the psychological torment that can easily occur if the people are captive and also if they believe they are going to be killed. People do have such fears, and it would be callous to ignore them. But will you be able to farm humans (in preparation for any purpose at all) harmlessly? Forcing humans into local work projects or into military service creates serious moral issues. Suffering can be brought to humans by keeping them confined, repressing their individuality, interfering with their spontaneity, frustrating their desires, and ignoring their needs for improvement (whereas some nonhuman species are not susceptible to such adversity), regardless of whether they are subsequently killed.

If it is claimed that killing (and also letting die) is wrong because it violates the right to life of the person killed, then what is to be said about the survivors who are the ones who suffer because a person important to them has been taken from them? We must be cautious to not privilege an abstraction and end up discounting peoples' suffering. That would be callous. Here is an example:

> To pass by on the street a person bleeding to death as a result of a hit-and-run motor accident, to ignore a child's cries for help as it drowns in a backyard swimming pool, to allow a blind man to step into the path of a car, is to show a grave lack of respect for the right to life. [H. J. McCloskey, "The Right to Life", 421]

I would have thought that the sentence ought to end: "show a grave lack of respect for those *persons*." Even if only persons had a right to life, it is not the alleged right which is being contemned by the passerby but the unfortunate persons, because they are being allowed to suffer.

Another example: Some writers say that the fundamental property that gives an animal a right to life is the property of being sentient. Now suppose we notice that only sentient organisms can suffer. If we abstract our concern for suffering into some sort of respect for sentience, as though it were *sentience* which was of supreme value,[16] then we may lose touch with the suffering, because while

---

[16] "The total version of utilitarianism regards sentient beings as valuable only in so far as they make possible the existence of intrinsically valuable experiences like pleasure. It is as if sentient beings are receptacles of something valuable and it does not matter if a receptacle gets broken, so long as there is another receptacle to which the content can be transferred without any getting spilt" (Peter Singer, "Killing Humans and Killing Animals", 149).

sentience may be necessary for suffering, it is not sufficient. A sentient animal might be born, live for a while in a relatively benign environment, and then die painlessly. This would be an exception to our usual expectations about sentient beings, but it may be enough to encourage us to be mindful of the misery of particular persons (and animals) and not to the abstraction of sentience.[17] Indeed, the importance of a given person (or animal) to one or more other persons is not that the person is a sentient being, or that the life is sacred, because then the *particular* person would be a mere proxy for sentience or sacredness. It is rather persons in their particularities—in their bundles of disparate actual and expected, explicit and tacit, values to us—that most motivate *our* concern for *them* in *particular*. There are very good reasons why some people are closer and more valuable to us than others, and therefore why we find our concern more deeply intertwined with their lives than with others'.

It would be nasty, mean, disrespectful, and callous to threaten to kill a person who feared death, because such a threat would bring great anxiety and mental turmoil to the person. But it would not be a wrong to the person to kill her if she was unaware of any threat and if the killing was done without causing pain. Although a painless killing cannot be a wrong to the person killed, it can be a wrong to the survivors in much the same way (but usually differing in degree and in the reach of its consequences) that the unbidden destruction of a house is not a wrong done to the house but rather a wrong to the persons who are caused to suffer because something important has been taken away.

5 The significance of suffering

Let me emphasize and expand upon some points made earlier. If there is no right to life—if a person was not wronged by having been killed—then what shall we say of abortion, homicide, euthanasia, and other killings? These issues are now transformed. For example, in considering the morality of abortion (about which more later), it is no longer necessary to agonize, as very many writers have, over

---

[17] Similar considerations may be brought to bear on the attention given to the abstraction of "the sanctity of life", independently of whether any adversity is involved. Lord Devlin, for example, in his famous *The Enforcement of Morals*, says: "A murderer who acts only upon the consent, and maybe the request, of his victim is no menace to others, but he does threaten one of the great moral principles upon which society is based, that is, the sanctity of human life" (6). A generation later, Ronald Dworkin, in the preface to the Vintage edition of *Life's Dominion*, used a similar term in a similar way: "The main sustaining idea [of] this book [. . .] is our shared conviction that human life, in any form, has inherent, sacred value, and that whatever choices we have about birth or death should be made, so far as possible, to respect and not dishonor that profound value" (ix).

the question whether a fetus is a person whose right to life does or does not take precedence over the woman's right to life (or over her right to determine what shall happen in and to her body). And in considering the morality of euthanasia, it is no longer necessary to wonder whether, for example, a human being in an irreversible vegetative state is still a person with a right to life. But then how are such issues—for they are still of great moment—to be dealt with, if not in terms of rights to life?

It is no wonder that many people search long and hard (and ingeniously) for a justification for the claim that killing (or at least certain kinds of killings) of humans (and sometimes other animals) is wrong—in fact, one of the worst wrongs. But it is misguided to seek a justification in a right to life. The effects of the death of a person can be so very tragic in a way that few other events are. Specifically, the tragedy of death lies partly in its being the finality of something very precious to us. A very, very complex organism has been permanently taken away from us. We can replace stones, automobiles, trees, and perhaps even wonderful works of art. If a suitable duplicate cannot be found, manufactured, or grown, then there are almost always various alternatives. But a loved human is even more a part of our lives than trees and works of art, and even more difficult to replace, which is one reason why we suffer when someone we valued has died.

Some writers acknowledge that killing a person can cause great sorrow to other people, but that fact is usually swept aside as being either of little concern or else independent of the moral issue of killing. Here, for example, is Don Marquis:

> It might be said that what makes killing us wrong is the great loss others would experience due to our absence. Although such hubris is understandable, such an explanation does not account for the wrongness of killing hermits, or those whose lives are relatively independent and whose friends find it easy to make new friends. ["Why Abortion is Immoral", 189]

I agree that the wrongness of killing a person does not depend upon "such hubris", that is, the person's *own* assessment of his or her value to others. But I maintain that a person's value to others is nevertheless central. The important issue is a person's value to the survivors *as judged by those survivors*. Any person's death will have consequences, and, ignoring for the moment certain considerations about the case of the hermit, the important consequences will have to be dealt with by those people whose lives were connected to the one who died; that is, certain *living* people will be faced with suddenly important issues (whereas there can be no issues at all for a corpse). As for persons "whose lives are relatively independent and whose friends find it easy to make new friends", this differs from the first case only in the extent or intensity of the consequences for others. When killing is wrong, it is so precisely because it causes people to suffer. For most people, there is hardly anything more valuable than a few other people. If it is one of those few who was killed, then the survivors have been caused to suffer greatly. Other survivors, more removed in consequential space, suffer somewhat less. How extensive the anguish is and how intense it is, are contingent matters for each instance of death. But in addition (and this is important also for the hermit case) people are made to wonder whether the killer might kill again, causing similar or even greater grief.

Here is another example where the wrongness of death has been misidentified (and somewhat trivialized):

> It seems quite plain that it is wrong to kill people. What is not so plain is *why* it is wrong to kill people, especially when one considers that the person killed will not be around to suffer the consequences afterwards. [. . .] His friends, relatives, and dependents might suffer, but that does not seem to be enough to solve the problem; it is, in the Common Moral Consciousness, just as wrong to kill somebody who has no friends, relatives, or dependents. To think of the wrongness of killing somebody in terms of whether or not it will upset somebody else is to miss completely the somewhat obscure point. The Common Moral Consciousness is quite clear that the reason why it is wrong to kill somebody has something to do with him, not with his mother or maiden aunt. [R. E. Ewin, "What is Wrong with Killing People?", 126]

But the issue is the suffering—*suffering*, not merely being "upset"—which is experienced by children, parents, siblings, spouses, lovers, and all others who valued the one who died. Their grief is in fact what is most noticeable and what most calls for our attention when someone dies. It is a crisis that we want to remedy in some way. We may want to be with those who are grieving and help them through this terrible time. And then we want to do something so that this kind of thing does not happen again, causing similar suffering to still other people. In cases of deaths from old age or disease, we make medical inquiries, hoping to improve health care. In cases of accidental deaths we increase precautions, hoping to prevent further accidents. In cases of killings we seek out the killers, hoping to prevent further killings. We ought in all cases to be concerned with the actual (and possible future) suffering of living people.

Why is suffering the basis for moral reckoning? The issue is of course complex, but I have only a very brief account to offer. When one suffers, one is strongly motivated to do something about it. Suffering is therefore an important basis for egoistic reckoning. But humans (and to some extent some other mammals) are also capable of empathy—identifying or feeling with others. As our empathy develops, and as we begin more and more to feel its subtleties, we suffer when others suffer. Hence, as our empathic sense develops, so too does our moral sense.[18] Suppose one is scolded for an action. When some suffering of others is an immediate and visible consequence of the action, one does not ask "But what's so bad with what I did?" Even children can understand this. But if there is no obvious suffering, then children ask "What's wrong with it?", and we have to teach them that suffering is a possible or probable result of this kind of action. As children mature, we expect them to understand more and more elusive consequences of their actions—actions whose proximal consequences do not involve visible suffering, but whose more distant consequences do. And eventually they understand not merely "causes suffering" but also "could likely cause suffering" and "is the sort of thing that usually causes suffering". The refinements of such understanding are part of the measure of moral development.

Later on we generalize and abstract. That is both valuable and dangerous. Valuable, because we can be more easily attuned to the possible misery of others (both human and nonhuman); and dangerous, because we may be tempted to steal the suffering away from the people suffering and turn it into a principle no longer having much to do with suffering people, as I cautioned before. To attend so closely to the abstraction is to risk losing touch with the original motivators of pain and grief and to risk losing a clear vision of the goals of preventing and relieving pain and grief.

Empathy is necessary not only in the initial stages of moral development but also later on as a constitutive element in the adult's ongoing concerns for others. But if Epicurus is correct that we can learn to attenuate the natural fear of death, then mightn't we also be able to release ourselves from the natural pull of empathy, and in consequence pay little or no heed to the suffering of others? Perhaps we could. But would we want to? The unlearning of something so natural and fundamental must be warranted by awfully compelling reasons. We can profitably unlearn the fear of annihilation; the profit comes in being relieved of significant forms of anxiety and fear, as well as in the unfettering of our appreciation of the good things in our experiences. But if we did not empathize, what would we be left with? In the absence of empathic response to others, there would seem to be no room for the kind of active and creative

---

[18] Gerald H. Paske makes a similar point ("Why Animals Have No Right to Life", 503) but uses it to develop a view quite different from mine.

attention to, and concern for, others' actual and potential adversity which a moral attitude involves. The risk of suffering both to ourselves and to those persons and animals who are valuable to us would be unacceptably increased were people's natural empathy to be extinguished, stifled, or left underdeveloped.

6 Policy

If one engages in an act that is the sort of thing known to risk causing difficulties for others, then one has a duty to take appropriate precautions. Suppose K wants to kill a person. Then he must take precautions against causing suffering. Perhaps K plans to shoot the person. Then he must shoot in such a way that the death occurs painlessly. He must make sure that the bullet does not harm others. He must know that the target has no family and friends, or, more generally, that the death will not cause undue hardship for others. Where can he obtain such assurance? It seems to me that it is in principle *possible*, but practically never, or at least seldom, to be had. When it comes to real life—when it comes to the world as we have experienced it—it is difficult to imagine anyone actually being able to provide such proof. And even if such proof were to be given in a particular case, we would want to know some very substantial facts about the killer, because we would probably not trust him not to kill again, next time without adequate precautions, so that any particular act of killing is easily seen as posing a risk of further killing, and further killings might cause suffering for the survivors. The burden of proof weighs heavily on K, because he is acting in a way that is usually very risky. In cases of emergency—that is, when action must be taken with few or even no precautions—the burden is on the actor to show that no less risky course of action was reasonably open.

A policy of condemning killings because of the risk of suffering which killing causes may be analogized to condemning theft because of the risk of hardship which theft causes. There are various policies which might be suggested in order to allow a person to make use of something without causing an undue burden for others. Here are two common ones: (1) a policy of requiring a survey of relevant people to see whether various proposed uses of that thing would meet with their approval, or would at least not cause them great inconvenience; (2) a policy of investing the final say in one person or a small group of persons (called the owner or owners of the item in question). Although on some occasions the former policy is thought to be useful for important, society-wide actions, the latter policy is very popular, and when it is in place, taking a person's property without permission is wrong because it is assumed to put the owner into a worse position by depriving her of something of value. But in judging the theft to be wrong, we understand that she may not at the moment know how some item of property would have been of use to her; that indeed she might be mistaken even if she does specify its use; and that even if she did value it in some particular ways, she might never get around to making use of her property in those ways or in any other ways. The value may be largely tacit and might remain only an unactualized potential. Just so, too, are some of the values of one person to others; such values are not always explicit, nor even always explicable. Some such values might remain unactualized potentials: a friend is one who *would* help out in time of need, even if that time never comes.

We may find another analogy with a policy of freedom of expression, for which Mill (*On Liberty*), among others, offers substantial support. It is a wise policy to refrain from forcibly interfering with the promulgation of opinions, not because an opinion is intrinsically valuable (whatever that would mean) but because the interference with the exchange of opinions can make our lives worse, or not as good as they could be, even if it is not known in advance what those opinions are, nor in what ways they might be useful to some people, nor who those people are. There are of course cases wherein one might reasonably argue that preventing a particular person's expressing a particular opinion on a particular occasion might be warranted. But the burden of proof should weigh heavily. We will need assurances that this interference, if allowed, will not encourage still further interferences in other cases that we do not wish to allow.

And so it ought to be in the case of killing. There are many ways to cause people to suffer. Although killing a person can be done without causing the person discomfort or anxiety, it is a *very reliable* way of bringing suffering to others, even if it is not known in advance who those people are. So a policy of condemning killing is a wise policy, although there might occasionally be exceptions, such as emergencies or other cases of having to respond to persons who pose credible threats to the well-being of others.

7 Abortion

The issue of abortion seems often to depend on whether the fetus is thought to have a claim-right to life, and whether that right takes precedence over the woman's right to control what happens in and to her body. But if there is no right to life, then the issue is transformed.

Michael Wreen finds it odd to say that a fetus has no right to life but a person who develops from that fetus has a right to not be harmed. That would imply, he says, that harming a fetus such that it matures into a harmed person is wrong, but killing a fetus (such that no person develops from it) is not.

> If we try to kill the fetus and fail, then, assuming that we harm it (and thereby the future person) in the attempt, we have done wrong; for the actual person that the fetus or infant develops into has rights, including the right not to be harmed. That's peculiar. Similarly, if I merely mutilate a fetus or infant (painlessly, we'll assume), I would be violating its and/or the future person's rights, but if I decide to kill it instead, I wouldn't be, as it would then have no rights at all, at that time or later. Again, if I maim a fetus or infant, I violate its and/or the future person's rights; but if I maim it and then kill it, I violate no rights at all. And still again, if I scramble a fetus's or infant's brain to the extent that it is permanently retarded but still a person when it grows up, I violate its and/or the future person's rights; but if I scramble its brains to an even greater extent so that it is not even a person at maturity, I do no wrong. ["The Power of Potentiality", 27–28]

Wreen means these gruesome examples to serve as *reductios*. His main point is that potentiality matters in ascribing certain rights (such as the right to life) to persons and even to potential persons.

I agree with Wreen that potentiality matters. A human baby, for example, has more potentiality (in certain important respects) than a dog. But I disagree on *why* it matters. Wreen thinks that potentiality can give an organism rights. I think that it gives us a motive. If, to modify one of Wreen's examples (29), either a puppy or a newly born human baby will die (painlessly) unless I act, and if I can save only one of them but not both, which one ought I to save? Surely it is expected that I would save the baby. And I would indeed make that choice, without hesitation, but not because the baby has a right to life and the dog does not, nor because the baby has a greater right to life than the dog, but rather because the human means more to me—is more valuable to me—than the dog. "But", a philosopher might ask, "suppose the dog meant more to you. Suppose you hated babies and loved dogs." I admit that I do not love babies; they are a nuisance. But then so are dogs. If I had to choose which one to be responsible for—that is, whether to adopt a baby (and raise it to maturity) or to adopt a dog (and tend to it for as long as it lived)—then I would choose a dog. But the question asks me to suppose that I must *save* one of them from destruction and that I hate babies and love dogs. Very well; in that case I cannot yet see why I ought to save the baby instead of the dog. If that sounds callous or at least very peculiar, then I agree; and it probably sounds that way because there is so much else which is presumed in the story but which has not been made explicit. The baby, for example, is probably in the care of someone (such as a parent) who values the baby more than the dog (most people are like that), and so to not save the baby would be to cause its parents considerable anguish. And even if I know that the parents have just been killed (which could be the reason why the baby needs saving), there might be other people who have placed this baby in their hearts. I remember the time a gust of wind blew the battered old hat off my friend's head. I rushed to retrieve it, not because I valued the hat but because my friend did.

The dogged philosopher huffs and puffs. "You", he says, "and the baby and the dog are the last living things in the universe. You loath babies but absolutely adore dogs. *Now* would you save the dog and not the baby?" That is an interesting question, and I know what the answer is. It might not be the answer you think I would give. Or maybe it is. In any case, I would be the last adult left alive (not even you, Dear Reader, could be there as witness), so no one could complain if I chose the dog.

The issue of abortion is (or, rather, ought to be) not whether a human being or a human fetus does or does not have a right to life, based on certain properties (such as consciousness or potentiality for moral agency), but rather how important the putative right-bearer is to beings who can suffer. Consciousness and potentiality for higher orders of living are certainly important, because such animals figure more richly in our lives, and so their harm or destruction causes us to suffer. Living beings (but also nonliving things and states of affairs) that are important to our lives are to be treated with special care, lest they be damaged, causing them to suffer and/or causing other beings to suffer. The more valuable something is to someone, the more careful one must be in one's dealings with it. For most people, other people are the most valuable things they deal with, and so people must be treated with special care. Mishandling my heirloom vase, such that it falls and breaks, will certainly cause some great annoyance to me, and so if you are given the opportunity to handle that vase, you must take care, according to its nature and environment. If you have any dealings with friends of mine, you must take even greater care—care of the kind corresponding to the nature of those beings and their value to others.

The later in the pregnancy the abortion occurs, the more likely people are to complain. Why? It may be because they believe that a later fetus has more vested in its life, and hence that its termination is worse for it than had it been aborted earlier. Or it could be that the developing fetus is more clearly a human person—a "baby"—the closer to birth it is; it looks and acts more like a person, and so it would be no wonder that many people, finding the idea of killing babies to be horrible, slide down a slippery slope (sometimes all the way back to conception). People might think this way, in spite of what we know, namely, that death cannot be bad or a misfortune or a wrong to whatever has died.

Both the woman and her mate, among all persons, are the ones most likely to have a stake in the fetus's life; they have "mixed their labor" together, and now a fetus is growing. The development of a fetus into an independent human being is a project, and should the fetus die, we should grieve with the woman and the man (but of course not with the fetus) for their loss. But if they do not want to continue the pregnancy, and if no one else can plausibly be said to have a major stake in the fetus's continued existence, then there seems no grounds to raise a moral objection to the abortion. Rather than requiring a justification for aborting an unwanted pregnancy, there is on the contrary a greater requirement to make a compelling case for *not* aborting, because if the woman is forced to continue the pregnancy, she will experience months of various inconveniences for some purpose against her own choices. It should be unconscionable to force a person into such servitude. Even worse would be a case where it is known in advance of birth that the baby will be such as to suffer from medical problems or from life in a perilous environment, because then not only will the woman suffer but so will a new person. And this is to ignore the impact the new person will have on the immediate family, the community, and beyond, at least in terms of the natural and human resources that will be consumed and altered by a new presence for many years.

8 Reorientation

This chapter has been a call to reorient some of our ethical concerns, and it is a reminder of what is fundamental to them, namely, suffering, or, in general, adversity. Let me return to the first, and main, point: There is no claim-right to life. But its absence from moral discourse would not be a bad thing. If we attend to an organism's alleged right to life and wonder in what it consists, whether this or that species can have such a right, whether this particular member of a species measures up to the preconditions for a right to life, whether we are justified in interfering, invading, or annulling this particular animal's right to life—because it is too evil to retain such a right, because it is too old or too sick to continue, or because some other rights have taken precedence—then we are peering down through a narrow lens as we dissect a moral corpse. If instead we lift our heads and look around, we might see the living faces of grief and hear the cries of suffering, and we may come to realize that these are the very issues of morality that we had been neglecting.

8

Immortality

Prelude

In 1965 Burl Ives recorded a number of popular Christmas songs that are still heard each year.

1 Kinds of immortality

Epicurus says that "death is nothing to us"; one's attitude about the prospect of one's own death ought to be indifference. We are to understand this as implying a pair of claims: one's own death will not be bad for one, and one's own death will not be good for one. Earlier chapters supported the first of the pair. This chapter will investigate the second. Some writers claim that our mortality is a good thing, because if we were immortal, then we would not have many of the things we now believe are good to have; moreover, immortality would bring with it not simply the lack of the good things of mortality, but some positive disadvantages of its own. I find such claims to be unconvincing.

What is meant by "immortal"? If I were immortal, would it be impossible for me to die? If I were unconditionally immortal—the sense of immortality as a kind of invulnerability—then there is no telling what life would be like. If I could set off a nuclear blast in my hand and still survive, then many of the familiar regularities of existence would have to be other than they are now. Similarly, if I were physically invulnerable by being a pure spirit or a disembodied soul existing apart from, and unaffected by, material things and processes, there would be no telling what such an existence would be like.[1] We can distinguish

---

[1] Also, we might wonder whether invulnerability need imply immortality. Even if people could not be killed, maybe they would perish anyway, perhaps at pre-established times. This might be similar to Leibniz's hypothesis about the indestructibility of souls. They are indestructible, he says, because they are ultimate simples, and only composites can be destroyed. Or, rather, only composites can be

between two types of invulnerability. The first kind would be invulnerability to all sorts of harm and damage, including psychological troubles such as anxiety or frustration. In our mortal lives, as Epicurus says, our basic concerns are about pleasures and pains—satisfaction and dissatisfaction. But for a person who was invulnerable to all possible interferences, the concepts of desire, threat, or mattering would seem to have no place. Such a being would have to be entirely emotionless; at least there would seem to be no point to emotions. Because that kind of invulnerable person could never be faced with the threat of any dissatisfactions at all, it would be so far beyond our ken that it would make no sense to try to evaluate it from our mortal perspective.

A second kind of invulnerability would allow for psychological suffering but exclude physical damage. A being not subject to physical harm might nevertheless not always be able to get (or get in a timely manner) those things which are desired, thereby causing frustration. Still, the notion of a physically invulnerable being is hard to square with our usual views of the nature of the physical world.

But practical immortality need not entail invulnerability; we can imagine a second, weaker sense of immortality, which we may call conditional immortality. Even if normal biological activity begins to stumble and fail, I might go on indefinitely with a replacement heart (natural or artificial), fresh bone marrow, invigorated neurons here and there, and so on. This is immortality in a weak sense because I would still be subject to death from some violent cause, such as a nuclear blast if I set one off in my hand.[2]

If I could be maintained by occasional repairs, then perhaps there could be a way of being entirely rebuilt all at once. If so, there is a third sense of immortality. There is a curious sense of "going on" if I can be recreated after death, as when, after that nuclear blast, frantic doctors rush to catch all those atomized bits of me and stitch them together again in the way they had been before. Humpty Dumpty might be immortal if all the King's technicians were very clever. Lucretius (*De Rerum Natura* 3.845–869) hypothesized that on the basis of Epicurean atomism, it would be possible that all of one's atoms which were dispersed at one's death might later on accidentally recombine in precisely

---

destroyed in any natural way. According to Leibniz, there is a deity who can make it the case that a soul exists or make it the case that a soul no longer exists.

[2] The distinction between conditional and unconditional immortality is similar to Hunter Steele's distinction between contingent and necessary immortality ("Could Body-Bound Immortality Be Liveable?").

the way they had been just prior to death.³ Or instead of being rebuilt, I might be copied—cloned in both body and mind. Let the old "me" perish; a new (and perhaps slightly improved) version can be created. Let this copying take place whenever necessary. Recombination and copying might be thought to provide for conditional immortality via a kind of death and resurrection, except that death would not have its usual meaning of permanent annihilation, but only a temporary falling apart or a temporary period of transitional absence. But we might well wonder whether there could be immortality in these ways. Each recombination or copy might better be considered to be the creation of a different person rather than a continuation of the earlier person. Lucretius thought that in the case of recombination (he did not consider cloning) there would be no continuity of memory between the earlier person and the later person.⁴ It is possible that the atoms that now comprise me comprised some former person. It is possible that these very same atoms comprised an infinity of previous perfect instances of me. But such copies are nothing to me without the continuity of memories. That, anyway, was Lucretius's conclusion, and for my purposes here, I will not take issue with him.

2 Conditional immortality

Given our present conceptions of what life is and what it can be in the foreseeable future, the kind of immortality I have called conditional immortality seems to be the most plausible, if any of them are. This kind of cautious immortality would involve our being continually repaired and upgraded as and when necessary—small sins periodically forgiven—but still being subject to permanent annihilation if precautions are not taken or if some catastrophe befalls us. The point is that if we were immortal in that sense, we would not face the *inevitability* of death which we believe we now face in our actual lives; we would not be confident that someday we would die, unless of course we purposefully arranged for it.⁵ This

---

³ It would be easy to be carried away and think that not only is such a recombination of atoms possible, but, given the Epicurean view of an infinity of atoms moving in an infinity of space in an infinity of time, all possible combinations of atoms must necessarily recur infinitely. But that conclusion is unwarranted. There is no necessity that each possible combination will occur even once, much less reappear, much less reappear infinitely. So Lucretius was right to speculate only on the possibility of recombination.
⁴ It is not clear how, if everything is composed of atoms, all memories would not be recreated along with the rest of the body. But let that pass.
⁵ On the other hand, the universe might be finite in time, at least in the sense that there might be a "Big Crunch", which will destroy everything (perhaps followed by another "Big Bang"). If so, we will

kind of immortality would be similar to the way many people (at least those of us who have the leisure to read philosophy) lead their lives much of the time. In our younger years we are seldom concerned with the prospect of our deaths. We occasionally get sick or sustain some injury, but we usually take it for granted that we will recover, either naturally or with the help of medical technology; and those injuries which are permanent are usually not serious enough to stop us altogether from continuing with an enjoyable life. We take precautions to avoid very serious injury or disease, and most of the time such precautions work. The preconditions for survival are usually not an issue; we manage to find enough food, water, shelter, sanitary conditions, social comforts, and recreation. Mortal life for us is not a series of emergencies. So conditional immortality might be something like an extension into the indefinite future of our usual inattention to the prospect of annihilation.

But how shall we judge whether conditional immortality would turn out to be troublesome? As children we had some values that were abandoned and replaced as we grew into adulthood. Is it therefore a bad thing to become adults? Adulthood is not necessarily a bad thing even from a child's point of view, for children are sometimes anxious to grow up, or at least to grow further up. Even if there are some values that we now have and appreciate as mortals but that we would not have and appreciate if we grew up to be immortals, that would be a weak reason for condemning immortality. Is there any way to find an assessment of the values of both mortality and immortality in order to compare the two? Perhaps we could find some important values, or ways of valuing, that seem to be central to us whether we were mortal or immortal—values which any valuer would have. Once apprised of those core values, we could then examine other values specific to mortality or to immortality and see whether they were or were not consistent with the core values. As far as I can make out, the only plausible candidates for basic values for organic beings rely on pleasure and pain and what is derivative from them. If we took away pain and pleasure, then it is hard to see that there could have developed any values at all. That is what I take Epicurus to mean when he says (as Cicero claims to quote him):

> Nor do I know what I could understand that good to be, if I set aside the pleasures we get from sex, from listening to songs, from looking at [beautiful] shapes, from smooth motions, or any other pleasures which affect any of man's senses. [*Tusculan Disputations* 3.41–42]

---

all be annihilated in the cosmic crush anyway in so many trillions of years, no matter what we do or do not do for the sake of our otherwise immortal selves.

And (from a fragment from Athenaeus)

> the principle and root of all good is the pleasure of the belly; and the sophisticated and refined [goods] are referred to this one.

(See also *Letter to Menoeceus* 128–29.)

Each organism might be understood as building other values from the core in a manner specific to that organism and its environment. The result would be that members of the same species would have similar values because pleasure and pain come to them in roughly similar ways; but other species will be slightly different. Humans, for example, learn early on to value social interactions in ways (or in additional ways) that domestic cats do not; mammals seem to enjoy play, cooperation, and risk-taking, whereas lizards seem not to; humans enjoy creating, decorating, and embellishing tools, whereas bats do not. Perhaps, then, mortals and immortals would differ in their higher values. And the question at issue is whether we mortals would have good reasons to think that some or all of the higher values of immortals would be inconsistent with mortals' important higher values. If so, then we would have some reasons to prefer not to be immortal; we might even find such reasons to be a kind of therapy for the fear of death.

So the issue is: If death were not inevitable, why might such an arrangement be thought to be bad (or mortality thought to be better)? I will present a number of answers, and I will raise problems for each.

3 Lucretius's replacement argument

I start with the weakest argument. It comes, surprisingly, from Lucretius, the most famous of Epicurus's admirers. He reminds us that death is both natural and necessary. Not only is it part of the cycle of nature, but the destruction of some beings is necessary in order to make way for (and to provide the material for) new ones.

> For the old order always passes thrust out by the new, and one thing has to be made afresh from others; but no one is delivered into the pit of black Tartarus: matter is wanted, that coming generations may grow; and yet they all when their life is done will follow you, and before you, no less than you, these generations have fallen and shall fall. [*De Rerum Natura* 3.964–971]

Immortality, then, would be both unnatural and an impediment to the existence of future generations.

The claims are weak because Lucretius's view seems to rely on rather simplistic ideas about what might eventually happen were population to continue to increase without limit (which is conceivable whether or not people were immortal). If the universe is infinite in matter (Lucretius follows the Epicurean teaching that matter, space, and time are infinite: DRN 1.951–1051), then people might always be able to find places which are not too crowded already, provided that they can work out appropriate technologies for interstellar travel, for building habitable structures on or off planets, and for energy conversion. And even if the universe (or an isolated portion of it) is finite in matter and energy (i.e., finite in terms of how many simultaneous lives it can support), it is possible that in response to the press of larger and larger populations, immortal beings would have fewer and fewer children, so that the population might eventually stabilize, even as it has among some portions of mortal civilization. It may even happen that immortal beings would come to appreciate life without children, just as some mortals do.

Still, any optimism ought to be cautious, for even if the universe is infinite, immortals might be able to make use of less and less of it as time goes on, in which case it would be as if the universe were finite. Suppose, for example, that the infinite material of the universe continues to expand without end, so that all things tend to move further and further apart. Then more and more energy would be required in order to travel from one galaxy or galactic cluster to another. Eventually such travel would require more energy than could be found locally, and groups of immortal beings would be separated, each effectively confined to a finite living area. Even if that area were large by our present standards—say, a collection of a few thousand galaxies—it would eventually fill up, or its usable energy would be dissipated to a point below the level necessary for continued life. So perhaps there is something to be said for Lucretius's replacement argument after all.

There may be room for a different kind of replacement argument. Death forces people to "step aside" so that newcomers can assume control of societies, which otherwise might become stale. A social system wherein people die and are replaced by new members might be a social system which is better overall than a social system of immortals who do not step aside. On the other hand, immortals can of course allow new members to assume control; they needn't die in order to do so; they might do so voluntarily. It might be that here, as in many other social contexts, voluntarism is best. Anyway, if immortals cannot step aside by dying, and if they do not willingly step aside when they ought to, then they might be made to step aside by threat of pain. Immortality, it seems, has little to do with the issue. Yes, some people might refuse to step aside, just as they do now when appointments are made for life. So immortals are well advised (and perhaps we, too, are well advised) to avoid policies of lifelong appointments.

Lucretius's replacement argument might be stood on its head. The trouble with mortals is that the new *does* replace the old. Each new person learns only so much and then dies. Some of what has been learned is passed on to others. Still, the passing on is done with culture and not with genes, and so each new generation must learn the most important things for itself. Perhaps a new war erupts. (Given the history of mortal humankind, future wars seem inevitable.) Fighting is bitter, complete with attacks on ethnic/racial/religious undesirables. We (we who have learned our lessons) shake our heads or perhaps recoil in horror: "When will they ever learn?" Well, even if *we* have learned, this new generation has not. The people of the new generation do not have the experience of the older generation; they know of prior cruelties only from historical records; they might not have the wherewithal to compare their present gut-wrenching outrage with their ancestors', and consequently they might not appreciate at first what they will come (they ought to come) to appreciate after their slaughtering of each other has reached a temporary truce. Perhaps immortals, once having learned the lesson, could be better off.

4 Evolution

Evolution has provided us with rationality. We can solve some kinds of problems because our biological predecessors managed to deal with earlier versions of them. Evolution by natural selection has brought this about by creating variations of simpler problem solvers and then killing off most of the unsuccessful of them. But if we were immortal, environmental pressures on us might not have the same survival-of-the-fittest effect, and so random genetic mutations, which would be sure to continue, would no longer be selected or rejected. The progress of genetic mutations might eventually create not better and better persons, but more and more monsters, some of which, such as pathological liars, might be undesirable because of what they do, and some of which, such as undying carrot-like beings, might be undesirable because of what they do not do. Do we want to live amid immortal carrots?

But that is a very weak indictment of immortality, amounting to a caution only. It is true that we got where we are first of all by means of natural evolution. But why should we continue to accept nature's natural course? We mortals already make significant improvements and enhancements to ourselves and to our environments without waiting for nature to chance upon such changes for us. We build huts and houses; irrigate land and sow seeds; mine ore and oil and salt; make and wear clothes; make fire for warmth, for cooking, for smelting, for destroying; wear vision-correcting and -enhancing spectacles, hearing-correcting and -enhancing aids, walking-correcting and -enhancing shoes. We use artificial hearts and hips and legs and teeth. In short, we construct tools for manipulating ourselves, our environments and even other tools according to our own designs. We are now rummaging around in the internals of DNA in order to effect medical improvements, avoid the birth of tragedies, and grow replacement parts for ourselves. We may expect that these and other innovations will allow us to gamble with changes to our basic structure without waiting for the roll of nature's dice. We could have evolution by artificial selection—or, rather, by artificial *design*. What? Are we still convinced that we are the Center of Existence? Are we to assume both that life evolves and that evolution stops here, with us as we are now? (Do we shout with Nietzsche "this and this forever more"?)

Nature, in her wild abandon, in her zeal for sheer spectacle, and in her blind thrashing about, can wipe out whole species (including us) by something as simple as a large meteor. We might do better and try to anticipate and avoid such excesses. Of course, we are bound to make some mistakes. But unlike meteors, we are also capable of reflecting on our actions and their consequences, understanding the underlying principles, and putting them to our uses. So evolution needn't end with immortality. Rather, it might change its shape, its means, and its modes. I think that could be a Good Thing.[6]

5 Avoiding pain

If we knew that we were immortal, we would not have a fear of death. But a fear of death is very useful. Hence, immortality would be a problem. This is the position apparently held by Martha Nussbaum among others. Nussbaum maintains that "Lucretius has completely failed to consider the possibility that the fear of death may have [. . .] some good consequences in human life" (*The Therapy of Desire*, 235). What good consequences might those be? Well, a fear of death motivates us to act prudently, and acting prudently can lead to self-preservation, and self-preservation obviously gives us a longer life. But of course

---

[6] For an extended discussion of some of the ethical issues, see John Harris, *Enhancing Evolution*.

if that were all there were to it, then we would not have arrived at an answer about whether immortality is good or bad; rather, the argument would have gone in a circle. Why would we want a longer life? If, as Epicurus claims, death is not bad, then there seems to be no reason to act only in order to extend life by any amount. Nussbaum realizes that a good Epicurean does not seek self-preservation, and so she suggests that self-preservation is linked to other values which are important to us—for example, the avoidance of pain. That is, if we are motivated to actions which preserve us, then we are motivated to actions which avoid pain. And so the fear of death may actually make for a less painful life.

A. O. Rorty makes a similar claim. The fear of death, she says in a nod to Epicurus, might be irrational "by appropriate canons of argument and inference"; nevertheless, it may be helpful to develop certain fears: "There might be rational grounds for acquiring a disposition whose exercise is admittedly often irrational" ("Fearing Death", 178). Even if the fear of death is not justified, that fear is helpful in avoiding pain, and "it is by no means always easy in the moment to distinguish debilitating from mortal dangers" (181).

Granted the distinction is hard to make—perhaps even impossible in many situations. But it does not follow that a fear of death is any more useful than a fear of pain. Rorty says that "the fear of death seems more efficient than an indefinite number of particular fears we would have to have: fear of exposure in very low temperatures, fear of dehydration, fear of this and fear of that" (181). Of course. But while it might be efficient to replace all such possible, particular fears with one overarching fear, that one fear needn't be the fear of death. Rather, the fear of pain will do just as well, graded in proportion to the perceived possible pain.

Darryl Reanney joins Nussbaum and Rorty in making a similar, but stronger claim. Whenever an animal flees, he says, it is fleeing from a threat to its own existence. "Quite literally, it is running away from death" (*After Death*, 6).[7] But it seems to me that an animal that flees from a threat is not fleeing death (or what it takes as a threat of death), but rather from a threat of damage, of pain. While humans can conceive of their future demise, I am not convinced that any other animals can. And if they cannot, then they cannot fear death. Moreover, not all threats of injury or pain are threats of death. Any organism's body has repair mechanisms, so that many—perhaps most—injuries are easily accommodated. Yet even threats of minor pain can cause flight responses. My cat fidgets and struggles to get away whenever I try to give him his medication, because I am

---

[7] Similarly, Philip Devine speaks of an "'animal' horror of annihilation" (*Ethics of Homicide*, 20).

causing him some discomfort. But he is capable of far more serious struggles; if he were fully determined to flee, I would not be able to hold him.[8]

The upshot is that what may appear to be an animal's fear of death is more likely a normal fear of pain. And that means that we might rid ourselves of the fear of death yet retain the usefulness of the fear of pain.[9]

6 Cherished values

Even if the fear of death is not necessary to avoid pain, perhaps it is the fear of death, and not the fear of pain, that makes us aware of particularly human values. That is to say, if some of our most cherished values depend upon our mortality, then realizing that fact might help us to appreciate the brevity of our lives and hence help to rid us of certain fears concerning death. It might also be used against Epicurus's claim that "death is nothing to us", for if what we most value is what it is because of our finite life, then death must be very important indeed.

But what important values would be lost if we were immortal? Nussbaum argues that "friendship, love, justice, and the various forms of morally virtuous action get their point and their value within the structure of human time, as relations and activities that extend over finite time" (*Therapy of Desire*, 226). But we must be careful here and not take "finite time" to mean "finite life". I see an analogy with H. L. A. Hart's point ("Positivism and the Separation of Law and Morals", 623) that if we were invulnerable, it would be idle to have laws against homicide. Yes, but even invulnerable beings might want other laws, because there could be many concerns about social order; such beings could be tricked or diverted from their goals, causing frustration or other forms of dissatisfaction. Immortality is compatible with having only finite time for a particular action or project, some of which can periodically recur: a beautiful sunset, a game of charades, pregnancy and birth.

My suggestion is that appreciating pleasure, having and pursuing goals, and being subject to pain and thwarted goals, are enough to provide grounds for most, if not all, of our values, including love, justice, and so on. Let us look at the

---

[8] "The fact that an animal struggles when an attempt to capture or kill it is made does not show that it desires to live; all it can show is that the animal in some way perceives the situation as undesirable, and tries to escape from it" (Peter Singer, "Killing Humans and Killing Animals", 156 n19).

[9] Rorty seems to recognize something like this later on: "Epicureans might argue that the propriety of danger-averting behavior does not affect the impropriety of a generalized metaphysical fear of nonbeing" ("Fearing Death", 183–84).

virtue of courage. Nussbaum says that courage would disappear for immortal beings (*Therapy of Desire*, 227). But that is implausible. We may say that the risk of death (for unconditionally immortal beings) would disappear, and so courage in the face of the threat of death would also disappear. But courage is not limited to cases involving the risk of death. Risk of pain will do just as well. Nussbaum seems to acknowledge this ("This will vary, however, with the amount and type of pain [...]. Prometheus's suffering is in certain ways worse because immortal": *Therapy of Desire*, 227 n. 36) and then to ignore it, for she goes on to link courage and friendship; and friendship, she says, would be nonexistent or else radically different for immortals:

> In heaven there is, in two senses, no Achilles: no warrior risking everything he is and has, no loving friend whose love is such that he risks everything on account of his friend. Friendship so differently constituted will not be the same thing, or have the same value. [228]

But in our own mortal existences, the risking of our lives is so extraordinary that it could only implausibly be said to form an important part of friendship. For mortal beings (and also for conditionally immortal beings), a willingness to die might be one indication of true friendship, and of course that measure will not be available for beings who cannot die. Very well, then; let them recognize some other test—in fact the very test which we ordinarily employ: the risk of pain. An immortal person might risk pain for a friend—perhaps great and long-lasting pain. And even if it is temporary, such as a headache, it is still undesired. There is also psychological suffering, which can be acute and long-lasting. But usually it is the many little things which show our friendships. I give up something I want so that my friend might have it instead; if I am to have it, it will have to be later on, if at all.

Could it be said, as Socrates does in the *Phaedo*, that death concentrates our attention on how we ought to live—that it puts the virtues in strong relief? Perhaps it can do that for some people, but we are able to concentrate our attention in other ways too. We can come to appreciate what we do and do not have without focusing on our prospective deaths; we might rather focus on other sorts of losses (even if we assume, what I earlier denied, that death is a loss in any sense at all for the one who died). In fact, losses are quite common in our experience, so if we can truly appreciate values in life only by attending to actual or possible losses, then we might do so without attending to the prospect of our own death. Perhaps, for example, my friend has been lost to me—has gone away and will never come back. That is painful to me even if I know that my friend is living well elsewhere.

If I do not yet have what I want, then I am valuing it. After getting it, I can still value it in my wish to keep it—not only keep it as contrasted with losing it but also keep it as it is, whole and intact, undamaged, functioning as it used to. Even immortal beings might be damaged, made ugly, or stop functioning in desirable ways. Suppose a human being is in desperate need of food. We might be concerned about the possibility of the person's starving to death, but there is much more to be concerned about, namely, suffering. A being who could not die could not starve *to death*, but might nevertheless starve *to great pain*. It is, after all, not mere life which we are usually after but rather life of a certain kind, and it is the threat to that kind of life which can be more severe than the threat of death even for people who fear death. One might be willing to permanently give up a certain kind of life for the sake of one's friend. Is that not to be accounted real friendship? We can and do understand love, friendship, courage, and all the other virtues quite well against the background of pleasure and pain. The risk of death in our own mortal lives is comparatively exceedingly rare; so rare is it, that if mortality were the measure, it would be a wonder that we ever developed the virtues we have.

> In general, the intensity and dedication with which very many human activities are pursued cannot be explained without reference to the awareness that our opportunities are finite, that we cannot choose these activities indefinitely many times. In raising a child, in cherishing a lover, in performing a demanding task of work or thought or artistic creation, we are aware, at some level, of the thought that each of these efforts is structured and constrained by finite time. [*Therapy of Desire*, 229]

I do not agree that, in general, "we are aware, at some level" that our values are structured by finite time, if by "finite time" it is meant that we are aware, at some level, that we are mortal. For it would do as well, so far as I can make out, that we could have finite time for any given project, or with any given lover, and so on, and still be immortal. Being immortal does not entail having everything you want whenever you want it. You practice playing clarinet in order to become better, but being immortal does not mean that you will be able to become a virtuoso, nor even to practice without end, for you might be immortal and yet at some point lose the use of your hands.

When works of art are created, when children are conceived and reared, when experiments are conducted and examined, what are the motives? No doubt they are many and varied. So the question is whether we would have sufficient motives in the absence of the prospect of death. And the answer, so far as I can see, must be: Yes. Why may not immortals create works of art? Is beauty, for example, forbidden to immortals? May not immortals profit from insight, creativity, new views and attitudes? We mortals have children, create art, and discuss science and philosophy for plenty of reasons having to do with enjoyment of the moment, or the surprising thrill of bringing something new into the world, or the expectation of happiness, fame, or comfort. We create for money, for revenge, for love, for hate, for jealousy, for practice, for power, for the relief of suffering. We create for countless reasons having nothing to do with our deaths, and immortal beings could have those sorts of motivations too.

Perhaps it is the transitory nature of some things and events which is a precondition for finding beauty in them, or value of any sort. If so, there is nothing to prevent immortal beings from both witnessing and appreciating such values, because, as I mentioned earlier, a person's own immortality would not entail the continued existence of all other things and events, so that the concepts *special*, *beautiful*, and *valuable* need not be useless for immortals.

What we are aware of, at some level, is not our mortality—finite time for the whole of our lives—but rather our more general finitude. Immortality does not entail omnipotence. Immortal beings could feel pain and pleasure; such beings could have desires and hopes, some of which might be achieved and others not. That, as far as I can tell, is what we are aware of, at some level. Even if, as immortals, we would not face the inevitability of losing immortal friends, we might nevertheless lose things we value, such as other animals, natural objects and events, and things we create.[10] There is nothing about immortality that makes all the things which we value immortal as well. Our present fundamental values involving love, courage, friendship, justice, beauty, and honesty could have a firm foundation in the lives of immortal beings in the same way that they have a firm foundation in us mortals. So far as I can see, nothing in such virtues requires a knowledge of mortality.[11]

7 Boredom

Immortality might be unwanted because if we were immortal then eventually all important things would have been done. All art would have been made,

---

[10] In my opinion, no right-minded person could fail to regret the destruction of the sole surviving print of the 1956 film *Invasion of the Body Snatchers*.
[11] Nussbaum softened her position a bit in her "Reply to Papers"; see especially 812–13; also see her "The Damage of Death", especially 37.

all possible symphonies written, all possible chocolate confections invented and savored. After that, we would be bored, and eternity spent in boredom is certainly not an attractive prospect. Of course, boredom would not arise on account of immortality as such. Some people become bored with a short life, or with a life of average length. The length of life seems to be irrelevant, except that it must be long enough for the person to become bored; and since an immortal life will eventually become "long enough", an immortal person would eventually become bored.

But whether life might be boring will depend on how one appreciates one's life. The Christmas season comes each year, and eventually some of us get bored and even annoyed by the same old Christmas tunes. But immortality need not be a condition in which it seems that you will have to listen to Burl Ives forever and ever. Even if, after centuries of seasons, one more winter or one more spring would seem to be just another winter or spring, an immortal might find release in other pleasant changes. Perhaps spring on Mars would be a wholesome adventure. After visiting a thousand planets, one might return to Earth, refreshed and eager for springtime in Paris. Even among mortals there is a kind of selective forgetting between generations, such that clothing styles come and go and come again. Musical, artistic, religious, political, and social styles wax and wane. These sorts of changes, even if cyclical, might continue to be pleasant, just as, for many people, a yearly change of seasons is pleasant. As we mortals mature, many of the activities which we enjoyed in our younger years become uninteresting. I no longer want much to play with toy trains or build model airplanes. (I prefer the full-sized things now.) From the point of view of a child, an adult's not wanting to construct an elaborate model train system might be a curiosity. And from a child's point of view, spending a large portion of time just sitting in quiet conversation might seem quintessentially boring. It may be that an immortal being would find satisfaction in constant pure contemplation, with little attention paid to the physical side of things. That probably strikes most ordinary mortals as boring. What is understandable, and even plausible, is that if we were immortal, we might have somewhat different sets of interests, and take somewhat different kinds of satisfactions in things and events which in our mortal lives we are less apt to. But it is difficult to anticipate just what the differences would be. It seems to me, therefore, that on this score the goodness (or, if it comes to that, the badness) of immortality is mainly an empirical issue. Would, for example, an immortal's brain start to fill up, such that it would become more and more difficult to incorporate new experiences? Are persons so constituted, and is the universe such that, there is only a limited number of kinds of experiences possible, such that after having enough of all of those kinds, there would be nothing new left to experience?

It is useful in this connection to mention Bernard Williams's view ("The Makropulos Case") that immortality would be boring. He uses as an example a somewhat altered version of a character, EM (Elena Makropulos), in Karel Čapek's play *The Makropulos Affair* (or the opera by the same name by Leoš Janáček). EM has managed to live for several centuries by drinking a magic elixir. But she grows bored with life, refuses the elixir, and dies. So EM's immortality was of the conditional type. There are two interesting features of EM's case. She remained (and, with the help of the elixir, might forever have remained) at the enviable age of thirty-seven.[12] Second, she grew bored with her life.

What would it mean to live eternally at the age of thirty-seven? Certainly one cannot remain thirty-seven years old for more than a year. Perhaps it would mean that one's biological age—the maturity of the organs, say—would remain at a stage normally found in thirty-seven-year-olds, as though, if one were to suddenly die and be autopsied, the investigators would declare the body to be that of a thirty-seven-year-old. But then what else would have to change in order for a biological system to be maintained indefinitely at a certain stage? What would happen in and to the brain? The brain ought not to be thought of as storing memories, habits, and experiences in the way a photo album stores discrete photos, or a (contemporary) computer's memory stores binary strings. Nevertheless the brain does become altered in various ways in the normal business of learning and changing, and it is to be supposed that the brain can do only so much of that, perhaps only so much of that until what has gone before becomes less and less distinct, more and more muddled. Perhaps, then, a normal human brain would become saturated within a few hundred years. One might expect that evolution would not have avoided such a possibility, given that the rest of the organism does not survive for so long. So a person surviving for centuries (not to speak yet of eternity) might need a much larger brain, or else some artificial enhancements (implanted devices, or new external storage devices to supplement those, such as written languages, that we already rely on). If there are to be biological accommodations, then the larger the brain, the more the other features of the body will have to change in order to accommodate it: the skeletal and muscular systems must be strengthened; the heart must be enhanced; glands must be enlarged. Some secure methods for drawing more

---

[12] Williams says that her age was given as forty-two, but, although the play is ambiguous on this point, thirty-seven seems to be a more reasonable reading.

energy from the environment would have to evolve, because a normal human's respiratory and digestive systems would be too meager. Perhaps a person capable of surviving for several millennia would already have to be the size of a redwood. This will have some impact on the person's social life.

An alternative would be to reuse portions of a normal brain. Perhaps there could be a kind of selective forgetting, as though portions of the brain were wiped clean. It would not, however, have to take the form of periodic massive strokes, each rendering the person largely incapable of normal functioning. It could take the form of episodes of peripheral amnesia so transient that not even the person herself would notice. We all forget things, and often we give little notice to that fact. I do not remember the name of my fifth grade teacher, although I do remember that I had a school boy's crush on her and that her name began with "S". But I do not wonder why her name is not easily available for recall. It's just one of those things; one does not remember all the details of one's life. So perhaps a woman who lived for several millennia would have forgotten most of the details of those many years, retaining only a relatively few of the more important facts and episodes; the rest would have vanished away in an unextraordinary, even expected, way, little by little. The brain, being of normal ability (or even being significantly enhanced by clever devices), would not, we may suppose, be able to retain all the languages she learned, all the music she appreciated, all the stories she cherished, all the science she studied, and all the memories of people she knew. As new skills become refined, older ones would mix together or fade away, but she would perpetually have skills and memories at the level of a (normal) thirty-seven-year-old.

Williams says that the defender of the desirability of immortality must show "something that makes boredom *unthinkable* [. . .] something that could be guaranteed to be at every moment utterly absorbing" ("The Makropulos Case", 94–95). But there is certainly nothing even in our own mortal lives that could meet that high standard. In fact when we recommend activities, we advocate their temporary employment. When I encourage you to try the chocolate cake, I do not mean that you should put your whole being, now and forever more, into eating chocolate cake; I am not claiming that if you did nothing other than eat chocolate cake, you would never become bored. I am merely saying that here is a little, or a temporary, pleasure. Try it now, and you won't regret it; you may even wish to do the like on some future occasion. John Martin Fischer rightly criticizes Williams for focusing on a *single* thing:

> But why suppose that any one supposedly absorbing activity must be pursued *at the expense of all others*? Why can't such activities be part of a *package* in

an immortal life, just as we suppose that they should be in a mortal life? ["Introduction", 11]

And as Hunter Steele points out, it is one thing to claim that a life is occasionally boring, but a different thing to maintain that the life would be constantly or always boring ("Could Body-Bound Immortality Be Liveable?"). Yet Williams does not distinguish between the two. Boredom is not a sufficient condition for rejecting a life, just as it is insufficient for rejecting activities in life, unless of course boredom is unrelieved. Sometimes there are stretches of time within the playing of a chess game which can be said to be boring. But one might accept such boring intervals for the sake of the overall pleasure of playing. People still play cricket. The existence of boredom does not bring with it the guarantee that the boredom is unrelieved, any more than the existence of high pleasure brings with it a guarantee that the pleasure will be eternal and uninterrupted.

Immortality might be unbearable for the kind of person who would eventually find it all to be "more of the same". I used to enjoy crossword puzzles, but now I do not much care for them. We all go through such stages. Suppose a person goes through one such change after another. At some point he might go "meta" and the next stage may seem to be just another one of those phases. His eyes are no longer held fast by the activities in some new stage; rather, he gazes further into the future than he ever did before, and he sees . . . one stage changing into another, stage after stage. Certainly one wants variety. But would variety itself eventually seem to be pointless? One of the reasons why the issue of becoming bored is important is because boredom leaves us wondering "What's the point?"

We have already seen that conditional immortality could include values that are fundamental for us mortals and could include as well some higher values such as courage. Whether an immortal life would be meaningless can be investigated in the same way that we consider whether a mortal life is meaningless. I have little to offer on that score, except to suspect that some writers are in search of an *ultimate meaning*. But must there be such a thing? Or are we merely extending, in a natural and understandable way, the idea of meaning (but extending it beyond its ordinary use)? The idea of "ultimate meaning" is apparently the idea that the business of drawing or noticing or constructing meanings must have a stop, and wherever this stop is, it is "ultimate".[13] Still, that will not satisfy most people who quest for "ultimate meaning", because the stop could occur immediately. I reach

---

[13] Must there be only one "ultimate meaning"? If I am pursuing various instrumental goods, leading off this way and that, along with some intrinsic goods of this or that sort, why suppose that everything meets up conveniently at a single point?

for a glass of wine. What is the meaning of my action? I am intending to have a little pleasure, that's all. But suppose the issue is pressed, and it is claimed that the very idea of meaning is the idea of pointing to, or referring to, or having some regards to, something beyond. Beyond what? Beyond the present action, or beyond the present simple pleasure. So perhaps my reaching for the wine has a social meaning: I am participating in a dinner party, and drinking a glass of wine is an agreeable part of it. But it might be asked what the meaning of the dinner party is. Perhaps the attitude is: "Invited to dinner, arrive, eat dinner, chat with other guests, drink some wine, chat some more, then leave. But is that it? Is that all there is to it? If the dinner party has no *further* meaning and significance, then why bother?"

It seems that one would be in search of the instrumental value of drinking the wine and the instrumental value of the dinner party. It is somehow unsatisfying to say that the wine and the party provided some pleasures, and such pleasures are their own rewards, pointing to nothing beyond, except for the possibilities of further social interactions.

Perhaps there are, then, two kinds of intrinsic goods: those which are trivial and those which are not. A simple pleasure is an example of something which may be appreciated without further ado; insofar as it is considered only in itself, it has no meaning. One can always ask: "So what? What does it profit me to engage in such simple pleasures?" Well, in one sense, if a simple pleasure is merely good in itself, then it is being conceived as something whose meaning or significance is either absent or irrelevant. So let us suppose that the having of a simple pleasure does some work—has some further significance. Then we are conceiving of that simple pleasure no longer under the aspect of intrinsic good; we now want to know its instrumental value for something "higher". Imagine, then, that someone conceives of himself, his life, all his actions, as somehow bound up into a Cosmic Plan for the universe. Then some of or all of these actions carry an instrumental value; they are instrumentally good for the fulfillment of the Plan. May one now ask about the Plan? I am participating in the Plan. But so what?

It appears that to ask after the meaning or significance of the Cosmic Plan is to ask a silly question. Probably for most theists the Plan is intrinsically good, and momentously so. But then it appears that *that* intrinsic good—*that* momentous intrinsic good—functions simply an end to all inquiry about goods. "The Cosmic Plan" is a way of stopping the conversation. One could certainly ask, "That's it? That's all there is? There is no further or higher significance? Then isn't it all meaningless?" One could ask these questions, but some people will find it very odd because they take the Plan to be that than which no higher Plan can be conceived, so that the issue of *its* meaning and significance simply cannot arise.

To suppose, then, that there is an ultimate source of significance is to refer all meaning to it. And such an ultimate source must be such that there logically cannot be anything beyond. This is, I gather, what Aristotle meant when he said that the truly final good is that which is never taken as instrumentally good; it would be odd or logically meaningless to take that something as instrumentally good, as though there could be something beyond.

But our question comes again: Is there something to which all other things must point, or must refer or must be instrumentally useful for, and yet which is itself impossible of being instrumentally good? Even human happiness can be thought of as instrumentally good, because one can think that human happiness serves some function in a "larger scheme of things". Happiness seems not to be the ultimate, because people are born, they are happy, and then they die. So happiness seems to be transitory. When one looks for an ultimate source, one might want the ultimate source to be permanent, that is, immortal. So perhaps William G. Vrasdonk is correct when he says "The search for ultimate meaning is in itself a search for immortality" ("Beyond Thanatology: Immortality", 283), although the immortality need not be *our* immortality, but rather the eternity of the ultimate source of meaning.

When "the meaning of life" is made into a Big Question, then there is a search for meaning writ large, and if we do not find it, we may experience despair or forlornness. But instead of supposing that there is *a* meaning of life, why not attend to meaning writ small—meaning in the trivia of life, in the fine print of everydayness, which we can appreciate whether we were immortal or not? Why suppose that there must be something more? Who was the thief who stole our sense of humor? Who told us that life itself is to have a meaning, and why did we not laugh at the very idea?

8 Pointlessness

James Van Evra says that if we were immortal,

> then no *particular* history would be more relevant than any other for determining the value of events in that life. Taking into account everything that has taken place in such a life, that is, what basis would there be for assigning, say, less

significance to one act than to another? Were the future without bound, I suggest that there would be none. Also, in such a life, everything would count equally as a prospect, and the order of our desires would be a matter of indifference. ["Death", 204]

I assume that when Van Evra speculates about a "future without bound", he is imagining a condition of endless possibilities, so that an immortal being might say of any possibility, "my life has not included that thing or event, but it *could*; I could structure my life so as to include that possibility"; and in doing so, such a being would not shut out any other possibility, for, given unlimited time, that other possibility could also eventually be included. There would then be an unlimited number of ways of continuing, yet all those ways would be equivalent in an important respect, namely, that each would eventually contain all the possibilities, and there would be no reason to choose one over the other, and so nothing would have significance or specialness.

But it seems to me that, on the contrary, there could be important valuational differences among histories and prospects, so that there would not be the kind of indifference or insignificance that Van Evra imagines. As I mentioned earlier in note 4, if some thing or event exists at one time, there is no guarantee that it will ever occur again, unless events are considered in general terms and not their specifics. If I say of my life that it is merely one thing after another, then I can say the same thing for any other life, so that, under *that* description, one life is the same as any other.

Van Evra seems to conceive of possibilities without regard to the order of events. For some activities and procedures, different orders will have the same results. Multiplying 56 by 4 yields the same product as multiplying 4 by 56. But some activities and procedures are ordered. Dividing 56 by 4 is not the same as dividing 4 by 56. Filling the swimming pool with water and then diving in is not the same as the reverse order. One could read the sentences of a novel in any order, but most of those orders would yield silliness; order is important, because the sentences are not isolated projects. Van Evra mentions "events", "everything", and "act", as though such things were to be appreciated independently of each other. Yet context is crucial, and the ordering is part of the context. To explain something is to give its patterned context. To expect something is to extend a pattern. To be surprised is to find a datum that does not fit the extended pattern. These and other forms of significances are parts of patterns that one learns, and many patterns are ordered sequences. Nothing makes sense outside of a context which embraces it as part of a pattern. Pure chaos would be pure meaninglessness because then the context of any one thing, or any group of things, would be as pointless as any other, hence of no more significance than any other. So if the elements (Van Evra's "events", "acts", etc.) could be jumbled into any order at all and have no more significance than any other order, then the elements themselves would be as interchangeable as grains of sand on a beach— interchangeable, that is, if the large picture were to be only "Grains of Sand on a Beach". But life, whether mortal or immortal, is not a bricolage of isolated events.

9 Ersatz immortality

Some people, even though not yearning for true immortality, might think of themselves (and others) as participating in a kind of postmortem meaning or value.

> It was good for Darwin that his ideas on evolution were vindicated by modern genetics; good for Mallory that Everest was eventually climbed and good for those who died fighting the Nazis that the Nazis were finally defeated. [James Lenman, "On Becoming Extinct", 262]

No doubt for some people it is comforting to imagine their projects being continued or fulfilled postmortem. Unless we are brain damaged in certain ways, it is natural that we imagine a future and what it might hold, and so it may have seemed good to Darwin that his ideas might find postmortem vindications (even if he could not anticipate the details), and Mallory may have thought it good that Everest would eventually be climbed (even if at some time beyond his death by someone unknown to him), and so on. But we cannot jump from there to the claims that it was good *for Darwin* that modern genetics eventually vindicated some of his ideas, or that it was good *for Mallory* that Everest was eventually climbed.

We could say that it is good that people have some kinds of concerns for others and for the extension of their projects. And people may indeed feel comfort in participating in something that goes beyond themselves in time. And we can say that such lives have "greater depth", if we want ("On Becoming Extinct", 262). But for the people who take comfort in that "greater depth", the future is speculation. The postmortem future is a special kind of speculative future, because, unlike their own lived futures, their postmortem futures can affect them in no way at all, and so we may wonder whether people are taking comfort in something that, on closer examination, can reasonably make no difference to them. "Whereas it would be good for me if my theories are vindicated now, or at some time during my life", an Epicurean might say, "vindication after I have ceased to be will then be neither good nor bad for me, since there will be no me at that time. I care that my theories are the *sort* that will be vindicated and the *sort* that will continue to be taught and used after I am gone; but that they *will* live on is mere speculation and is in any case nothing to me."

But if *he* lives on, what then? When the technology becomes available to extend life indefinitely, as I assume it will, a host of new practical and moral problems will arise. One of them will be taken up in Chapter 10: Would an Epicurean reasonably commit suicide? The issue of suicide arises in the case of practical immortality because if ever one did find life meaningless or unbearable, one would face an *unending* life that would be (or would seem to be) unbearable, and in order that it end, one would have to choose to end it. A mortal being, on the other hand, has only to let nature take its course.

Will He Nill He

Prelude

Little Tony is standing near the fence in his back yard, looking out over a field of clover and considering what he wants for his birthday. He approaches a genie. (I don't know where the genie came from. But I don't know where Tony came from either.)

"Please, sir", Tony says. "I want a pony."

The genie smiles condescendingly. "You want a pony, do you? Aren't you a little young for that?"

"I guess. But that's what I want."

"Where will you keep it? Shouldn't your wish include a barn?"

"OK. I want a pony and barn to keep it in."

"Very well", says the genie. "If you're sure that's *exactly* what you want . . . ." He pauses and looks at Tony, who nods enthusiastically. The genie snaps his fingers. "It is so. You own a pony and a barn."

Tony looks around, not seeing a pony or a barn. "But where are they? You're not a very good genie."

"Oh", says the genie nonchalantly. "They're half-way around the world, where taxes on the barn are much less than here."

"But that's not what I wanted."

"You said you wanted a pony and a barn. I fulfilled your wish. Stop complaining."

"But that wasn't my wish. I wanted them *here*."

The genie shakes his head. "Oh, I *do* wish you would tell me *precisely* what you desire. Or maybe you don't even know yourself what you want."

"I do so! I want a pony right here in this field next to where I live."

"Then you should have told me that. And you want the barn here too, I take it."

"Yes."

"Are you finished now? That is precisely your wish? You've told me everything?"

"Yes."

"Because I could just as easily give you a chocolate cake, or—."

"No. I want a pony and a barn. Right here in this field."

"Very well." The genie snaps his fingers. "There they are. I hope you're satisfied now, because I have a full schedule today."

Tony looks at the just-materialized pony. It is scrawny, sick, and lying on the ground in front of an old barn that is obviously no more sturdy than the pony is. Tony clenches his fists and stomps his foot. "But I want a pony I can ride!"

"There you go, changing your wish again. Look, kid, I'm really rather busy. You can ride the pony if you can manage to get him healthy. Go find a vet. Shouldn't be difficult."

"What's a vet?"

"If you want to change your wish yet again, then please tell me precisely—I mean in full detail—what you want. I won't have you complain that I gave you a brown pony when you wanted a spotted pony. Tell me how old the pony should be, whether male or female, whether blind or sighted, how long its tail should be, whether it is even-tempered or mischievous, and so on. Tell me *everything*."

"Oh, never mind! You knew what I wanted, so if this is the best you can do, I don't want one of your stupid ponies. And you're a stupid genie."

The genie sighs wearily. "So now you *don't* want a pony. Are you sure about that? Do you want a chocolate cake instead, or . . . ?"

Tony turns and walks back to the house.

The genie shrugs and then disappears in a puff of smoke. He reappears eighty years later in another puff of smoke when Tony is lying dead in a casket.

"Sorry I'm late with this", says the genie, gesturing to a fine, healthy pony standing next to him. "I've been busy. But your wish has now been fulfilled."

1 Problems

The Epicurean view as I have expressed it in the Indifference Conclusion ("I cannot reasonably care about anything that will occur when I am dead") is not without significant problems.

Epicurus left a will.[1] So did the later Epicurean Diogenes of Oenoanda.[2] Perhaps most Epicureans made wills. But a will is a statement of a wish that one's property be disposed of in certain ways after one's death; how can an Epicurean both be concerned with the postmortem disposition of property and at the same time claim that death is nothing? It would seem that according to the Indifference Conclusion an Epicurean ought to say "After my death I will necessarily not care

---

[1] Diogenes Laërtius, *Lives* 10.16–21; Diskin Clay, "Epicurus' Last Will and Testament"; James Warren, *Facing Death*, 162–99. (Complete bibliographic information on this and all other sources in this book is provided in the Bibliography.)

[2] Diskin Clay, "A Lost Epicurean Community".

what happens to my property then, and so I cannot care about that now". And if so, why would a good Epicurean bother to draw up a will? So my first query is this: Did Epicureans misunderstand their own doctrine?[3] Or is there some way in which making a will can be consistent with Epicureanism?

On the other hand, if an Epicurean does not draw up a will, because he holds that "death is nothing", then will he not have an uncaring attitude toward the fate of others after his own death? If he accepts the Indifference Conclusion, won't the welfare of his survivors be nothing to him now? Must he not say sincerely that he does not now care what might or might not happen to them after his death? Will he not refuse to invest in life insurance of the sort that cannot benefit him, but can benefit only his survivors? Will he not now care a whit whether their present hopes and desires, dreams and projects reach fruition after his death?

Sometimes a will is made concurrently with another person's promise to fulfill the testator's wishes postmortem. There is a common conviction that if we make a promise to a person before his death to do something after his death (bury him in a certain place, for example, or dispose of his property in certain ways), then we are under an obligation to fulfill that promise. Yet according to the Indifference Conclusion, whether or not such a promise is kept *ought* to make no antemortem difference to the testator, and *cannot* make any postmortem difference to the deceased (who will then be only an ex-testator). Would Epicurean survivors feel justified in ignoring a dead person's antemortem desires?

2 Contracts and promises

A usual view is that promises must be kept; when a promise is broken, someone is wronged. This common view is put to work frequently in people's lives; they complain about such harms when they are the victims, and they may even want to take action against the perpetrators. It is understandable that this view would easily be applied to the postmortem keeping of promises made antemortem; without reflection people suppose that such promises continue as promises postmortem and therefore should be honored. This is especially the case when they think of such a promise made to themselves. It rankles them to think that at some later time (which in this case will be after they are dead) the promise

---

[3] Cicero raises this objection to Epicureanism in *De Finibus* II.99–103. See also the discussion in Warren, *Facing Death*, 162–99.

might not be kept; they think about that kind of broken promise in the same way they think about all other broken promises, namely, that they will have been betrayed, wronged, harmed, duped, or treated with contempt.[4]

But the rational supports for such sentiments no longer hold when an attempt is made to stretch them beyond the grave, for the simple reason that in that singular and unusual kind of case there is no longer a promisee, even if there is still most of a human body which used to be part of a promisee. Here is one sort of case: a promise made antemortem and "broken" postmortem. Livvy promised sincerely to Diane that after Diane died, Livvy would bury her (or, to speak more precisely, bury her body) on the farm. Diane died. But now Livvy decides to bury the remains elsewhere. Here is another sort of case. Diane died, after which Livvy promised the corpse to bury it on the farm. But now Livvy decides otherwise. Was Diane wronged in either sort of case? It should be clear that in the second case (the case of the alleged postmortem promise) there was no promise to be honored, because there was actually no promise at all, even if Livvy thought she was making one, because there was no promisee to whom a promise was given. But then in the first case—the antemortem promise—we can reasonably say that after Diane's death there was no longer a promise to be honored because there was no longer a promisee to whom fulfillment of an earlier promise was owed. Consider familiar cases where the fulfillment of an earlier promise is not required even though the promisee is still alive: the promisee has a change of mind, vacates all interest in the promise, no longer wants the promisor to act on the promise, and explicitly absolves the promisor of any obligation in the matter. In such a case there continues to exist a person who is now a former promisee, but there is no longer a promise to be satisfied. Death is something like vacating all interests in everything, because a decedent is only a former person—a collection of body parts that used to form a person to whom fulfillment of promises was owed. The former promisee had interests, but the actual decedent has no interests at all and is no longer the sort of thing which can be a promisee.

In the postmortem "promise" case, talking to a dead body in promissory ways was *like* making a promise. But if it was not really promising, then what was it? It seems to me that it was the making of a resolve; we should interpret Livvy as having resolved to herself to bury the corpse on the farm. If Livvy does not now

---

[4] "When a promise is broken, someone is harmed, and who if not the promisee? [...] If there is no 'problem of the subject' when we speak of wronging the dead, why should there be when we speak of harming them, especially when the harm is an essential ingredient of the wrong?" (Joel Feinberg, "Harm to Others", 182–83).

carry through with the resolve, she is revealed not as a wrongdoer, but rather as a person of unreliable resolve. So, too, in the first case, where there was a promise that Livvy made to Diane before Diane's death. Because of Diane's death, any interest that she had in Livvy's earlier promise was vacated. Assuming that no other persons' interests became entangled with Livvy's promise, the promise by Livvy is, if anything, now a mere resolve, and something of her character may be revealed by her subsequent actions.

Here is another way to consider the matter. Some promises are voided by changes in circumstances. Livvy and Diane discussed the beauty of a particular ocean beach, and Livvy promised to take Diane there on the weekend. But in the interim an industrial waste accident poisoned the beach and surrounding areas. Livvy is now relieved of the promise because, through no fault of her own, conditions have changed such that the promise cannot be fulfilled. Now consider a similar case, but with a different change in circumstance. Livvy and Diane discussed the beauty of a particular ocean beach, and Livvy promised to take Diane there on the weekend. But Diane died in the interim. Does Livvy now have an obligation to fulfill the promise? Must she take a dead body to the beach? (What for? Would she prop up the body for a good view of the ocean? Would she adorn Diane's corpse with a straw hat and sunglasses?) Livvy's taking Diane's body to the beach would be *like* fulfilling the promise, but it is actually now something sentimental, something perhaps in memory of Diane, something only for Livvy's own benefit. There may be a resolve to live up to, but there is no longer a promise to fulfill.[5]

Now consider a life insurance policy. We may understand it as a contract or a set of promises made between one person and an insurance company. The person agrees to pay premiums, and the insurer agrees to pay some amount to a beneficiary upon the insured's death. But it is an unusual contract in this respect, namely, that when it comes time for the insurer to make good on the promise, there is no longer a promisee. Since the promise died with the promisee, the promisor (the insurance company in this case) cannot reasonably be held to the defunct promise.[6]

---

[5] H. L. A. Hart says, "This is an intelligible development of the figure of a bond (*vinculum juris: obligare*); the precise figure is not that of two persons bound by a chain, but of *one* person [the promisor] bound, the other end of the chain lying in the hands of another [the promisee] to use if he chooses" ("Are There Any Natural Rights?," 181). But what shall we say if the promisee dies? If the chain is annihilated as well, then there is no longer a promise. Or does the end of the chain drop loose and become available for anyone to pick up? (And if so, then why not the promisor, in which case it is a "promise" of one person to himself, which is not a promise at all, but rather a resolve.)

[6] In a contract between two persons, each person plays dual roles of both promisee and promisor. Suppose you paid premiums to a company, but later, while you were alive, the company died. In the

Joel Feinberg, adumbrating Ernest Partridge's concerns ("Posthumous Interests and Posthumous Respect"), raises an objection:

> There would be no point whatever in buying life insurance policies if the vendors could not be trusted to keep their promise made to the deceased when he was alive to pay his beneficiary at the appropriate time. Life insurance companies, in the absence of such trust, would be forced out of business, and all of us who *care* about our dependents would be left insecure and the dependents themselves highly vulnerable. ["Harm to Others", 189]

One response to this is: Tough! Perhaps life insurance companies *should* go out of business, or at least change the way they do business. Perhaps there is nothing for it but to give up the old practice and settle for something more enlightened, even if it means that some people will not be able to have the kind of assurance that they wish they could have and in the manner they were accustomed to having it. Let them find some different, more reasonable method of obtaining assurance, even if it seems at first to be more cumbersome. The history of contracts—how they are made, what they can be, and how they can be enforced—is filled with such instances of people having to change their ways.

But why predict that life insurance companies would be forced out of business? Here is a weak suggestion. Leave things more or less as they are now, excluding the fiction that there can be a contract even when one party to the contract does not exist. Diane, for example, paid premiums to some insurance company and named Livvy as beneficiary. Diane died. Now Livvy goes to the insurance company to collect. Feinberg's worry is that the insurance company could claim that because Diane is dead, they are no longer under any contractual obligation to her. That makes good sense to me. Still, the company might be willing to pay Livvy—as willing, anyway, as they might be under our current interpretation—for a very simple reason: they want to stay in business, and they are going to get a bad reputation if they have not changed the now defunct contract into a firm resolve. If they do not pay Livvy, then she will not buy her own insurance from them, and anyone else who learns of this company's practice may decide to shop elsewhere.

Of course, one ought not to be sanguine about the resolves of corporations. So here is a better possibility for people seeking contractual assurances. Let the intended beneficiary herself make a contract with an insurance company; let Livvy

---

absence of contractual obligations requiring you to switch to some other vendor (the original contract might be interpreted in some way as your having made an agreement with both the original and the replacement vendor), the contract has been extinguished. It would be silly to suggest that you ought to continue paying premiums to a nonexistent company.

spend her own money to buy insurance against Diane's death. Such insurance will then be more clearly known for what it is, namely, a gamble against Diane's life. If Diane dies before Livvy does, Livvy receives a handsome payoff. But if Diane outlives Livvy, then Livvy has paid premiums without financial reward. If Livvy does not want to spend her own money (or does not have the money) to pay the premiums, and if Diane wants her to have such insurance (we will investigate that issue in Section 6 "Attenuated transitivity of concern"), then Diane can give Livvy the money for the premiums while she, Diane, is alive. That is to say, let Livvy sign a contract with the insurance company, and let Diane sign a contract with Livvy to pay the premiums. Then upon Diane's death, her contract with Livvy is extinguished, but Livvy's contract with the insurance company remains and can be enforced if necessary. In this way something of the kind of assurance that potential survivors seek can be preserved, and the very reasonable claim that no contract can survive the death of one of the contractees can be sustained.

But this does not answer a more fundamental question. If Diane is an Epicurean, will she *want* to arrange for such insurance—insurance whose benefits necessarily accrue only after she is dead? This is a variation on the desire that one's survivors fare well, which seems to be an aspect of friendship.

3 Friendship

Epicureanism is often characterized as a variety of egoistic hedonism (see again premise α in Chapter 1), which is thought to be incompatible with true friendship, because true friendship requires that a person has a disposition to act for the friend's own good. In the space of six brief points, let us see why egoists can have, and be, friends. Then we will apply what we have learned to the matter of making wills.

(1) I often act for the sake of some tool without regard to its practical use (even if, when I am questioned about it, I agree that it is an instrument). So I can maintain the tool or repair it for its own sake even though at the same time I have a retrievable purpose for it. "For the sake of" is therefore ambiguous. When I act for the sake of the tool, I am acting as though it were only an end in itself, because any instrumental value of the tool might at the moment be unnoticed or irrelevant, as when I clean the lawn mower and bring its engine cover up to a like-new shine even though I am not anticipating that a shiny engine cover will make for a better mower. I can in this way act for the sake of another person.

(2) Consider the difference between tools that are merely opportunistic and those that are not. It takes a more imaginative mind than a chimp's to invest

time and energy into the production of a tool-for-keeping; one must be able to temporarily set aside the purpose of such a tool and then to later recollect that purpose. One engages in the making of such a tool because one has a tacit, but retrievable, use for it. To be able to defer gratification and to see more subtle, future values are marks of a higher intelligence. In important ways friends can be like tools-for-keeping.

(3) Simple tools, such as hammers, can be described pretty much completely in advance; that is to say, there are usually few surprises. But when tools increase in the complexity and in the richness with which they interact with their environment, including us the users, it becomes more and more difficult to be acquainted with all of the variations and to know how well each will serve various ends. One's purposes for a very rich tool become very rich themselves, and so new instances of such tools hold out the possibility of significant surprises. Humans are some of the richest, and most unpredictable tools we have.

(4) Simple tools may be easily replaceable, but the more sophisticated the tool, the more difficult it is to adequately replace. Strictly speaking, of course, nothing is replaceable without residue by something else; that holds for pencils and snowflakes just as much as for persons. But as a practical matter, when I want to replace the spark plug in my lawn mower, I do not care about Leibniz's law. What I want is some device that can produce an efficient spark to ignite the compressed fuel-air mixture in the combustion chamber. I might not care about the make or model of the spark plug, except as such considerations give me some information about how well it is likely to do its work. So it is with friends. The crucial difference is that I believe that I know well enough (and if I do not know, I can consult authorities) what is important about spark plugs for my purposes, and, further, that my purposes for the spark plug are very clear, whereas in the case of persons, I only sometimes know what some of my purposes are for another person, and I only sometimes know what it is about a person that will likely satisfy my purposes. Humans are far more complex than spark plugs, not only in how they can satisfy my desires but also in how they can ignite new desires (and sometimes go wrong by frustrating my desires). Friends are useful not merely for a few explicit purposes but rather for a lifestyle of ends. If one can specify, in advance, a final set of attributes which one's friend is to have, such that any instantiation of all the items in that set will do as well as any other, then one simply is not appreciating the richness of human beings.

(5) Because friends are not easily replaceable, I do not discard them, but rather I try to assure them a safe place from which I might later draw on them for satisfaction of some or many of my desires. A safe place for a tool depends

on the tool. Metal tools ought to be kept away from corrosive conditions. Cotton tools, such as shirts, ought to be kept away from damp or very high temperature conditions. Edible tools, such as carrots, ought to be kept in low-temperature storage. And so on. How should friends be kept? They should be allowed to roam about on their own but with regular (and sometimes lengthy and costly) attention to their well-being.

So if it is thought that the Epicurean attitude makes some people out to be mere "things", to be used and discarded willy-nilly, then one is misunderstanding the matter. Friends are very valuable, and very valuable things are not dealt with willy-nilly. They are pampered and cared for, and they are not given up without some attempts to keep them whole and healthy. My friends can remain my friends even when, on occasion, they treat me ill. I will give them the benefit of the doubt, and should a friendship seem to be falling apart, then, as with any valuable instrument, I will make efforts to repair it. To grant this is to acknowledge that friends are rare instruments of high value.

(6) So I needn't give up egoism in order to have friends; I need only recognize that certain people are important parts of my life. In caring for them, I need not explicitly reckon what advantages or disadvantages come to me. It is not that there are no advantages to me, or that what I am doing is independent of my own interests. It is rather that the attention given to them is done out of a policy I have—a habit which I find has developed in me—which encourages me to care for the others' welfare, because their welfare has had effects on my own. That is to say, it is good policy to treat a person with special affection because he is my friend, but he became my friend because I came to see the value of treating him with special care. Something like this may be what Epicurus has in mind when he says "Every friendship is worth choosing for its own sake, though it takes its origin from the benefits [it confers on us]" (*VS* 23).

But what of the case of making wills? In that case, I seem to be acting for the sake of the friend but necessarily without being able to improve my life by doing so, since my friend's welfare will be affected only after I have died. How could an Epicurean justify *that* kind of apparently non-egoistic attention to a friend?

4 Wills

If promises are extinguished by death, then so are some obligations attached to wills. There can be nothing morally binding in a decedent's last will and testament which, after death, is merely the record of an earlier expression of interests now vacated. Fulfilling the former wishes of a former person cannot benefit the person (since there is no longer a person to benefit), and not fulfilling the former wishes of a former person can do no harm to the person (since there is no longer a person to harm).

Joan C. Callahan says that even though not honoring persons' wills after their deaths does not harm them, we can have duties to the heirs, and it is a useful fiction that we couch such duties in terms of duties to the deceased.

> The vast majority of us are greatly comforted now to know that after our death the law can be used to contribute to the good of the persons and causes we care about. If maintaining the fictions of harm and wrong to the dead in our legal institutions is the most effective way of securing this comfort [...] then keeping them is exceedingly well justified. [Callahan, "On Harming the Dead", 352]

But such fictions and the resulting comfort do not respond to the deeper question of the philosophical justification of such practices. They are no more justified than is continuing to endorse a fiction in, say, Santa Claus for the sake of one's children. That such fictions produce some kinds of comfort for some people is to be admitted, and so in that respect it is a nice thing to do. But it is not necessary to give children the idea of Santa Claus in the first place. If we accepted the Null Hypothesis, we would not need the fiction that expersons can be harmed by not honoring their vacated wishes.

Ernest Partridge maintains a different but still instrumentalistic view:

> If the casual voiding of wills became a general policy—that is, if it were understood that one might attempt to humor the living with empty promises to keep their wills, and that the promiser might do as he pleased after the death of the promisee—then, if such practices were generally known, the survivors would themselves be left with precious little assurance that any such promises could be relied upon in their own eventual cases. Without these assurances, few such promises would be made. ["Posthumous Interests and Posthumous Respect", 261]

True enough. But if it is, as Partridge says, a case of "empty promises", then the problem is one of fraud: anyone who knowingly makes such an empty promise is a liar. But there is a deeper issue. Why would the survivors want assurances that *their own* antemortem wishes would be carried out postmortem? Why would they have any wishes at all about what might take place after their deaths? The very basis for thinking that there could be expectations which survive one's death is a misunderstanding of death. A full understanding would mean that one would have no wishes whose objects exist necessarily only beyond one's death. If the survivors are themselves Epicureans they would understand that what happens beyond their deaths will make no difference to them, and so they will not care about such assurances.

So now we may ask: Why do people want to make wills, and why do people want to honor them? These are not conceptual or moral issues, but rather psychological ones. People make wills because there is an ongoing tendency in their lives to think of themselves in the future, and this habit easily perseveres even when thinking of that future which is beyond their deaths, so that their present care for their loved ones is imagined to continue beyond death. People tend to honor wills because they have the lifelong habit of honoring living people's wishes, especially those wishes which are important. If a person is recently deceased, it is easy to think of him, in spite of his nonexistence, as presently having wishes, so that whoever is in charge of his property will feel some compulsion to try to honor those wishes. Habits do not wink out all of a sudden, and so people naturally have a tendency to think of decedents in some ways as though they were still alive.[7]

Time will change that, of course. Suppose archaeologists unearth a fortune in gold and precious stones, buried with a corpse thousands of years ago in an area whose culture long ago disappeared. They also find a will which asks that the fortune be put to such and such uses, which evidently was never done. Even if people today could put that fortune to those uses, they will not feel the same kind of compulsion to do so that they feel in the case of a recently deceased person's estate. Occasionally ancient graves and tombs are unearthed, and what is found is taken to museums. Doing so would not honor the ancient wishes of at least some of those whose remains were found. Sometimes it is done anyway. Time can make a difference.[8]

There is another issue. What would a society of Radical Epicureans be like? If wills would not be made, how would the disposition of decedents' property be handled? There are various possibilities. All property might be claimed by the State. Something like that happens even now often enough anyway; the State can take a portion—sometimes a very large portion—of a decedent's estate even when doing so is contrary to the decedent's former wishes in the matter. If it is,

---

[7] The wishes, it is sometimes said, "are" the wishes of the person now dead, as though the present tense were still applicable. See how easy it is to confuse "his wish that *p*" in the sense of the subject of his wish (i.e., what his wish was about), which can exist postmortem, with a wish that he has gerundively (i.e., his wishing that *p*), which cannot exist postmortem.

[8] Modern archaeologists might reasonably be hesitant to unearth and remove ancient bones, not because doing so might be against ancient wishes but because living people—descendants and members of a still-living culture—might have wishes that (for whatever reason) the bones be left where and as they are.

as Partridge claims, wrong to not honor antemortem wishes, then the State acts immorally; or else people do not really have quite the respect for persons' former wishes that they like to say they have.

But it is more likely that a society of Epicureans could after all be a society in which wills are made and respected. How would that be possible? Very simply: An Epicurean could make a will according to the wishes of his loved ones, not so that his loved ones will be better off when he is dead, of course (he won't care about that), but so that his loved ones are better off now. They would be better off now, because, knowing that they are being appreciated now, and knowing that they will be the beneficiaries of some future goods, they will be pleased, comforted, thankful, and relieved *now*, and the beneficiaries' present happiness can affect the benefactor.[9] The same kind of consideration applies to life insurance. Of course, no Epicurean would make *secret* wills and *secretly* take out life insurance (unless there could be some *living* point to it; but I can't imagine what it might be).

But would wills be honored? Yes, and just as much as they are now, I expect, because it would be in the interest of the survivors to protect not their abilities to make their own wills for some future beyond their own deaths, as Partridge sees it, but rather to protect what had been promised to them. There could easily be rules (legal or otherwise) that if one had been promised a portion of someone's estate, then one would be protected in that expectation. Under this interpretation, it would not be a matter of respecting the decedents' vacated wishes, but a matter of protecting living persons' expectations.

5 Callousness and indifference

My comments so far suggest that as an Epicurean I see no point in spending my money or energies or, in general, my present care and concern on the fate of my loved ones (indeed, of the entire world) after I have died, and such an attitude seems to be very callous; it might be received with surprise or distaste, and so I think the notion of unconcern needs looking into.

---

[9] A similar point is made by James Warren (*Facing Death*, 189f), but Warren says that an Epicurean could justify writing a will for the benefit of the friend because he would know (or expect) that the friend would "reciprocate" (during the testator's life, of course). But the focus on reciprocation can be misleading, because the writing of the will need not be part of an exchange—a "this for that", or an "I'll do this for you if you do that for me".

Ordinarily when I discover that someone I know is unconcerned with me, I feel slightly threatened. Of course I know very well that right now most people (almost eight billion) are unconcerned about my welfare, simply because they do not know I exist. But if I learn that someone who knows me is unconcerned about my welfare, then I take that to be an indication not of some innocent and understandable lack (a lack of concern for my welfare) but rather of something more active, namely, a disregard, a contempt, or a wrongful neglect of my welfare—perhaps even a betrayal. It is one thing to accidentally bump into someone because of a coincidence of events I could not have anticipated, but it is quite another thing to accidentally bump into someone because I did not take due regard for the possibility. If I get drunk and then drive my car and accidentally smash into someone, I have done a wrong, because I did not have the proper concern for the damage my car could cause; I ought to have taken more care. Within a given society we set some (often vague) boundaries for the kinds of care which we ought to give to others and which we expect from others.

When I learn that someone who knows me has no concern for my welfare, my first impulse is to understand such a lack of concern as something the person has decided upon or else has been wrongfully negligent about. And when a person neglects to take due regard for me—or, worse, when a person intentionally disregards me—he is in a condition to harm me (by, in the first case, his inattentions, or, in the second case, his intentions). We are certainly social beings, and when our friends, our relatives, or our neighbors, and even strangers whom we encounter, do not pay us the attention we believe we deserve, we are naturally uneasy about it. One of the cruelest punishments is to be "sent to Coventry", a condition wherein our comrades intentionally pay no attention to us; we become nonentities, and as nonentities we cannot be the objects of concern. And that is threatening.

When, then, I say that I will have no concern for someone or anyone beyond my own death, it *seems* as though I am either intentionally or inattentively neglecting what is due them. If I say "I will care for you until I die, but thereafter whatever happens to you can be no concern of mine", it may seem as though it were something like "I shall care for you until midnight Saturday, but thereafter what happens to you can be no concern of mine", as though a choice had been made, and as though I might be persuaded to have a change of heart and continue caring even on into Sunday and beyond. It sounds as though I am planning to *withdraw* my concern at a certain, predefined time, after which I will be aloof, direct my attention elsewhere, and be indifferent to pleas for help. That would indeed be callous.

But that is not what the Epicurean is about. Rather, the Epicurean can say "I devote my life to you. I will love you until the day I die. You make my life full and exciting and meaningful". All that may sound a bit saccharine, perhaps; but in any case it is not in the spirit of a callous attitude. I make no decision to neglect my responsibility. My social pledge is rather that for as long as I live I shall have proper concern for any and all others who do or might come into my life in any way.

I disagree with Herbert Fingarette when he says that it is not enough to have concern for others now; we must also be concerned about the fate of others beyond our own death:

> Of course, it's true that the welfare of my sorrowing family won't matter to me when I'm dead. But it does and surely should matter now. My concern for their future welfare isn't based on the expectation of my own satisfaction in that postmortem future. There is satisfaction for me right now, life is more fulfilled for me right now, if I can think of them as faring well after my death. Surely such concern is part of what it means to love someone. [Fingarette, *Death*, 17–18]

I do not see that it is necessarily part of what it means to love someone, although I readily grant that it is usually thought to be so. Perhaps the idea of not caring for what happens to others after my death seems unacceptable because it is difficult to come to grips with the idea that my loved ones will have no effect on me nor I on them. After all, because they are my loved ones, they have had and continue to have very important influences on me and I on them, and so to imagine that such interaction will be extinguished is to imagine that the love will no longer be there, which I can do now only in the most abstract way: I can say with honesty that it is *possible* that at some time in my future I will not love those people and things I now love. But because I do now in fact love them, the bare possibility of not loving them is not a live one.

Why would it not be enough to say that their lives are crucially a part of mine and so I shall be concerned for my loved ones for as long as I live? I suspect that the "after my death" in the previous passage from Fingarette is not being fully appreciated—it does little work (although it should). We easily understand the sentence this way: "There is satisfaction for me right now, life is more fulfilled for me right now, if I can think of them as faring well." This is a sentiment which Epicureans share. That the "after my death" *ought* to do some work is given support by other adverbial phrases which plainly do make a difference, for example, "after they have taken all my money and spread vicious rumors about me", or "after they have been discovered to be homicidal maniacs". Should

I, under *those* conditions, wish them success in their endeavors? Wishing them well is of course conditional on such empirical matters. The Epicurean claims that one's own death is a more rigid limit than any contingent condition; one's death is a logically limiting condition on one's concern for others.

Steven Luper says that since a hedonist will not be concerned with the fate of someone who lives beyond the hedonist's death, "it is by no means clear" that the hedonist could be concerned about others "during *any* period of time" (*Invulnerability*, 147–48). I do not see how that conclusion follows. Our concern for other persons (and things and events) is not unconditional. There are limits which are almost always tacit, but I could make them explicit by saying, for example, "I shall have concern for your welfare unless you become a mass murderer". But that contingency does not mean that I am unable to be concerned about your welfare during any period at all. I might also discover a logical limit to my concern and announce "I shall have concern for your welfare until you die", simply because it does not make sense to be concerned about your welfare when there is no you to fare well. But I see no reason to conclude that therefore I am unable to be concerned about your welfare during any period at all. The logical limit of death is in some ways like other conditions which, if fulfilled, might block future concern but without preventing present concern. I can certainly be concerned with any person, event, or situation which has a bearing on my life. My family affects my life. So do my friends. Even many strangers will have a bearing on my life. During my life I should have some concern for other people's welfare, since their welfare might interact with my own. Of course, I will grade these likelihoods; I will probably take greater care for the welfare of my loved ones than for the welfare of strangers. That is what we do anyway, Epicurean or not. Epicureanism does not start out with the premise that one ought not to care what happens to others after one's death; that kind of indifference is an inference made from premises that advise us to care about what happens to us in life. This was the point of the Indifference Conclusion in Chapter 2. The limit of our concern is whatever puts a limit on what can affect us. There are probably very few empirical limits which would put a total stop for our concern for others, but, given the materialistic hypothesis that death is annihilation, we ought to realize that death is not an empirical limit (even though the *time* of death is an empirical matter) but a logical condition on all our concerns.

Could there be instructive analogies to help us understand the Epicurean position? They would have to fit a pattern such as this one:

P1: I care now about *X* (or what now happens to *X*).

P2: I know that after time *t*, *X* will continue, but I will then no longer care about *X* (or what will happen to *X*).

P3: So (using a version of the Indifference Conclusion) I do not now care what will happen to *X* beyond *t*.

Opponents of the Indifference Conclusion will maintain that P3 is a mark of a callous attitude, and that P1 and P3 are incompatible. But let me try some instantiations of *X* and *t* such that all three claims seem ordinary. (I will then comment on how the examples fail.)

Here is a simple instantiation of the pattern: I care now for my car; I take good care of it. I know that at some time *t* I will sell my car, after which I will no longer attend to whether it fares well or not. For the duration of my ownership I make regular appointments to have the car serviced, but I do not schedule such service beyond *t*. So I do not now care about whether it will fare well after I have sold it. It is not the case that I have a present concern for the welfare of my car beyond *t* and that selling the car is a way of arranging that someone else take care of it. No; I know in advance that selling the car is merely a way of recouping part of my investment, and what happens to the car after that will no longer be my concern.

Another example: I am enjoying a movie at the cinema. I care now that the projection equipment is in good shape and does not fail. But after the movie is over, I will leave the theater, and if the equipment then breaks down, I will not care. So I do not care now whether that happens then.

These examples, it must be admitted, are unconvincing, for two reasons. First, they involve conditions of indifference about nonpersons—about fairly easily replaceable things; it would usually be odd to accuse someone of having a callous attitude toward mere things, and so my examples do not rise to the level necessary to withstand a serious charge of callousness. So let me try still another example. I care now for my adult son. But he is on his way to apply for a job as a tax collector, one of the most immoral occupations legally available. I have been unable to change his mind, and so I have promised to disown him if he carries through on his mission. The *t* in this example is the condition of his becoming a tax collector; it is a limit to my concern for him.

This brings us to the second reason for the admission that my examples are rather weak. They do not take into account my concern for how other persons will be affected by *X*. If my car breaks down soon after selling it to someone, I might want to do something for that new owner. If the projector fails after I have left the cinema, I will sympathize with the people who came to watch the next showing. If my son becomes a tax collector, I will worry about all the misery caused to taxpayers. Moreover, the tax collector example falters because it is not unreasonable that I will continue to have *some* concern for my son, namely, that he change his ways and become a better person.

Weak as the examples are, they are the best I can do, because a closer look at the pattern P1–P3 above will reveal that it is significantly less than what is needed to construct an adequate analog. Specifically, P2 ought to include a mention that although X will continue in existence, I will not. But if the pattern included the stipulation that *t* is the time of my death, then all possible examples would simply be expressions of the Epicurean position, and I would not have argued for anything. The problem is that no example of P1–P3 can be a fully satisfactory analog, because death is a singularity for each of us. The consolation is that no instantiation of the pattern can be a fully satisfactory counterexample either.

I said before that the inertia of habits inclines people to think and act unreflectively in making and honoring wills. Taking note of that inertia, we can make a distinction between understanding and acting. During a storm one night the power in my house went out, yet when I entered a dark room to get a candle, I flipped up the light switch. Sometimes I can avoid such inappropriate actions if I am able to attend to what I am doing and why. Yet it is difficult to now attend to what was previously habitual, because habits are what have been formed such that my attention can be given elsewhere. Ordinary tendencies in important matters such as caring for others are in some respects like great and powerful addictions. Even when one has decided to give them up, one may have to spend time and effort—perhaps with the ongoing support of professionals, and sometimes with the aid of medication—in order to actually rid oneself of them. One may recognize the pull of a habit without at the same time having the emotional power to withdraw from it.[10] The Epicurean has come to have a different *intellectual* attitude about mortal things. Ways of reasoning which are suitable in and for one's life are no longer extended by habit into a future which is not one's own. But there is an *emotional* shift which does not occur immediately with the change in the intellectual approach. It is difficult to stop anticipating that a loved one now deceased continues to participate in important ways in one's life. We unreflectively give special attention to those things that belonged to the deceased, as though the person now dead still had concerns, wishes, and values. We can even be tender in our regard and treatment of the

---

[10] There is a parallel with optical illusions, although they may be less reliant on either intellectual or practical habits. One can know—because one can measure them—that the double-headed arrows in the Müller-Lyer illusion are equal in length, yet still perceive them as unequal.

corpse. My dearest friend loved this particular painting, although I did not. Yet now that she is dead, I do not throw the painting away; I do not sell it; I do not give it away. For a while at least I let the painting hang on the wall as it always did. I may even come to appreciate it more because she is no longer here to do so. Whatever else humans are, we are bundles of habits. My very central habits of care for important persons and things can still move me, even when I acknowledge that those persons and things no longer exist to be cared for. One's tendencies regarding care and concern for others can carry on into one's unexamined expectations of the future, not only into the time that is future to those persons' deaths but also into the time that is future to one's own death.

It is this otherwise admirable tendency which gives rise to the appearance that a Radical Epicurean, who seems to saying that he has no such tendency, is indifferent to people's welfare. A person whose lover has just died, but who very soon takes up with another lover, or who acts in ways that indicate that he no longer gives much, if any, thought to the former lover, seems to be acting in such a way as to indicate that he could not really have loved the previous person at all: How could grief be so short-lived? The Epicurean says that he should give no thought to what might happen to his loved ones after his death, and so it *seems* as though the proper habits of care and concern for his loved ones now, during his life, cannot be in place if he so easily dismisses what might happen to them after some condition obtains.

Although one's natural emotional attitudes are difficult to change on the basis of a change in conceptual understanding, it is expected that nearly anyone could have some success at that psychological task. People can give up undesirable addictions; children can overcome a fear of heights; soldiers can be trained to overcome a reluctance to kill. Some people no longer think that they will survive death as disembodied souls, even if, earlier in their lives, they had been tutored in religious ideas of an afterlife; they have now reached a point at which they can say that they have left such impulses behind—old shards of dashed expectations. But their having learned this lesson, and their having come to have different emotional reactions to the certainty of their own mortality, do not prevent them from caring deeply for themselves; nor are they prevented from caring deeply for others.[11] But such concern for oneself and for others now takes a slightly

---

[11] One does not like to envision bad things for those persons whom one holds dear. Even now, when I am confident that a friend is actually living contentedly, if I conjure up a graphic image of his suffering, with details of the kind of suffering, its intensity and its cause—an image invented for the sake of making this very point—I am given some discomfort, just as I would if I witnessed an obviously fictional video of his being put into agony. It is easier to think of the possibility only very abstractly, without details. Then, it seems, my concern is so mild that it might even be

different form because it no longer rushes headlong into the time after which one will not exist. Epicurus thought that philosophy was the proper way to provide training that would lead to a fuller emotional acceptance of the claim that death is nothing to us. One might quarrel with that empirical issue; perhaps psychoanalysis or behavioral conditioning would be more efficacious. In any case, that is a matter other than the question of the adequacy of the reasoning which supports the quest for an emotional acceptance.

6 Attenuated transitivity of concern

I said that the Epicurean view seems to shut out commonsensical concerns about events that will happen after one's death, and I have tried to show that upon examination some of the consequences of that view are more acceptable (or less problematic) than they might at first have appeared. But there is still the sticking point that a good person will somehow take into account at least some postmortem persons, things, or events. I have already indicated how the psychological or emotional aspect of concern for others can sometimes have enough inertia to carry over into one's feelings about postmortem futures. Can such sentiments be given at least some justification within the Epicurean view, or must they remain prereflective impulses only? I believe that there is after all some small justification; I mentioned it in the earlier discussion of whether an Epicurean would make a will. It is a simple point, and it does not take us very far at all, but it deserves a little elaboration.

You are of course concerned now for how you will fare in your own future. If I predecease you, then part of your future will be after my death. I can be concerned for you now, while I am alive, and so I can have concerns now about your present concern for how you will fare after I am dead. So I can have a kind of indirect concern about what will happen to you after my death.[12] Moreover, if you have concerns about others' concerns for what will happen to them after your

---

nonexistent. When a Radical Epicurean claims that he does not care what happens to his friends after he is dead, he must mean that this bare, abstract thought causes him no anxiety or distress. But he can also shy away from any detailed thought or image of a friend's suffering, because the more detailed it is, the more immediate it seems, and the more immediate it seems, the more present it seems, and the more present it seems, the more his emotional responses are evoked.

[12] I might participate in helping to remedy some environmental problems (and I might take care to avoid contributing to environmental problems), even if I can reasonably expect that such problems or solutions will have no significant effect on me but can be anticipated to have effects on future generations beyond my own expected lifetime. My concern will not be for the well-being of future generations, but rather for people I care about in the present generation who will continue to live beyond my own life; they have, now, some regard for their own future welfare, and my present

death, then you can have an indirect concern about what will happen to them after your death. That indirect concern of yours can figure into my concerns for your present concerns. So I can in this doubly indirect way have concerns about what will take place after—perhaps long after—my death.

This extension of concerns by means of overlapping of concerns might usefully be given a name. It is not quite transitivity, which would be of this form: If A is concerned for B, and B is concerned for C, then A is concerned for C. Moreover, concern is not an all-or-nothing affair (as are, for example, the usual notions of "to the north of" and "greater than"); concern tends to be weaker as its object becomes less certain and further removed in consequential space. So perhaps "attenuated transitivity" would be an apt name.

Attenuated transitivity often characterizes one's interest or concern for other persons and things, quite apart from the issue of death. I might not antecedently care in any special way how well some given person fares, but if I learn that the person is important to my friend, then my concerns for my friend will begin to include some additional attention to that other person. But such concern will be indirect only and so it will not be as motivating to me as is my more direct concern for my friend. Or perhaps my friend is an avid spectator of that damnable sport hockey. I might join my friend watching a hockey game on television, not because hockey itself holds any interest for me, but only because I can take some delight in my friend's curious tastes. We ought to see attenuated transitivity of care and value nearly everywhere in our lives, because it is, after all, a version of instrumental valuation, which participates in nearly everything we do. The world around us consists of rich interactions of differently attenuated values.

This notion of attenuated transitivity of care gives weak support to our prereflective sentiment that we can have some kinds of *indirect* concerns for what might happen after our deaths. But it is severely limited: It applies only to persons, because it is through their concerns that I come to have whatever indirect concerns I might have. I do not see any similar reason for caring now for the fate of my projects or my property or my reputation after my death, except as those issues might be important to my loved ones in their own present concerns about their futures subsequent to my death.

---

cooperation can make their present lives better (and therefore make my life with them better) by giving them hope for their own better futures.

10

Suicide

Prelude

Skylar wants to experience skydiving, so he pops out to a skydiving club at a small local airport, gets instruction, and has a go at it. He enjoys the experience, so he joins the club in order to participate regularly. One day, in a moment of philosophical leisure during a lull in a club meeting, he wonders aloud what it would be like to experience skydiving without a parachute. His fellow club members have no doubt that it would be very thrilling—until a very low altitude was reached, at which point it would become very terrifying. And they raise several cautions. Diving without a chute would not be the same as wearing one but not using it, because if a chute is worn, one would feel safe because one could always deploy it. Besides, club rules require the use of safety features such as automatic activation devices that deploy the main or reserve chutes below a certain altitude.

That issue is set aside, and the conversation turns to how to survive a fall from 12,000 feet. Could the required type and thickness of, say, a foam rubber mattress be accurately calculated so as to absorb enough kinetic energy to break the fall without undue stress on a human body? But what if the diver's aim was off, and what if there were wind gusts? There is little directional control without a chute. After a long discussion, they see no practical way to avoid death at the bottom.

Skylar agrees. But since he is an Epicurean with regard to death, it does not matter to him that such a leap would be his last. His only concern is that he would have to be confident that his contact with the ground would be sure to kill him more or less instantly and not cause him to suffer.

So Skylar plans to wear a chute as usual on the next dive (no pilot would take him up unless he was wearing the proper gear), but immediately after jumping from the plane, he will unbuckle the apparatus and continue the dive sans chute.

1 Some ethical issues in suicide

Suicide, which for our purposes can include what goes by the names of assisted suicide and voluntary euthanasia, can have a range of motivators: physical pain, romantic or other relationship problems, severe financial issues, feelings of acute shame or self-hatred, and others. Some people who arrange for their own deaths might take death to be if not a good thing, then at least a better alternative than what they expect continuing in life to afford. But my arguments in Chapter 5 against the deprivation theory of the evil of death are also arguments against the deprivation theory of the goodness of death. Many of the useful ways of talking about loss or deprivation (and also cure or relief) that apply in life cannot apply in the special case of death. It is on account of that irregularity that the issue of suicide can be perplexing.

The literature on suicide is vast, but I want to limit my discussion to some ethical issues and some prudential issues. (There is little that need be said here about any metaphysical issues, save a reminder that the death of a person is the annihilation of the person.) Let me first mention a few ethical concerns but without presuming to settle them; I want only to describe them from an Epicurean standpoint. The prudential issues are more difficult, so I will procrastinate.

If I have no right to not be killed (see Chapter 7), then no one does a wrong to me by killing me, provided other issues are neglected (the killing is without pain or warning, no one is caused to suffer, and so on). Am I one of the persons who does no wrong to me by killing me? On the other hand, if I had a claim-right to life, then all persons would be under a duty to not interfere with my living; that is, they would be under a duty to not kill me. Am I one of the persons who would be under a duty to not kill me? If I have a right to eat this apple, do I not have a right to refuse to eat this apple? If I have a right to continue eating this apple, have I not the right to discontinue eating this apple? And so if I had a right to continue living, would I not have a right to discontinue living?

Some people claim that there is only a limited right to suicide—that it is sometimes morally impermissible.[1] I find something a bit odd in such a claim. Perhaps it makes some sense to say to a person who is about to commit suicide, "You have important duties to others, and so you should rethink your intentions here." And perhaps a person can be forced to perform those duties before death. And perhaps it makes sense to say, to a person who tried unsuccessfully to die, that he or she was morally wrong to make the attempt because of certain duties

---

[1] Victor Cosculluela ("The Right to Suicide") elaborates on a view that one can have a right to suicide, depending, in part, on one's duties to others that can in some cases override one's right to suicide. In those cases, he argues, suicide is impermissible. (Complete bibliographic information on this and all other sources in this book is provided in the Bibliography.)

that were not fulfilled. And perhaps in the case of the successful suicide it makes some sense to hold the person's estate to account.

But can there be anything beyond that? Suppose that a person kills himself when he had important duties to others. If someone claims that the person did something immoral, we may ask "So what? What purpose does such a judgment serve?"

It seems to me that moral appraisals are for one or both of two purposes: (1) To justify the use of force of some sort, either to compel certain behavior or to prevent certain behavior. The use of force visits the person with some adversity such as pain or the withholding of some good, or the interference with the person's freedom. (2) A second purpose for moral appraisal is to teach, in order that future behavior is affected. We might learn that certain duties are expected of people, and we might learn to be more careful in the future to not let people in such situations kill themselves; or we may learn that were we to unsuccessfully attempt suicide, we might be punished. But if a person kills himself, there is no learning on *his* part; there is no edification for the one who died. The successful intention to die adequately extinguishes itself.

Aside from such consequences, it is rather idle to appraise a suicide as right or wrong. Perhaps we should say that a suicide, once successful, is morally neutral. However we now evaluate his action, our evaluation can have no relevance for him, because there is no him to have relevance for. There is no one who can be condemned (or praised) for what they did; we have only *post esse* counterfactuals.

But there may be moral issues that arise in connection with the intention to die.

> Take the case of Charlotte Hough who (as reported in *The Sunday Times* of 22 June 1986) promised an elderly woman that she would stay with her throughout a suicide attempt and, if necessary, make sure that she was really dead. When the woman's cocktail of pills apparently did not work, Charlotte Hough, reluctantly complying with the old woman's emphatic prior instructions, placed a plastic bag over her head. She did not want to, and had hoped that she would not have to when she first agreed to be with the old woman until she died. Charlotte Hough was found guilty of attempted murder and served six months of a nine-month sentence. [Rob Campbell and Diane Collinson, *Ending Lives*, 122]

I imagine myself in the old woman's position. Could I in good conscience request of Charlotte that she make sure of my death, if to do so would be to risk bringing down upon her possibly burdensome consequences? Ordinarily, to ask someone to do something which carries penalties is to place a burden on her, and so such a request must be weighed carefully. But in my case, as in the old woman's, where any consequences will occur only after my death, I will view those consequences as nothing to me. Still, Charlotte is now, before the event, aware of what could happen (or so we will suppose), and so my request could cause some anguish, now, in her. On the other hand, if she is completely ignorant of the possibility of such consequences, then I have no problem. Or, if there is a problem, it is a slightly different one: What if I do *not* die, in spite of Charlotte's assistance? Then I might be witness to her legal burdens.

If assisting a suicide raises ethical issues, what about preventing suicide? If death really is nothing, then interfering with a suicider does not save him from something bad; in fact, it saves him from nothing. But we might want a policy of interfering with a suicider (just as we might approve of a policy of preventing killing) if we have reason to believe that the death will cause others some adversity. If my friend is in such pain that he wants to die, I might interfere if I have reason to believe that his problem can be solved. I will have a strong motive to interfere, because I do not want to lose my friend. But if I see no solution to his problem, it would be cruel to interfere with his suicide, because not only will my friend suffer but I will also suffer because of his suffering.

Suppose that there were a general policy of not only not interfering with suicide, but positively promoting it, in the following curious way. Suppose that all persons alive at a particular time encouraged each other to not produce children. Absent immortality, the human species would die out as a result of such a universal choice, so it would amount to a kind of species suicide.[2] Would that be bad? Would it be immoral? My suspicion is that such a voluntary end of the human race would be thought to be bad for one or more of these reasons: (1) Human life would be worth less without children around; it would be a lower quality of life. In that case, though, it would not be the end of the species which would be bad, but rather a life without children. (True, many people choose—and we may suppose that they choose wisely—to have no children. But that choice is made in a context in which other people do have children. So many persons' choices to not propagate would be compatible with species survival.) (2) The end of *Homo sapiens* would seem very much like the *destruction* of *Homo sapiens*. That is, the end of humanity might not be appreciated as being completely voluntary. If the species stops, it might seem to have been caused to stop by the secret workings of some external cause against which humanity

---

[2] Samuel Scheffler gives us a very thoughtful discussion of a similar issue in *Death and the Afterlife*, 38–49.

waged an unsuccessful battle, such as a mind-altering virus that created child-aversion behavior. (3) It would be objectively bad for the universe to contain no humans. But perhaps only a human would claim that it would be objectively bad if there were no humans. This is not because only humans can appreciate such subjunctives; we may imagine an alien species, just as thoughtful as we, but not as prepared as we to revere humans. Or suppose all humans have the chance to elevate themselves into something above, higher than, but decidedly other than, human; perhaps evolution can be seen at work producing, over many millennia, a new species. Shall humanity stop that development, on the grounds that humanity is better than anything else, even that which evolves out of, and in some sense above, humanity? (4) Human life might be less than satisfactory if people thought that there would be no people in the future—people to carry on, to remember.[3]

Finally, (5) if the end of humanity were to occur suddenly and without warning, then there could be no complaint (by humans). But if the end were to occur like a long illness, with progressively fewer and fewer survivors, then at any given time most of those who remain would see the coming end with dread. Epicureans, on the other hand, would not care about the end per se, but they would care deeply about the continual loss of friends and even strangers as societies declined.

2 Some prudential issues in suicide

Many discussions of suicide focus on whether the intention or desire to die could be rational. The assumption seems to be that such a decision is suspect, unless special or extraordinary conditions obtain.

> [Considering] the difficulty of ascertaining the real will of someone who is either suffering from intense pain or who has been drugged to relieve it, the chances of securing valid consent *at the time of the administration of euthanasia* are severely reduced. [Philip E. Devine, *The Ethics of Homicide*, 189; emphasis in original]

But what is this thing "real will"? Why is a plea from a suffering person not their real will? Why is the expressed desire of a heavily drugged person not their real will? It might be said that a severely suffering person, wracked by intense pain, or made sometimes incoherent on account of massive doses of drugs, may

---

[3] See again Scheffler, *Death and the Afterlife*.

appear to express a choice; but later, should their condition improve, they will be able to give a different expression of their will. Yes, but why should we discount one expression and sustain another? Why not say, what seems obvious to me, that they changed their mind? So the question is not "What is their real will?" but rather "Will they change their mind?" In the case of everything else in life, prudence recommends that room be made for second thoughts. But a choice to die is unusual because, having been carried out, it cannot result in either regret or satisfaction.

Still, the rationality of suicide is the issue I want to look at here. Specifically, the question is whether an Epicurean, upon careful reflection, could prudentially choose suicide. It would be easy to infer from some passages that Epicurus advised against suicide. VS 38, for example, says that "he is utterly small-minded for whom there are many plausible reasons for committing suicide." And in his *Letter to Menoeceus* (125–26) he says:

> The many sometimes flee death as the greatest of bad things and sometimes choose it as a relief from the bad things in life. But the wise man neither rejects life nor fears death. For living does not offend him, nor does he believe not living to be something bad.

I see this and similar passages as raising two points. (1) They are not so much injunctions against suicide as they are reminders that neither life nor death is something to be feared; nor is either to be cherished. And (2) Epicurus is not pointing out the foolishness of suicide. Rather, he is commenting on the foolishness of a kind of life. But it is not suicide that makes the life foolish. Some people think of death as a great harm, a great ill, something to be feared, and that fear infects their lives. Epicurus is saying that they are not living very well if they are living under such a fear. There are other common fears as well, such as the fear of the gods, and the fear of what might happen after death. It is a real pity that people's lives are full of anxiety and suffering because of such fears. Epicurus recommends a serene life of stable satisfaction, and anything that seriously interferes with such a life is to be avoided. Suicide does not interfere with such a life (i.e., it ends a life, of course, but it does not make for a worse life), whereas the fears (which might lead some people to suicide) do. The focus of Epicurus's comments is not on suicide but on some of the reasons which drive some people to suicide. It would not matter if those reasons drove those people to something else instead; what matters is that they are not living well. Epicurus is not recommending that we change our attitudes *so as to avoid suicide*, but rather *so as to lead a happier life*. The Epicurean attitude is not "It's a pity that this fellow wants to die" but rather "It's a pity that this fellow is leading such a miserable life."

Still, there remains the puzzle: Is suicide ever consistent with prudence? Is it ever choiceworthy? If suicide is a choice, it might be perceived by the person as a choice for the better, or away from the worse. Life can seem to be worse than death (or death better than life) under the circumstances as perceived by the person making that choice. One tends to choose that which one thinks at the moment is better, comparatively, than perceived alternatives. That, anyway, would be a description of suicide if suicide were an ordinary act like eating or reading or walking or engaging in any other project, great or small. But suicide cannot be like that. For an Epicurean, at least, it cannot be the object of choice in the same way that all other choices are.

St. Augustine appears to understand the Epicurean view about choosing death. In *De Libero Arbitrio* (3.VIII.76–77) he says:

> See how foolish and inconsistent it is to say, "I would prefer not to be, than to be unhappy." The man who says, "I prefer this to that," chooses something; but "not to be" is not something, but nothing. Therefore, you cannot in any way choose rightly when you choose something that does not exist. [. . .] Furthermore, a man necessarily becomes better when he achieves what he rightly chose to seek. He who does not exist, however, cannot be better. No one, therefore, can rightly choose not to exist. [*On the Free Choice of the Will*, 104]

There is a way of choosing what looks like nonexistence, but it is actually a different kind of choice: An Epicurean can sign a Do Not Resuscitate order if he reasonably believes that if he is awakened, he might have to live in pain. This is not suicide (or "assisted suicide"), because he is not choosing to die. His DNR is the expression of a wish that he not be put into pain. He does not reason this way: "Better to be dead than to be in uncompensated pain." But he can say "If I were unconscious, then it could not matter to me if I died. But it could matter to me to be awakened into pain." This is unlike the person who chooses death as a response to pain already being experienced.

How about a wish in retrospect that one not have been in pain? Can one coherently want to die because "it would have been better to not have been born"? We could, of course, take "I wish I had never been born", or the equivalent, to be a dramatic way of meaning, "I am full of pain; I have not been enjoying the things and events in my life, and I have no expectation that things will go any better for me. I have neither fond memories nor pleasant anticipations." I understand such an attitude to be summarized in this way: "I take no satisfaction in the way things are. I wish they were different such that I could be satisfied." It is similar to "I wish I had never come to this party", which indicates a dissatisfaction with present circumstances and a confidence that an alternative should have been chosen. There is an implied "instead" in such a wish. Sometimes it is explicit: "I should have stayed at home or gone to the movies instead of coming to this party." But not having been—that is, nonbeing—is not an "instead" for a person who wants an alternative for an unsatisfactory life. Regardless of my present dissatisfaction, it would not have been better *for me* had I never been born. At least, it would not have been better *for me* in the way possible things and events (or their absence) in my life would have been better for me. To say that the presence or absence of some particular thing or event would have been better for me is to say that I had certain experiences (and expected others) that I wish I had not had; I would have been *better off* had I not had those experiences (but had some others instead). But to not have been born is neither to be nor to have been better off in that usual sense.[4]

Suicide (or euthanasia) is a response to a problem. Problems are always problems for someone (just as values are always values for someone), so in each case we must be careful to be clear about what the problem is, for whom it is a problem, and what a solution would be. An animal's suffering is a problem for it, and it may also be a problem for another animal. My dog's suffering is a problem for my dog, and it is also a problem for me. Perhaps it is not a problem for my nasty neighbor who hates dogs. Sometimes animals (and humans) are killed out of compassion for their apparently great and otherwise unending pain and suffering. Why would anyone think that death would in fact adequately deal with the problem? An important distinction must be made between two ways to end an animal's suffering: (1) Remedy (solve, cure, or fix) the problem. Something is relieved of a problem by making it the case that the problem-bearer no longer has the problem. (2) Kill the animal. In the first case we change the present and future experiential properties of the animal, but in the second case we destroy the bearer of experiential properties. Again, we must ask after the "instead". To relieve an animal of its suffering is to do something that gives the animal non-suffering experiences instead. But to kill an experiencing animal does not relieve it of any of its bad experiences. (It can, however, relieve us of our experiences of a suffering animal, in which case there would be an "instead" for *us*.) We should

---

[4] This is in contrast to David Benatar's provocative claims in *Better Never to Have Been*.

be reminded of the Fallacy of Misplaced Contingency: the mechanic at Reaper's Auto Repair does not solve your car's problem by destroying it.[5]

3 A note on duration

Epicurus says that a happy life is a life of pleasure; but pleasure, when interpreted as katastematic (see Chapter 3), is such that it is complete at all moments when it is experienced and cannot be made better by going on longer. Cicero criticizes Epicurus's hedonism for making the claim that a longer duration cannot add anything to pleasure:

> But if one thinks that happiness is produced by pleasure, how can he consistently deny that pleasure is increased by duration? If it is not, pain is not either. Or if pain is worse the longer it lasts, is not pleasure rendered more desirable by continuance? [*De Finibus* II, 88]

Cicero gets it wrong. Even if we confine our attention to pleasures and pains as sensations, and if we consider the dimension of intensity, then we cannot say that intensity of pleasure or intensity of pain increases by the sensation's lasting longer. Sometimes a sensation will increase in intensity over time, but sometimes not; in some cases intensity will decrease over time. Notice that Cicero switches from wondering why pleasure or pain would not be increased (*crescere*) by duration to a slightly different issue, namely, why pleasure would not be more desirable (*optabiliorem*) or pain become worse (*miserrimus*) by duration. An Epicurean can agree that a pleasure of longer duration is more desirable than a pleasure of shorter duration, while the opposite holds for pain. But there are two important cautions. First, we are to consider the pleasure or pains "in themselves" (as we sometimes say). Second, we must assume that we are speaking of pleasurable or painful sensations—or, rather, pleasurable or painful episodes.[6] But the issue is now trifurcated: (1) the episode comes to an end earlier, or (2) the episode comes to an end later, or (3) the episode does not end.

---

[5] Scheffler imagines an "Epicurean" torturer (*Death and the Afterlife*, 84; but how an Epicurean could possibly justify torture, we are not told) and suggests that if death as the end of life does not matter, then death as the end of pain ought also to not matter. But Scheffler thinks that it is reasonable for the torture victim to long for death, and it is on that premise that Scheffler finds fault with the Epicurean view. His discussion goes wrong, though. One wants the end of bad things (and the continuation of good things) *as part of one's experiences*. True, death puts an end to torture, just as it puts an end to happiness. But the death-end of torture is not the beginning of relief, and the death-end of happiness is not the beginning of unhappiness.

[6] Instead of pleasures and pains, we could speak of periods of happiness or of unhappiness.

Now, in the matter of pain, why would an earlier end be chosen over a later end or no end at all, if we ignore the dimension of intensity? A pain of shorter duration is usually to be chosen over a pain of longer duration (or over an unending pain) not because of duration, full stop. A pain is unwanted for as long as it lasts, but a difference in duration makes a difference to our choices because differences in duration are expected to have differences in consequences. Any pain has this consequence: Our lives are interrupted in an undesirable way; that is, pain comes to us as a problem. A mild headache of short duration is less of a problem than a mild headache of longer duration because of how our activities are interrupted. (But if I can adjust to the mild headache, as I might habituate to any other constant sensation, then I might be able to pursue my interests with little or no interference.)

Another, and more important, issue in matters of duration is this: There is a contrast between the conditions *during* an interval and the conditions *after* that interval. Always the question is, "What will subsequently happen?" That is why Epicurus puts so much emphasis on prudence.[7] It is obvious to anyone that pleasure is desirable and pain is not; that merely describes our natural constitution. But we have to learn to reason about these issues in order to engage in activities that are to our long-term benefit, which is why even a longer-lasting pain might be chosen over a brief pain if the longer-lasting pain is reckoned to better protect us from disturbances later on.

But when it comes to the issue of death, the previous considerations no longer apply. The crucial difference is that at death pains and pleasures end but without any of the consequences that their endings have in life. The death-end of pleasure cannot put us into a condition of frustration; and the death-end of pain cannot put us into a condition of relief. Hence, prudential considerations cannot cross the singular boundary of death. (This is simply a summary of Epicurus's argument in *Let Men* 124–125 that "death is nothing to us".) So although in life we may choose a pleasure of longer duration over a pleasure of shorter duration (because of the condition we anticipate that we will be in afterward), it makes no sense to choose any duration over any other when each ends in death. A longer *life* of pleasure is not prudentially to be chosen over a shorter *life* of pleasure, when in each case the result will be the end of life, that is, when the result will be such that prudential considerations can no longer apply.

---

[7] See, for examples, *Let Men* 128–130, 132, and *VS* 71.

Why then does Epicurus have us consider the ever-lasting happiness of the gods?[8] (This brings us back to an issue raised in Chapter 3.) He does so, first, to emphasize that the right kind of happiness is the kind of happiness that is not interrupted by unhappiness; and second, because it is by appeal to the everlastingness of the gods that our *ordinary* appreciation of happiness can be solicited—namely, that we do not want it to end. But we do not ordinarily distinguish between two kinds of endings, because we can have had experience of only one kind. So our experience of true happiness (*ataraxia*) ought to be like the gods' in that it does not end (in the way all other endings have been experienced by us). What we do not appreciate (unless we have the leisure to carefully examine the issue) is that there can be no difference, as far as our consequential experiences are concerned, between *ataraxia* that lasts for a year, at which point we die, and *ataraxia* that lasts for fifty years, at which point we die. Or, rather, in both cases we cannot experience the end of *ataraxia*. One can say "I have experienced *ataraxia* now for fifty years", but since there can be no experienceable consequences of the death-end, one cannot then continue with "and so I am better off than had I died earlier (or prematurely)". One can only say "and so I am better off than had I lost *ataraxia*—i.e., than had I continued to live but in a dissatisfied condition". If, then, we wish to ideally live like the gods—if we wish to avoid dissatisfaction—then we need not wish for immortality. An infinite time does nothing whatsoever to provide for *ataraxia* that a finite, death-end of *ataraxia* cannot. Nor can a death-end of *ataraxia* do anything to diminish *ataraxia* which an infinite time does not. There is no prudential choice between *ataraxia* of infinite duration and *ataraxia* of finite, death-ended duration.

4 How to solve the problem?

An important feature of Skylar's plan is that he is not intending to die; that is, he does not prepare for a chuteless dive in order to die. It would be just fine with him if he somehow ended up on the ground unhurt; he would still have had his thrill of falling chuteless. But if he is not concerned about his death, would he have the same thrill as a person who was afraid of death? Why do people enjoy parachuting? Skylar's experiences are consistent with those of his clubmates: Part of the enjoyment comes from the feeling of weightlessness during freefall; partly it is the fun of learning to maneuver as one is falling—to join up with others, for

---

[8] *Let Men* 123, 135; *PD* 1; *VS* 33; *Letter to Herodotus* 77, 78.

example; and partly it is the fun of the final portion, when one controls a gentle descent to a precise spot marked on the ground in the drop zone. Risk-taking is rarely a motivator. Indeed, the club places great emphasis on safety at each step, including periodic rigorous instruction in the use of equipment, along with inspecting, maintaining, and occasionally upgrading equipment, and thorough rehearsals of all maneuvers.

Except for the pleasure of a gentle, controlled landing, Skylar would enjoy the activities mentioned earlier. In facing death, he might experience something like a *degma* as mentioned by Philodemus—a natural fear (in this case, a fear of death) that would be, for a good Epicurean, only a temporary sting (see Chapter 3). On his way down he might feel a natural but brief worry, followed by his usual philosophic awareness (assuming that he could overcome the excitement in order to have a moment of reflection) that death is nothing. In any case, although Skylar is not on a suicide mission, his plan is suicidal in the sense that he chooses to do something for which his death is a reasonably certain consequence. But he does not care about the death part of it, since the death will have no consequences *for* him (because it will be the end *of* him).

Skylar can be contrasted to Payne, who, suffering greatly, considers killing himself. Payne might choose some method of death that will operate quickly and without ceremony. Or he might choose skydiving without a parachute as a way of experiencing a temporary respite from pain (the thrill of falling being fairly certain to provide a distraction) followed by death as a way (so he supposes) of escaping further suffering.[9]

Payne's agony has been unrelieved by any drug or medical procedure that has been tried. He is now offered a recent pharmaceutical discovery that will cure him of the medical problem, thus relieving the pain, allowing his life to return to a satisfactory status. It represents a familiar kind of cure, akin to any other analgesic: you're in pain, you take a pill, and a bit later on you're no longer in pain. Happens all the time. I will assume that most people in Payne's condition would find such a restorative pill attractive. An Epicurean, too, would have the same motive as Payne to take the pill.

But suppose instead that the medication is pill #2. It will relieve the pain, but it will have a side effect of bringing on a painless death a few years later. Most people would hesitate and then probably refuse the pill; they want the relief of

---

[9] Contrast Skylar's and Payne's cases with Dyan, who wishes to experience what it is like to die—not to be dead (for she agrees that death is annihilation) but rather to undergo the process of becoming dead. What, she wonders, would the final few moments of dying be like, in a case where death would be fairly quick but not instantaneous?

pain, but not the death, especially if they are not already old and feeble enough to expect death at any time. Although most people would refuse the pill, an Epicurean would not. As he would see it, the death that comes later, whether natural or drug-caused, is nothing to him. So he would understand the alleged alternatives as take the pill and be relieved of pain or else continue in pain. Prudence would recommend taking the pill.

Pill #3 will relieve the pain but will have a side effect of bringing on a painless death a few minutes later. Most people would refuse the drug (and might even classify it as a suicide pill), whereas an Epicurean would reason just as before.

Pill #4 will bring on a painless death immediately. Most people would refuse the pill (which is obviously a suicide pill and nothing more). Would an Epicurean reason as before? No, because in this case the drug will not relieve pain; there is no prudential reason to choose it. Why would an Epicurean wish to do something that, so far as his experiences can be concerned, will yield no experiences? Epicurus, who, we know, was suffering at the end of his life,[10] would reason this way about pill #4:

> I am being offered a choice between (a) having pain and (b) nonbeing (where neither "being in pain" nor "being without pain" can apply). Since the nothing of nonbeing does not come into prudential reckoning, this is a degenerate choice, equivalent to asking if I would like to have (a), i.e., some pain. Ordinarily the answer would be "No", but this is no ordinary situation. For, what is the "instead" that must be the alternative choice? Would I like to have some pain instead of... of what? Not "instead of nothing", because death is not an "instead" for me. There is actually no prudential choice for me here. True, I can choose to end my existence, but that—to repeat—is nothing for me. Death cannot take my suffering away from me.

Clearly, he would not choose the pain. It is not that he wants (b), which is nothing; rather, he does not want (a), pain. But disjunctive syllogism cannot operate here.

So the prudential problem has not been solved, yet I am at a loss to know how to continue, except to affirm that prudence is in no position to recommend suicide.[11] Prudence is alive when practical choices are available; it recommends

---

[10] For an interesting presentation of the details, see Maria Bitsori and Emmanouil Galanakis, "Epicurus' death".
[11] A rational calculation will give a game-theoretic "maximin"—maximize the minimum payoff. Wallace Matson says (speaking of the Cyrenaic attitude), "Now, what action in particular does the maximin strategy dictate for life as a whole? Well, what gives complete assurance of no negative payoff? Only one thing: suicide" ("Hegesias the Death-Persuader", 556). This is an example of the Fallacy of Misplaced Contingency. If one wants to follow a maximin strategy in the playing of a

actions that seem to be productive of, or continuations of, or changes toward, stable satisfaction. There is a contingency in living: sometimes with pain and sometimes without. But in the case of extraordinary pain, when suffering has become so intense and overwhelming that one is left alone with only it, the contingency has vanished, and in its place there appears, larger than life, the eidolon of pain itself—the very thing that must be annihilated because it is now everything.

---

game, one is confused if one thinks that the strategy calls for *not playing the game*. If one does not play, one is using no strategy at all to play the game. One cannot possibly lose a game that one is not playing. Nor can one win. There is no game outcome for a non-player.

Bibliography

Annas, Julia, *The Morality of Happiness* (New York: Oxford University Press, 1993).

Aristotle, *Nichomachean Ethics*, H. Rackham (trans.) (Cambridge: Harvard University Press, Loeb Classical Library, 1934).

Armstrong, David, "All Things to All Men: Philodemus' Model of Therapy and the Audience of *De Morte*," in J. Fitzgerald, G. Holland, and D. Obbink (eds.), *Philodemus and the New Testament World* (Leiden: Brill, 2004): 15–54.

Athenaeus (excerpts), in Brad Inwood and L. P. Gerson (trans.), *The Epicurus Reader* (Indianapolis: Hackett Publishing Co., 1994): 78.

Augustine, *On the Free Choice of the Will*, Anna S. Benjamin and L. H. Hackstaff (trans.) (Indianapolis: Bobbs-Merrill, 1964).

Baxter, Stephen, "Last Contact," in Gardner Dozois (ed.), *The Year's Best Science Fiction: Twenty-Fifth Annual Collection* (New York: St. Martin's Press, 2008): 270–79. First published in George Mann (ed.), *The Solaris Book of New Science Fiction* (Oxford: Rebellion, 2007).

Belshaw, Christopher, *Annihilation: The Sense and Significance of Death* (New York: Acumen, 2009).

Benatar, David, *Better Never to Have Been: The Harm of Coming Into Existence* (New York: Oxford University Press, 2008).

Bennett, Jonathan, *A Philosophical Guide to Conditionals* (Oxford: Clarendon Press, 2003).

Berger, Peter, *A Rumor of Angels* (New York: Doubleday, 1970).

Bitsori, Maria, and Emmanouil Galanakis, "Epicurus' Death," *World Journal of Urology* 22 (2004): 466–69.

Braddock, Glenn, "Epicureanism, Death, and the Good Life," *Philosophical Inquiry* 22 (2000): 47–66.

Bradley, Ben, "When is Death Bad for the One Who Dies?" *Noûs* 38 (2004): 1–28.

Bradley, Ben, *Well-Being and Death* (New York: Oxford University Press, 2009).

Bradley, Ben, "Eternalism and Death's Badness," in Joseph Keim Campbell, Michael O'Rourke, and Harry S. Silverstein (eds.), *Time and Identity* (Cambridge: MIT Press, 2010): 271–81.

Brandt, Richard B., "The Concept of a Moral Right and Its Function," *Journal of Philosophy* 80 (1983): 29–45.

Brandt, Richard B., *Morality, Utilitarianism, and Rights* (Cambridge: Cambridge University Press, 1992).

Brueckner, Anthony, and John Martin Fischer, "Why is Death Bad," *Philosophical Studies* 50 (1986): 213–21; reprinted in Fischer (ed.), *The Metaphysics of Death*: 221–29.

Brueckner, Anthony, and John Martin Fischer, "The Asymmetry of Early Death and Late Birth," *Philosophical Studies* 71 (1993): 327–31.
Callahan, Joan C., "On Harming the Dead," *Ethics* 97 (1987): 341–52.
Campbell, Rob, and Diane Collinson, *Ending Lives* (New York: Blackwell, 1988).
Cave, George P., "Animals, Heidegger, and the Right to Life," *Environmental Ethics* 4 (1982): 249–54.
Cave, Steven, *Immortality* (London: Biteback Publishing, 2013).
Chandler, M., "Doubt and Developing Theories of Mind," in J. W. Astington, P. L. Harris, and D. R. Olsen (eds.), *Developing Theories of Mind* (New York: Cambridge University Press, 1988): 387–413.
Cicero, *On Ends (De Finibus Bonorum et Malorum)*, H. Rackham (trans.) (Cambridge: Harvard University Press, Loeb Classical Library, 1914).
Cicero, *Tusculan Disputations* (excerpts), in Brad Inwood and L. P. Gerson (trans.), *The Epicurus Reader* (Indianapolis: Hackett Publishing Co., 1994).
Clark, E. V., "Lexical Meaning," in E. L. Bavin (ed.), *The Cambridge Handbook of Child Language* (New York: Cambridge University Press, 2009): 283–300.
Clay, Diskin, "Epicurus' Last Will and Testament," *Archiv für die Geschichte der Philosophie* 55 (1973): 252–80.
Clay, Diskin, "A Lost Epicurean Community," *Greek, Roman and Byzantine Studies* 30 (1989): 313–35.
Cosculluela, Victor, "The Right to Suicide," *Journal of Value Inquiry* 36 (1996): 431–43.
Daniels, Chas, and James Freeman, "An Analysis of the Subjunctive Conditional," *Notre Dame Journal of Formal Logic* 21 (1980): 639–55.
Darwall, Stephen, *The Second-Person Standpoint* (Cambridge: Harvard University Press, 2009).
Descartes, René, *Replies to the Second Set of Objections*, in John Cottingham, Robert Stoothoff, and Dugald Murdoch (trans.), *The Philosophical Writings of Descartes, Vol II* (Cambridge: Cambridge University Press, 1984): 93–120.
Devine, Philip, *The Ethics of Homicide* (Ithaca: Cornell University Press, 1978).
Devlin, Patrick, *The Enforcement of Morals* (New York: Oxford University Press, 1965).
Draper, Kai, "Disappointment, Sadness, and Death," *The Philosophical Review* 108 (1999): 387–414.
Dworkin, Ronald, *Life's Dominion* (New York: Vintage Books, 1994).
Epicurus, *Letter to Herodotus*, in Inwood and Gerson (eds.), *The Epicurus Reader*: 5–19.
Epicurus, *Letter to Menoeceus*, in Inwood and Gerson (eds.), *The Epicurus Reader*: 28–31.
Epicurus, *Letter to Pythocles*, in Inwood and Gerson (eds.), *The Epicurus Reader*: 19–28.
Epicurus, *Principal Doctrines*, in Inwood and Gerson (eds.), *The Epicurus Reader*: 32–36.
Epicurus, *Vatican Sayings*, in Inwood and Gerson (eds.), *The Epicurus Reader*: 36–40.

Erler, Michael, and Malcolm Schofield, "Epicurean Ethics," in Keimpe Algra, et al. (eds.), *The Cambridge History of Hellenistic Philosophy* (Cambridge: Cambridge University Press, 1999): 642–74.

Ewin, R. E., "What is Wrong with Killing People?" *Philosophical Quarterly* 22 (1976): 126–39.

Feinberg, Joel, "Harm to Others," in Fischer (ed.), *The Metaphysics of Death*: 171–90.

Feinberg, Joel, "Voluntary Euthanasia and the Inalienable Right to Life," *Philosophy and Public Affairs* 7 (1978): 93–123.

Feldman, Fred, *Confrontations with the Reaper* (New York: Oxford University Press, 1992).

Feldman, Fred, "The Termination Thesis," *Midwest Studies in Philosophy* 24 (2000): 98–115.

Fine, Kit, "Critical Notice: *Counterfactuals*," *Mind* 84 (1975): 451–58.

Fingarette, Herbert, *Death: Philosophical Soundings* (Chicago: Open Court, 1996).

Fischer, John Martin (ed.), *The Metaphysics of Death* (Stanford: Stanford University Press, 1993).

Fischer, John Martin, "Introduction," in Fischer (ed.), *The Metaphysics of Death*: 3–30.

Fischer, John Martin, *Our Stories* (New York: Oxford University Press, 2009).

Frankfurt, Harry, "Moral Responsibility and Alternate Possibilities," *Journal of Philosophy*, 66 (1969): 829–39.

Freud, Sigmund, "Thoughts for the Times on War and Death," in *The Standard Edition of the Complete Psychological Works of Sigmund Freud*, Vol. 14 (London: Hogarth Press, 1957).

Frey, R. G., *Interests and Rights* (New York: Oxford University Press, 1980).

Frey, R. G., *Rights, Killing, and Suffering* (New York: Blackwell, 1983).

Frey, R. G., "On Why We Would be Better to Jettison Moral Rights," in H. B. Miller and W. H. Williams (eds.), *Ethics and Animals* (Clifton: Humana Press, 1983): 285–301.

Furley, David J., "Nothing to Us?" in M. Schofield and G. Striker (eds.), *The Norms of Nature* (Cambridge: Cambridge University Press, 1986): 75–91.

Glover, Jonathan, *Causing Death and Saving Lives* (London: Penguin Books, 1977).

Goldman, Alan, "Abortion and the Right to Life," *The Personalist* 60 (1979): 402–6.

Görler, W., "Storing up past pleasures," in K. A. Algra, M. H. Koenen, and P. H. Schrijvers (eds.), *Lucretius and his Intellectual Background* (New York: Koninklijke Nederlandse Adademie van Wetenschappen, 1997): 193–207.

Grey, William, "Epicurus and the Harm of Death," *Australasian Journal of Philosophy* 77 (1999): 358–64.

Griffin, James, *On Human Rights* (New York: Oxford University Press, 2008).

Harris, John, *Enhancing Evolution: The Ethical Case for Making Better People* (Princeton: Princeton University Press, 2007).

Hart, H. L. A., "Are There Any Natural Rights?" *The Philosophical Review* 64 (1955): 175–91.

Hart, H. L. A., "Positivism and the Separation of Law and Morals," *Harvard Law Review* 71 (1958): 593–629.

Hetherington, Stephen, "Where is the Harm in Dying Prematurely?" *Journal of Ethics* 17 (2013): 79–97.

Hobbes, Thomas, *Leviathan*. Various editions.

Hohfeld, Wesley, "Some Fundamental Legal Conceptions as Applied in Judicial Reasoning," *Yale Law Journal* 23 (1913): 16–59.

Hynes, Samuel, *Flights of Passage: Reflections of a World War II Aviator* (Annapolis: Frederic C. Beil/Naval Institute Press, 1988).

Invasion of the Body Snatchers, Don Siegel (dir.) (Allied Artists, 1956).

Inwood, Brad, and L. P. Gerson, (trans.) *The Epicurus Reader* (Indianapolis: Hackett Publishing Co., 1994).

Ives, Burl, *Have a Holly, Jolly Christmas* (Decca Records, 1965).

Kastenbaum, Robert, "A World Without Death? First and Second Thoughts," *Mortality* 1 (1996): 111–21.

Kaufman, Frederik, "Thick and Thin Selves: A Reply to Fischer and Speak," *Midwest Studies in Philosophy* 24 (2000): 94–97.

Kaufman, Frederik, "Comments on [James Stacey Taylor's] *Death, Posthumous Harm and Bioethics*," *Journal of Medical Ethics* 40 (2014): 636–37.

Keller, Simon, "Posthumous Harm," in Steven Luper (ed.), *The Cambridge Companion to Life and Death* (Cambridge: Cambridge University Press, 2014): 181–97.

Kim, Seahwa, and Cei Maslen, "Counterfactuals as Short Stories," *Philosophical Studies* 129 (2006): 81–117.

Kment, Boris, "Counterfactuals and Explanation," *Mind* 115 (2006): 261–310.

Koestenbaum, Peter, "The Vitality of Death," *Journal of Existentialism* 5 (1964): 139–66.

Laërtius, Diogenes, *Lives of Eminent Philosophers*, R. D. Hicks (trans.) (Cambridge: Harvard University Press, Loeb Classical Library, 1925).

Lampe, Kurt, *The Birth of Hedonism: The Cyrenaic Philosophers and Pleasure as a Way of Life* (Princeton: Princeton University Press, 2014).

Lenman, James, "On Becoming Extinct," *Pacific Philosophical Quarterly* 83 (2002): 253–69.

Lesses, Glenn, "Happiness, Completeness, and Indifference to Death in Epicurean Ethical Theory," in Lawrence J. Jost (ed.), *Eudaimonia and Well-Being: Ancient and Modern Conceptions* (Edmonton: Academic Press & Pub, 2002): 57–68.

Lewis, David, *Counterfactuals* (Oxford: Blackwell, 1973).

Lewis, David, "The Paradoxes of Time Travel," *American Philosophical Quarterly*, 13 (1976): 145–52.

Lockwood, Michael, "Singer on Killing and the Preference for Life," *Inquiry* 22 (1979): 157–70.

Lucretius, *On the Nature of Things (De Rerum Natura)*, W. H. D. Rouse (trans.), revised by Martin F. Smith (Cambridge: Harvard University Press, Loeb Classical Library, 1992).

Luper, Steven, *Invulnerability: On Securing Happiness* (Peru: Open Court, 1996).

Luper, Steven, "Exhausting Life," *Journal of Ethics* 17 (2013): 99–119.
Marquis, Don, "Why Abortion is Immoral," *Journal of Philosophy* 86 (1989): 183–202.
Matson, Wallace, "Hegesias the Death-Persuader; or, the Gloominess of Hedonism," *Philosophy* 73 (1988): 553–57.
McCloskey, H. J., "The Right to Life," *Mind* 84 (1975): 403–25.
McMahan, Jeff, "Death and the Value of Life," in Fischer (ed.), *The Metaphysics of Death*: 233–66.
McNamara Robert S., in Errol Morris (dir.), *The Fog of War* (Sony Pictures, 2003).
Merriman, W. E., L. L. Bowman, and B. MacWhinney, "The Mutual Exclusivity Bias in Children's Word Learning," *Monographs of the Society for Research in Child Development* 54 (3–4, No. 220, 1989): 1–132.
Mill, John Stuart, *Utilitarianism*. Various editions.
Miller, Fred D. Jr., "Epicurus on the Art of Dying," *Southern Journal of Philosophy* 14 (1976): 169–77.
Mitsis, Phillip, "Epicurus on Death and the Duration of Life," in John J. Cleary and Daniel C. Shartin (eds.), *Proceedings of the Boston Area Colloquium in Ancient Philosophy*, Vol. 4 (Lanham: University Press of America, 1989): 303–22.
Mitsis, Phillip, "Happiness and Death in Epicurean Ethics," in Lawrence J. Jost (ed.), *Eudaimonia and Well-Being: Ancient and Modern Conceptions* (Edmonton: Academic Print and Pub., 2002), 41–55.
Mothersill, Mary, "Death," in James Rachels (ed.), *Moral Problems* (New York: Harper & Row, 1971): 372–83.
Nagel, Thomas, "Death," in Fischer (ed.), *The Metaphysics of Death*: 61–69.
Nagel, Thomas, *The View From Nowhere* (New York: Oxford University Press, 1986).
National Transportation Safety Board Aviation Accident Final Report. http://app.ntsb.gov/pdfgenerator/ReportGeneratorFile.ashx?EventID=20100125X25502&AKey=1&RType=Final&IType=LA, accessed 25 November 2016.
Nearing, Scott, and Helen Nearing, *Living the Good Life* (New York: Schocken Books, 1970).
Nietzsche, Friedrich, *Beyond Good and Evil*. Various editions.
Nussbaum, Martha C., *The Therapy of Desire* (Princeton: Princeton University Press, 1994).
Nussbaum, Martha C., "Reply to Papers in Symposium on Nussbaum, *The Therapy of Desire*," *Philosophy and Phenomenological Research* 59 (1999): 811–19.
Nussbaum, Martha C., "The Damage of Death: Incomplete Arguments and False Consolations," in James Stacey Taylor (ed.), *The Metaphysics and Ethics of Death* (New York: Oxford University Press, 2013): 25–43.
Parfit, Derek, "Future Generations: Further Problems," *Philosophy & Public Affairs* 11 (Spring 1982): 113–72.
Partridge, Ernest, "Posthumous Interests and Posthumous Respect," *Ethics* 91 (1981): 243–64.
Paske, Gerald H., "Why Animals Have No Right to Life: A Response to Regan," *Australasian Journal of Philosophy* 66 (1988): 498–511.

Philodemus, *On Death*, W. Benjamin Henry (trans.) (Atlanta: Society of Biblical Literature, 2009).

Pitcher, George, "The Misfortunes of the Dead," in Fischer (ed.), *The Metaphysics of Death*: 159–68.

Plato, *The Republic of Plato*, Alan Bloom (trans.) (New York: Basic Books, 1968).

Plutarch, "That Epicurus Actually Makes a Pleasant Life Impossible," *Moralia XIV*, Benedict Einarson and Phillip H. De Lacy (trans.) (Cambridge: Harvard University Press, Loeb Classical Library, 1967).

Rafetseder, Eva, Maria Schwitalla, and Josef Perner, "Counterfactual Reasoning: From Childhood to Adulthood," *Journal of Experimental Child Psychology* 114 (2013): 389–404.

Reanney, Darryl, *After Death: A New Future For Human Consciousness* (New York: William Morrow, 1991).

Reinhardt, Tobias, "The Speech of Nature in Lucretius' *De Rerum Natura* 3.931–71," *Classical Quarterly* 52 (2002): 291–304.

Rorty, Amélie Oksenberg, "Fearing Death," *Philosophy* 58 (1983): 175–88.

Rosenbaum, Stephen, "How to Be Dead and Not Care: A Defense of Epicurus," *American Philosophical Quarterly* 23 (1986): 217–25. Reprinted in Fischer (ed.), *The Metaphysics of Death*: 119–34.

Rosenbaum, Stephen, "Epicurus on Pleasure and the Complete Life," *The Monist* 73, 1 (1990): 21–41.

Rosenbaum, Stephen, "Review of Feldman, *Confrontations with the Reaper*," *Philosophy and Phenomenological Research* 55 (1995): 233–37.

Rosenbaum, Stephen, "Appraising Death in Human Life: Two Modes of Valuation," *Midwest Studies in Philosophy* 24 (2000): 151–71.

Rosenbaum, Stephen, "Concepts of Value and Ideas about Death," in James Stacey Taylor (ed.), *The Metaphysics and Ethics of Death* (New York: Oxford University Press, 2013): 149–68.

Rosenthal, Abigail L., "What Ayer Saw When He Was Dead," *Philosophy* 79 (2004): 507–31.

Rubio-Fernández, Paula, and Bart Geurts, "How to Pass the False-Belief Task Before Your Fourth Birthday," *Psychological Science* 24 (2013): 27–33.

Sainsbury, Mark, *Fiction and Fictionalism* (New York: Routledge, 2009).

Sanders, Kirk R., "Philodemus and the Fear of Premature Death," in Jeffrey Fish and Kirk R. Sanders (eds.), *Epicurus and the Epicurean Tradition* (Cambridge: Cambridge University Press, 2011): 211–34.

Scheffler, Samuel, *Death and the Afterlife* (New York: Oxford University Press, 2013).

Silverstein, Harry S., "The Evil of Death," *Journal of Philosophy* 77 (1980): 401–24. Reprinted in Fischer (ed.), *The Metaphysics of Death*: 95–116.

Silverstein, Harry S., "The Evil of Death Revisited," in P. A. French and H. Weinstein (eds.), *Midwest Studies in Philosophy* 24 (2000): 116–34.

Silverstein, Harry S., "'The Evil of Death' Defended: Reply to Burley," *International Journal of Philosophical Studies* 16 (2008): 569–79.
Silverstein, Harry S., "The Time of the Evil of Death," in J. Campbell, M. O'Rourke, and H. Silverstein (eds.), *Time and Identity* (Cambridge: MIT Press, 2010): 283–95.
Silverstein, Harry S., "The Evil of Death One More Time: Parallels between Time and Space," in James Stacey Taylor (ed.), *The Metaphysics and Ethics of Death* (Oxford: Oxford University Press, 2013): 83–99.
Singer, Peter, "Killing Humans and Killing Animals," *Inquiry* 22 (1979): 145–56.
Steele, Hunter, "Could Body-Bound Immortality Be Liveable?" *Mind* 85 (1976): 424–427.
Strawson, Galen, "Against Narrativity," *Ratio* 17 (2004): 428–52.
Striker, Gisela, "Commentary on Mitsis," in John J. Cleary and Daniel C. Shartin (eds.), *Proceedings of the Boston Area Colloquium in Ancient Philosophy*, Vol. 4 (Lanham: University Press of America, 1989): 323–28.
Suits, David B., "Really Believing in Fiction," *Pacific Philosophical Quarterly* 87 (2006): 369–86.
Suits, David B., "Death and Other Nothings," *Philosophical Forum* 43 (2012): 215–30.
Taylor, James Stacey, *Death, Posthumous Harm, and Bioethics* (New York: Routledge, 2012).
Thomson, Judith Jarvis, "A Defense of Abortion," *Philosophy & Public Affairs* 1 (1971): 47–66.
Thomson, Judith Jarvis, "Rights and Deaths," *Philosophy and Public Affairs* 2 (1973): 146–59.
Thoreau, Henry David, *Walden and other Writings*, J. W. Krutch (ed.) (New York: Bantam Books, 1971).
Tooley, Michael, "Abortion and Infanticide," *Philosophy and Public Affairs* 2 (1972): 37–65.
Tsouna, Voula, "Rationality and the Fear of Death in Epicurean Philosophy," *Rhizai: A Journal for Ancient Philosophy and Science* 3 (2006): 79–117.
Tsouna, Voula, *The Ethics of Philodemus* (New York: Oxford University Press, 2007).
Unger, Peter, *Identity, Consciousness and Value* (New York: Oxford University Press, 1990).
Van Evra, James W., "Death," *Theoretical Medicine* 5 (1984): 197–208.
Velleman, J. David, "Well-Being and Time," in Fischer (ed.), *The Metaphysics of Death*: 329–57.
Velleman, J. David, "Narrative Explanation", *Philosophical Review* 112 (2003): 1–26.
Velleman, J. David, "Comments on John Martin Fisher's *Our Stories*," *Philosophical Studies* 158 (2012): 515–21.
William G. Vrasdonk, "Beyond Thanatology: Immortality," *Journal of Value Inquiry* 6 (1972): 280–85.
Warren, James, "Epicurean Immortality," in David Sedley (ed.), *Oxford Studies in Ancient Philosophy* XVIII (New York: Oxford University Press, 2000): 231–61.

Warren, James, "Lucretius, Symmetry Arguments, and Fearing Death," *Phronesis* 46 (2001): 466–91.

Warren, James, *Facing Death* (New York: Oxford University Press, 2004).

Warren, James, "Removing Fear," in James Warren (ed.), *The Cambridge Companion to Epicureanism* (Cambridge: Cambridge University Press, 2009): 234–48.

Williams, Bernard, "The Makropulos Case: Reflections on the Tedium of Immortality," in Fischer (ed.), *The Metaphysics of Death*: 73–92.

Wimmer, H., and J. Perner, "Beliefs about Beliefs: Representation and Constraining Function of Wrong Beliefs in Young Children's Understanding of Deception," *Cognition* 13 (1983): 103–28.

Wreen, Michael, "The Power of Potentiality," *Theoria* 52 (1986): 16–40.

Young, Robert, "What Is Wrong with Killing People?" *Philosophy* 54 (1979): 515–28.

Index

abortion 151–4
addiction 10, 11
adversity 8, 111–12, 143–50, 154
annihilation 2, 7, *see also* nonexistence
aponia 4, 44
ataraxia 4, 44
Athenaeus 159
atomism 5
attenuated transitivity of concern 195–6
autonomy 139–40, 143–4
Ayer, A. J. 11 n.7

Bennett, Jonathan 72 n.5
Berger, Peter 10
boredom 167–73
Bradley, Ben 30–2, 91, 104–9
Brandt, Richard 132
Brueckner, Anthony 26 n.1

Callahan, Joan C. 186
Cambridge change 34
Campbell, Rob 199
Čapek, Karel 169
causal explanation 67–70
Cave, George P. 137–8
Cave, Steven 19 n.9
choice 17, 203, 206, 209
Cicero 43, 47–8, 158, 205
Collinson, Diane 199
complete life 38–9, 41–2, 44–6, 49–50, 52, 59–64
contingent
    attributes 6, 96–8, 106, 109
    in ethics 127–30
continuity 32–5
contract, *see* promise
counterfactuals 12–14
    comparisons 12–14, 19–20
    in esse 78–9, 109–11
    plausible 70–4
    possible worlds 71–4
    post esse 78–9, 109–11

courage 165
Cyrenaics 39 n.1

Darwall, Stephen 132
death
    defined 2, 5–6
    denial of 10
    fear of 2, 8–9, 62–3
    no situation 13, 15, 87, 91, 109
    premature 16, 38–42, 46, 59–64, 83
    relevance of 3, 8, 25
    solution 14–15
deprivation 12–14, 35, 54–5, 59–62, 83–95, 99–108, 110–12, 137–8
desires 28, 49–50
    interference with 135
    vacated 135
Devine, Philip E. 201
dissatisfaction 8
Do Not Resuscitate order 203
Draper, Kai 84
duration 205–7

egoism 4, 149
emotion 9, 193
empathy 76, 149
Epicureanism 27
    Radical 27, 187–8, 194
Epicurus
    Letter to Menoeceus 3, 4, 42–3, 47, 49–50, 202
    Letter to Pythocles 29 n.4
    PD-19 42
    PD-20 42, 44, 49–50, 54
    PD-21 50 n.18
evil 21, 25
    problem of 72
    standard and non-standard 34
evolution 161–2
Ewin, R. E. 148
experience 3, 17–18, 25, 99
experson 6

Fallacy of Misplaced Contingency 96–8, 109
false belief task 77
fear 8, 9, 55–7, 62–3
Feinberg, Joel 41 n.9, 182
Feldman, Fred 5 n.5, 33 n.7, 100–1
fiction 76
Fine, Kit 75
Fingarette, Herbert 190
Fischer, John Martin 26 n.1, 32–5, 170–1
fog 70, 74–5, 78, 79
Frankfurt, Harry 128–30
friendship 165–6, 183–5

Glover, Jonathan 16
Goldman, Alan 140–1
good life 4–5, 53, 61
Grey, William 88–9
Griffin, James 131–2

Hart, H. L. A. 181 n.5
hēdonē 4
hedonism 4, 100–1
Hobbes, Thomas 44–5, 45 n.13
Hohfeld, Wesley 125
Hynes, Samuel 2 n.2
Hypothesis of Prudence 25

immortality 15–16, 155–62, 164–71, 173–6
 conditional 156, 157–8
 ersatz 175–6
 invulnerability 155–6
 unconditional 155
indifference 27, 108, 188–95
Indifference Conclusion 27, 29, 30, 191–2
 problems 178–9, 182, 185–8, 190–1, 195
Instead Requirement 130–1, 136

Kastenbaum, Robert 15
Kaufman, Frederik 143
Keller, Simon 104–5
killing 123–5, 127, 131, 133–43, 145–8, 150–3
Kim, Seahwa 74
Kment, Boris 76
Koestenbaum, Peter 18

lacuna 68–70
Laërtius, Diogenes 43
Lampe, Kurt 39 n.2
Leibniz, Gottfried Wilhelm 71–2
Lenman, James 175
Lewis, David 73–4
life insurance 181–3
Lincoln, Abraham 96
loss 19, 136–7
Lucretius 47
 recombination 156–7
 replacement argument 159–61
 Speech of Nature 50–4
Luper, Steven 28, 191

McCloskey, H. J. 145
McMahan, Jeff 99
Marquis, Don 147
Maslen, Cei 74
materialism 5
meaning
 in life 18
 ultimate 171–3
Mill, John Stuart 132
moral appraisal 199
mortality 2, 38
myth of Er 11

Nagel, Thomas 94, 112
narratives 40–1
National Transportation Safety Board 68
Nietzsche, Friedrich 133 n.11
nonexistence 2, 7, 26
"no subject" problem 87, 114–15, 121
nothing, *see* nonexistence
Null Hypothesis 24, 25, 26, 30
Nussbaum, Martha 83, 162, 164–6

otherwise 19–20, *see also* counterfactuals; Instead Requirement
"ought" implies "can" 127–30

pain 4, 8, 162–4, 205–6
paradox 62–4
Parfit, Derek 70
Partridge, Ernest 186
Paske, Gerald H. 138–9

Philodemus of Gadara 54–9
    degma 57, 208
    deprivation 54–5
phronesis, see prudence
Pitcher, George 41 n.9
Plato 11
pleasure 3, 42–3, 45
    katastematic 43–5
    kinetic 43–5
pointlessness 173–5
policy 143–4, 150–1
possible worlds, *see* counterfactuals
postmortem events 41 n.9, 83–4
potentiality 152
problem of evil 72
problem of the subject, *see* "no subject" problem
promise 179–83
prudence 20, 25, 49, 206

Reanny, Darryl 163
Reinhardt, Tobias 52, 62
Rescue arguments 38–65
    critique 46–65
respect for persons 138, 145
rights
    claim 126–7
    honoring 141–2
    liberty 125–6
    to life (*see* killing)
    negative 140
    positive 140
    violation 141
Rorty, A. O. 163
Rosenbaum, Stephen 44 n.12

St. Augustine 203
Sanders, Kirk 59 n.27, 62–3
satisfaction 4, 29, 48, 50, 54
sense experience 3, 7
sentience 7, 145–6
Silverstein, Harry S. 114–21
singularity 21, 98

slave 139
space-time framework, *see* Silverstein
spatial analog 101–3
Steele, Hunter 171
Striker, Gisela 38–9, 41
suffering, *see* adversity
suicide 15, 197–204, 208–10
    ethical issues 198–201
    pill 209
    prudential issues 201–5
    species 200–1

telos 5, 42
tenseless verbs 91
tetrapharmakos 48, 61 n.30
theory of mind 77
Thomson, Judith Jarvis 142–3
Thoreau, Henry David 61 n.29
threat 133–4
tool, *see* values (instrumental)
Tooley, Michael 134
Tsouna, Voula 55, 57–8

Unger, Peter 17–18

values
    cherished 164
    connect with feelings (VCF) (*see* Silverstein)
    core 158
    instrumental 172–3, 183–5
    intrinsic 172–3
Van Evra, James 173–5
Velleman, J. David 40, 98
Vrasdonk, William G. 173

Warren, James 46 n.15, 53, 63 n.33
well-being 104–9
Williams, Bernard 169–71
wills 29, 178–9, 185–8
Wreen, Michael, 152

Young, Robert 136

www.ingramcontent.com/pod-product-compliance
Lightning Source LLC
Chambersburg PA
CBHW052039300426
44117CB00012B/1889